THE NEW WORLD DISORDER

ALSO BY SHASHI THAROOR

NON-FICTION

The Hindu Way: An Introduction to Hinduism
The Paradoxical Prime Minister: Narendra Modi and His India
Why I Am a Hindu
An Era of Darkness: The British Empire in India
India Shastra: Reflections on the Nation in Our Time
India: the Future is Now (ed.)
Pax Indica: India and the World of the 21st Century
Shadows Across the Playing Field: 60 Years of India-Pakistan Cricket (with Shahryar Khan)
India (with Ferrante Ferranti)
The Elephant, the Tiger, and the Cell Phone: Reflections on India in the 21st Century
Bookless in Baghdad
Nehru: The Invention of India
Kerala: God's Own Country (with M. F. Husain)
India: From Midnight to the Millennium and Beyond
Reasons of State

FICTION

Riot
The Five Dollar Smile and Other Stories
Show Business
The Great Indian Novel

ALSO BY SAMIR SARAN

NON-FICTION

Pax Sinica: Implications for the Indian Dawn (with Akhil Deo)
Financing Green Transitions (ed.)
The Future of Work in India: Inclusion, Growth and Transformation (with Terri Chapman, Rakesh Sinha, Suchi Kedia, and Sriram Gutta)
The Road to Universal Health Coverage (with Anjali Nayyar, Dhruv Pahwa, and Oommen C. Kurian)
The New India-US Partnership in the Indo-Pacific: Peace, Prosperity and Security (with Abhijit Singh, Aparna Pande, Sunjoy Joshi, and Walter Lohman)
Our Common Digital Future: The Global Conference on Cyberspace Journal, 2017 (ed.)
Prospects for EU–India Security Cooperation (with Eva Pejsova, Gareth Price, Kanchi Gupta, and John-Joseph Wilkins)
India's Climate Change Identity: Between Reality and Perception (with Aled Jones)
Re-imagining the Indus: Mapping Media Reportage in India and Pakistan (with Hans Rasmussen Theting)
BRIC in the World Order: Perspectives from Brazil, China, India and Russia (with Nandan Unnikrishnan)

THE NEW WORLD DISORDER

AND THE

INDIAN IMPERATIVE

SHASHI THAROOR
& SAMIR SARAN

ALEPH

ALEPH

ALEPH BOOK COMPANY
An independent publishing firm
promoted by Rupa Publications India

First published in India in 2020
by Aleph Book Company
7/16 Ansari Road, Daryaganj
New Delhi 110 002

ISBN: 978-81-942337-3-2

1 3 5 7 9 10 8 6 4 2

For sale in the Indian subcontinent only

Printed at Parksons Graphics Pvt. Ltd, Mumbai

...Things fall apart; the centre cannot hold;
Mere anarchy is loosed upon the world...
The best lack all conviction, while the worst
Are full of passionate intensity.

Surely some revelation is at hand;
Surely the Second Coming is at hand...
The darkness drops again; but now I know
That twenty centuries of stony sleep
Were vexed to nightmare by a rocking cradle,
And what rough beast, its hour come round at last,
Slouches towards Bethlehem to be born?

—W. B. Yeats, 'The Second Coming'

To my grandson, Eliseo Kailash
May he grow up in a better world.
—Shashi Tharoor

To two individuals who inspire me—my dear mother, Sunita, who ensured
that her children grew up among books, and her passion to learn became
theirs; and to Katharina, my dear wife, with whom I look forward to many
years of love, travel, and discovery.
—Samir Saran

CONTENTS

PROLOGUE

3 May 2016: Donald Trump is nominated as the Republican presidential candidate. Campaigns to 'Make America Great Again'. Promises withdrawal from the Trans-Pacific Partnership (TPP); opposition to the Paris Climate Change Agreement; to build a wall on the border with Mexico; and withdrawal of American troops in the Middle East. Donald Trump is elected president on 8 November 2016.

23 June 2016: The United Kingdom holds a referendum on withdrawal from the European Union (EU). 51.9 per cent of those voting support the decision to leave the EU.

14 May 2017: China hosts the Belt and Road Forum (BRF). President Xi Jinping presides over a gathering of thirty heads of state as they sign onto the most ambitious global connectivity initiative in history. Two months earlier, China's parliament approved the removal of the two-term limit on the presidency, in effect allowing Xi Jinping to remain in power for life.

17 November 2018: The yellow vest movement erupts in France—with widespread agitation against austerity, inequality and 'business as usual' politics. Just two months earlier, President Emmanuel Macron delivered a landmark speech calling for a more global French diplomacy.

10 May 2018: Mahathir Mohamad assumes office as Malaysian prime minister—after campaigning on a strident anti-China platform. Renegotiates a Belt And Road Initiative (BRI) project deal with China in April 2019.

26 May 2019: Populist, far-right and Eurosceptic parties in Europe win a quarter of all seats in the European Parliamentary elections—their best ever performance.

INTRODUCTION

As we approach the end of the second decade of the twenty-first century, it is clear that the international liberal order is facing a moment of crisis. The political, economic and security fundamentals that underpinned it are invalid, with no consensus on others. Globalization is now being confronted by economic nationalism. Attempts are being made to close open borders. Strongmen politicians are leveraging multiple grievances—real and perceived—to legitimize populist rule. And international norms and institutions appear less relevant to managing the global commons. There is a sense that the global order is once again becoming more Westphalian—that the gains of interdependence are being undone. There is a visible reassertion of sovereignty—from democracies and otherwise. And, above all, there is an uncertainty about what this century has in store for our societies.

Within the punditry that seeks to understand why the world is as it is today, the overwhelming sentiment is that popular and populist leaders have undermined what was a well-meaning and well-functioning international order. Our book seeks to engage with and perhaps correct this narrative. From our perspective, the world has fundamentally been defined by the spirit of Darwinism: the 'survival of the fittest'. The processes of global governance merely legitimized what was otherwise coercive state diplomacy. It provided a means to amass and maintain power and wealth without the use of military force. As our book will show, the crisis of global governance is, in many ways, a comeuppance for the custodians of the post-1945 world order. The story of decline does not begin with populist leaders trampling on an existing world order—although they certainly are. These leaders are the product of the contradictions that have always defined the liberal order.

Before we detail this any further, it is useful to set the context. Where are we now? For one thing, the guarantors that once evangelized the liberal international order are themselves being swept away by the undercurrents of these shifts. American elites remain dismayed that the US elected Donald Trump—an individual with no interest in global partnerships or liberal posturing. European elites are mortified by the rise of the Alternative für Deutschland (AfD), the National Rally, Viktor Orbán, and others who represent values ostensibly antithetical to those of the EU. Those who would stand for globalization and multilateral values, on the other hand, are struggling for relevance. Macron is fighting a wave of popular discontent over his 'business friendly policies', while Angela Merkel will have demitted office after fighting a losing battle against a populist resurgence in the EU. From the perspective of Western elites, the norms, institutions and partnerships that were so carefully crafted in the post-war period can no longer sustain their peace, freedoms or security. On the contrary, it is these very ideals that are seemingly the root cause of the problem. The wave of popular anger in the transatlantic community is directed at free movement and open borders; towards globalization and the volatility of interdependence; and towards the elites in politics, business, academia and media that support these policies. Local identity and sovereignty—both of which the international liberal order was thought to have subsumed—are reasserting themselves everywhere.

This domestic turbulence has also shaken the security foundations of the international liberal order—the transatlantic and transpacific partnerships of the United States. A core diplomatic mantra of the Trump administration appears to be irreverence for all that was revered. His administration has adopted economic and security policies that are bordering on hostile towards the EU and Japan. It has been relentless in compelling both to 'pay more for their own defence'. More than this, Trump has also been willing to raise military tensions in these regions—with Iran in West Asia, and North Korea in East Asia. His willingness to use unilateral force and pressure in lieu of multilateral negotiations has caused much anguish in Europe, Japan and South Korea. More consequentially, perhaps, Trump has been more than willing to undermine the institutional frameworks of the global order—namely the United Nations (UN) and the World Trade Organization (WTO). He sees both organizations as captured by actors inimical to American interests that infringe on the absolute sovereignty of the US.

Amidst this turbulence in the West, there is also a resurgence of the East. The old empires and civilizations of Asia, especially China and India, are beginning to impress upon the world their size and weight. China, undoubtedly, is leading this charge. While the West is thinking local, China is going global. At the World Economic Forum (WEF) in 2017, President Xi emerged as the unlikeliest defender of globalization, stating, in a very statesmanlike fashion, that the international community 'should adapt to and guide economic globalization, cushion its negative impacts and deliver its benefits for all countries'[1]. More important, the Middle Kingdom is investing in infrastructure projects across Asia and Europe in an unprecedented effort to connect the two continents. The Belt and Road Initiative (BRI) is a multi-billion dollar geopolitical and geoeconomic thrust that will see China emerge as the chief arbiter of an Eurasian political, economic and security arrangement. In doing so, Beijing is steadily undermining the efficacy and legitimacy of the post-war alliance arrangements. In Europe, the China-led 17+1 arrangement is eroding the EU's influence over its eastern borders. China's aggressive naval build-up in the South China Sea (SCS) is displacing American military power in the Pacific, and sowing discord among the member states of Association of Southeast Asian Nations (ASEAN). Its investments in G7 nations like Italy have divided and derailed any potential Western response.

Equally significantly, China's rise is being accompanied by an alternative proposition for global governance. Remember, China

---

[1] Matt Clinch, 'China President Xi Jinping: "No one will emerge as a winner in a trade war"', *CNBC*, 17 January 2017.

bears an enduring grudge against those who profess to lead the international order. China's political histories are stories about humiliation, subjugation and suffering at the hands of outsiders. There is some disagreement in international affairs literature about exactly what change, and how much of it, China actually seeks. This line of thinking, however, misses the point. China is large enough that the influence of its domestic arrangements will be felt organically in other parts of the world. Beijing has only grown more authoritarian at home and more assertive abroad under the presidency of Xi Jinping. And China is certainly exporting bits and pieces of this model. The most obvious manifestation is surveillance technologies that China's massive technology companies are selling in developing countries around the world. China's propositions are certainly international; they are infused, however, with Chinese characteristics. It is a proponent of globalization—but a morphed version that prioritizes state-led capitalism with the People's Republic of China in command. Beijing favours international institutions, but seeks to subvert their original purpose. In the UN, for example, China has attempted to introduce human rights language that privileges and protects state interpretations, as opposed to more universal (read, in Chinese eyes, Western) international values.

The myth of the liberal order is caught between these shifts in domestic attitudes and the balance of global power. And it is crumbling under these pressures because it is unsuited to balancing internationalism and sovereignty, or to managing a more multipolar international system. Many write and speak about the international liberal order with rose-tinted glasses and a sense of nostalgia. This could not be further from the truth. It was hardly international—premised as it was on America's system of post-war alliances. While it did guarantee sovereign equality, it is difficult to argue that decision-making authority was sufficiently diffused. Instead, important institutions were run by the largest and most powerful countries. The fabled Washington Consensus, meanwhile, privileged the commercial interests of a handful of geographies, often to the detriment of emerging economies, the environment and the blue-collar worker.

Nor was this order truly 'orderly'. If institutions could realistically impose limits on the unilateral actions of all countries, we would not have seen disastrous Western interventions in the Middle East. Perhaps the only legitimate claim the international liberal order can truly have is to liberalism itself. It certainly helped that the victors of World War II were all open, democratic societies—even though much of the world was not. With the original guarantors of this order themselves in disarray, it is understandable why its resilience is fraying. The idea of global governance, then, was ultimately a consensus building framework for the global political, economic and security elite. As a popular right-wing Indian commentator tweeted, 'The entitled elites don't believe in the survival of the fittest but the survival of the fatuous, frivolous and the feckless.'[2] In other words, pedigree, privilege and personal networks have defined who is at the high table—and more important, who isn't. This may be a Trumpian statement to make—but as our chapters on development and cyberspace will show, both twentieth and twentieth-first-century debates have been monopolized by small but vocal and influential communities. The backlash we are seeing today is driven by a groundswell of grassroots opposition to many of its central tenets and philosophies.

Where, then, does the world go from here? What happens to the liberal international order? In all the criticism, one shouldn't lose sight of the fact that there did exist a period of democratic resurgence, of massive reductions in poverty and disease, and a rise in wealth of new communities and nations. But if there is a new world order in the making it will still require legitimacy. The answer to 'what next' lies in the problem: there are no alternative stakeholders in the existing international order. The Western assumption that China would be one such stakeholder has proven misplaced. Instead, it is offering an alternative world order altogether—even though its propositions may still be in beta-phase. Many developing countries certainly find this

---

[2]Sushant Sareen, Tweet on 27 May 2019, accessed 15 June 2019, https://twitter.com/sushantsareen/status/1132925746454753280.

attractive—especially those that are in dire need of infrastructure finance. However, China's behaviour over the past decade has given us very little cause to believe that it will be any less imperial and self-serving. It privileges the diktat of the Communist Party of China (CPC) above all—and it is difficult to see China designing global norms and institutions that would allow for a diffusion of decision-making power. And more to the point, for those of us who have lived our lives in free and open societies, there is still a desire to see democracy flourish and to see a functioning international system that minimizes conflict and prioritizes stability.

To be able to do this, however, requires a long exposition and inquiry into what we call 'the New World Disorder'. Essentially this describes global governance in the late twentieth and early twenty-first centuries. Our central effort in the book is to try and describe and understand this phenomenon and provide some suggestions on how the crisis that currently prevails might be resolved. India should, in our view, be part of the solution; we go deeper into the Indian imperative in the last chapter of the book. The book is divided into an introduction and six chapters. We first lay out the groundwork itself—identifying the crisis in global governance. Our next chapters—particularly on the history of the peace and security debate, the global development agenda and the governance of cyberspace—offer a detailed study of how global governance has been captured by Western elite consensus-making, from the early forays in the development sector to the more contemporary efforts around managing the bounties available on the internet. We then highlight the normative shifts underway in the global order—from international to national; from real to virtual; and from West to East. These processes will alter the assumptions that will underwrite a new world order. Finally, we ask the question: where do we go from here and what role should India play?

In our book, we look to India for answers and alternatives. It is not lost on us that it might seem opportunistic for two Indians to make a case for Indian leadership. But the appeal is too strong to ignore. A soon-to-be relatively wealthy, democratic, multicultural state with an instinct that privileges multilateralism and rules-based order, is the perfect antidote to the increasingly parochial and unilateral mood defining global politics. The rules-based order is shared commitment by all countries to conduct their activities in accordance with agreed rules that evolve over time, such as international law, regional security arrangements, trade agreements, immigration protocols, and cultural arrangements. Its identity as an Asian power gives it a sense of responsibility to ideate and execute equitable global rules that protect the interests of the marginalized. And its civilizational philosophy of Vasudhaiva Kutumbakam—the whole world is one family—have tempered its willingness to use force as a means to achieve its political interests. This is not to say that India itself is insulated from the disruptions underway around the world. We see strident nationalism increasingly defining the Indian political space as well. Nor is an Indian 'rise' inevitable—inequality remains persistent and social risks and economic mismanagement, as well as the risk of divisive politics, continue to daunt the nation. However, providing solutions for the world at large is a fine motivation for Indians to get our house in order. And India's phenomenal transformation over the past seven decades gives us much to be optimistic about. Of course, we are conscious that Indian leadership is not an end in itself, but a means. The twenty-first century requires this new ethic in order to revive the legitimacy and efficacy of global governance. The rise of India must catalyse methods for governance that are more inclusive, democratic and equitable than before and its own national experience must temper the mercantilism embedded in today's market-led growth and development models to one where markets are made to serve humankind. It may be time for a New Delhi Consensus, which is not a metaphor for Indian exceptionalism but a call for a more inclusive and participatory world order. This is the most pressing Indian imperative.

CHAPTER 1

GLOBAL GOVERNANCE AND
ITS DISCONTENTS

Much of the first half of the twentieth century was marked by civil unrest, strife, and war, culminating in the horrors of the Holocaust and Hiroshima—the mass extermination of an ethnic minority and first use of nuclear weapons, that too against a civilian population. Following the devastation of World War II, a few far-sighted leaders were determined to prevent such a state of affairs ever again. Their answer lay in the creation of institutions to manage world affairs after the cataclysm—anchored in an emerging idea that came to be called 'global governance'.

Global governance is a concept that is used to describe the processes and institutions by which the world is governed, and it was always intended to be an amorphous idea, since there is no such thing as a global government to provide such governance. 'Global governance' is a term that tries to impose a sense of order, real or imagined, on a world without an organized system of government. To describe it more precisely we intend to focus on four essential aspects.[1]

The first is history. The institutions of global governance today are those that emerged after the disasters of the first half of the twentieth century. In the first half of the twentieth century, the world saw two world wars, countless civil wars, mass expulsions of populations, and the extermination of civilians whether in gas chambers or through nuclear bombing. Leo Tolstoy had already written the memorable line that if you were not interested in war, it didn't matter; war was

---

[1]Shashi Tharoor, *Pax Indica: India and the World of the 21st Century*, New Delhi: Penguin Books, 2012.

1

interested in you. In the first half of the twentieth century, man's fate seemed to be ineluctably caught up in conflict and war.

Then things changed. In and after 1945, a group of far-sighted leaders were determined to make the second half of the twentieth century different from the first. So they drew up rules to govern international behaviour, and they founded institutions in which different nations could cooperate for the common good. That was the idea of 'global governance'—to foster international cooperation, to elaborate consensual global norms and to establish predictable, universally applicable rules, to the benefit of all.[2]

The principal foundation of the new world order—the keystone of the arch, so to speak—was the United Nations itself. The UN was seen by world leaders as the only possible alternative to the disastrous experiences of the first half of the century. It stood for a world in which people of different nations and cultures could look on each other, not as subjects of fear and suspicion but as potential partners, able to exchange goods and ideas to their mutual benefit. The UN was seen by visionaries like former US President Franklin Delano Roosevelt as the only possible alternative to the disastrous experiences of the first half of the century. As Roosevelt stated in his historic speech to the two US Houses of Congress after the Yalta Conference, the UN would be the alternative to the military alliances, balance-of-power politics and all the arrangements that had led to war so often in the past.[3]

His successor, the US president who presided at the birth of the UN, Harry Truman, argued passionately in San Francisco, when the Charter of the United Nations was signed, that the sacrifices that soldiers had made in World War II would only be justified if you had an arrangement in which all countries felt they had an equal stake. Truman put it clearly: 'You have created a great instrument for peace and security and human progress in the world,' he declared to the assembled signatories of the Charter of the United Nations

---

[2]Id.
[3]Shashi Tharoor, 'Is the United Nations Still Relevant?', Asia Society, 14 June 2004.

in San Francisco on 26 June 1945. '…If we fail to use it, we shall betray all those who have died so that we might meet here in freedom and safety to create it. If we seek to use it selfishly—for the advantage of any one nation or any small group of nations—we shall be equally guilty of that betrayal.'[4]

'We all have to recognize,' Truman declared, 'no matter how great our strength, that we must deny ourselves the license to do always as we please. No one nation…can or should expect any special privilege which harms any other nation… Unless we are all willing to pay that price, no organization for world peace can accomplish its purpose. And what a reasonable price that is!'

That was a very clear and strong vision, but between vision and fulfilment there inevitably falls a shadow. Paradise did not descend on earth in 1945. We all know that tyranny and warfare continued, and that billions of people still live in extreme and degrading poverty. But the overall record of the second half of the twentieth century is one of amazing advances. A third world war did not occur. The world economy expanded as never before. There was astonishing technological progress. Many in the industrialized world now enjoy a level of prosperity, and have access to a range of experiences that their grandparents could scarcely have dreamed of; and even in the developing world, there has been spectacular economic growth. Child mortality has been reduced. Literacy has spread. The peoples of the developing world threw off the yoke of colonialism, and those of the Soviet Bloc won political freedom. Democracy and human rights are not yet universal, but they are now much more the norm than the exception. And yet we all know there is still a long way to go.[5]

The second important feature is the global nature of the determining forces of today's world. There are broadly two contending and even contradictory forces in the world in which we live today:

---

[4]'1945: The San Francisco Conference', United Nations, accessed 15 June 2019, https://www.un.org/en/sections/history-united-nations-charter/1945-san-francisco-conference/index.html.

[5]Shashi Tharoor, 'India's Role in the Emerging World Order', Indian Council of World Affairs, 26 March 2010.

on the one hand are the forces of convergence, the increasing knitting together of the world through globalization, modern communications and trade, and on the other are the opposite forces of disruption, of religious polarization, of the talk of the clash of civilizations, and of terrorism. The two forces, one pulling us together, the other pulling us apart, are both concurrent phenomena of our times, and these are taking place in a world in which—to take an Indian example—the terrorist attacks in Mumbai on 26/11 were in many ways emblematic of this paradoxical phenomenon. The terrorists of 26/11 used the instruments of globalization and convergence—the ease of communications, GPS systems and mobile telephone technology, five-star hotels frequented by the transnational business elite, and so on—as instruments for their fanatical agenda. Similarly, on 9/11 in New York, rather than as forces to bring the world closer together, the terrorists also used similar tools—the jet aircraft being crashed into those towers emblematic of global capitalism, while the doomed victims of the planes made frantic mobile phone telephone calls to their loved ones.[6]

Both 9/11 and 26/11 were grotesque moments of disruption exploiting and undermining convergence. At the same time, 9/11 had already reminded us of the cliché of the global village, because it proved that we are living in a village in which a fire that started in a dusty cave somewhere in Afghanistan, in one corner of the world, could be strong enough to melt the steel girders holding up two of the tallest skyscrapers at the opposite end of the global village. We have to recognize both the positive and negative forces of the world today, and from it, a consciousness of the increasing mutual interdependence that characterises our age.[7]

Global governance therefore rests on the realization that security is not indeed just about threats from enemy states or hostile powers, but that there are common phenomena that really cut across borders and affect us all. In fact, in Kofi Annan's days at the UN, he used

---

[6]Id.
[7]Id.

to use the phrase 'problems without passports'[8]—the notion that the world is full of problems that cannot be solved by any one country or any one group of countries, however rich or powerful, and which are unavoidably the shared responsibility of humankind.

This idea had gained much currency through the 1990s and through the first decade of the twenty-first century. There is an obvious list of such problems: terrorism itself, the proliferation of weapons of mass destruction, of the degradation of our common environment, of climate change (quite obviously because we cannot put up a fence in the sky to sequester our own climate), of persistent poverty and haunting hunger, of human rights and human wrongs, of mass illiteracy and massive displacement. There are financial and economic crises (because the financial contagion becomes a virus that spreads from one country to others), the risk of trade protectionism, refugee movements, drug trafficking. And we must not overlook epidemic disease: the SARS epidemic in China a few years ago, the Ebola virus in Africa thereafter. With SARS, initially there was an attempt to keep it quiet, but it was very easy for the virus to hop on a plane and arrive in Toronto, and suddenly it became a global phenomenon, no longer something that could be contained in any one country. The same is true of AIDS, the same was true of swine flu (H1N1) and is true of Ebola today; and the recent scare of a global epidemic of incurable influenza points to the continuing need for responses and solutions that transcend all divisions.[9]

Today, whether one is from India or from Indiana, whether one lives in Narita or Noida, it is simply not realistic to think only in terms of one's own country. Global forces press in from every conceivable direction; people, goods and ideas cross borders and cover vast distances with ever greater frequency, speed and ease. The internet is emblematic of an era in which what happens in New York or New Caledonia—from democratic advances to deforestation to the fight against AIDS—can affect lives in New Delhi. As has been

---

[8]Kofi A. Annan, 'Problems Without Passports', *Foreign Policy*, 9 November 2009.
[9]Id.

observed about water pollution, we all live downstream.[10]

Indians therefore realize they have a growing stake in international developments. To put it another way, the food we grow and we eat, the air we breathe, and our health, security, prosperity and quality of life are increasingly affected by what happens beyond our borders. And that means we can simply no longer afford to be indifferent about the rest of the world, however distant other countries may appear.

The third aspect is the emergence of institutions and processes that reflect this reality of increasing global convergence. Global institutions benefit from the legitimacy that comes from their universality. Since all countries belong to it, the UN enjoys a standing in the eyes of the world that gives its collective actions and decisions a legitimacy that no individual government enjoys beyond its own borders. But the institutions of global governance have been expanding beyond the UN itself. There are selective inter-governmental mechanisms like the Group of Eight (G8), military alliances like the North Atlantic Treaty Organization (NATO), subregional groupings like the Economic Community of West African States (ECOWAS), one-issue alliances like the Nuclear Suppliers Group (NSG). Writers connect under PEN International, soccer players in Fédération Internationale de Football Association (FIFA), athletes under the International Olympic Committee (IOC), mayors in the world organization of United Cities and Local Governments (UCLG). Bankers listen to the Bank of International Settlements (BIS) and businessmen to the International Accounting Standards Board (IASB). The process of regulating human activity above and beyond national boundaries has never been more widespread.[11]

This is occurring at a time when we have this huge list of problems without passports that call for solutions that cross frontiers. Individual countries may prefer not to deal with such problems directly or alone, but they are impossible to ignore. So handling them together internationally is the obvious way of ensuring they

---

[10]Id.
[11]Id.

are tackled; it is also the only way. Perhaps we can call for 'blueprints without borders': some scholars of international affairs have begun to speak of an idea they call 'responsible sovereignty', the notion that nations must cooperate across borders to safeguard common resources and to tackle common threats. As far back as 1992, former UN Secretary General Boutros Boutros-Ghali in his report 'An Agenda For Peace' stated that 'the time of absolute and exclusive sovereignty has passed'.[12] The issue of sovereignty will have to be faced.

In parallel is emerging a fourth idea, that there are universally applicable norms that underpin our notion of world order. Sovereignty itself, however understood, is one, and linked to that idea is the principle of non-interference in other countries' internal affairs, equality and mutual benefit, non-aggression and coexistence across different political systems, the very principles originally articulated by India's first prime minister, Pandit Jawaharlal Nehru, in his Panchsheel doctrine with the People's Republic of China in 1954. (Today's China does not speak very much of the Panchsheel, the Five Principles of Peaceful Co-Existence, but its principles are embedded in the Chinese concept of a 'harmonious world'.) At the same time, there has evolved a new set of global norms of governance that complement these principles, including respect for human rights, transparency and accountability, rule of law, equitable development based on economic freedom, and at least to most nations, political democracy. These are seen as broadly desirable for all countries to aspire to, and while no one suggests that they can or should be imposed on any nation, fulfilling them is seen as admirable by most of the world and broadly accepted as evidence of successful governance.

Now these four broad aspects are descriptive of global governance, rather than prescriptive. But we would suggest that we should examine them in the context of a significant change in the way the world has evolved since the end of World War II. While we have all benefited from the global governance structures that evolved since 1945, we still have to recognize that these reflect the realities of 1945 and

---

[12]R. C. Longworth, 'End of Sovereignty', *Chicago Tribune*, 19 September 1993.

not of today, when a large number of emerging powers have begun asserting themselves on the world stage. That is why the time has come to think seriously about the challenges and the opportunities in global governance in the future, at a time when we are witnessing the weakening of traditional power centres in the world.

As we look around the world of today, we cannot fail to note the increase in the number of major powers across the world since the structures of the international system were put in place in 1945. It is an undeniable fact that the emerging powers have moved very much from the periphery to the centre of global discourse and global responsibility, and they have now a legitimate and an increasingly voluble desire to share power and responsibility in the global system. The dominance of a handful of small industrialized Western countries, especially in the international financial institutions (the so-called Bretton Woods Institutions), looks increasingly anomalous in a world where economic dynamism has shifted irresistibly from the West to the East. (In arguing the case for more democratization of the international system, we would like to add here, parenthetically, the increasing role of what are called social forces—NGOs, civil society movements, multinational corporations, transnational terrorist groups—which we must also take note of in our discussion on global governance.) With all of this, and the emergence of new powers and forces which, unlike China, were omitted from the high table in 1945, we have clearly reached a point where there is need for a system redesign of global governance to ensure that all countries benefit. Clearly, what we in India are looking for is a more inclusive multilateralism, and not, as some American and Chinese observers once suggested, a G2 condominium.[13]

As Indians, we have no doubt that we must be proactive on issues that are being agitated across the world if we are to create and maintain the society we want at home. And our success at home is the best guarantee that we will be respected and effective abroad.

Because the distinction between domestic and international is

---

[13]Shashi Tharoor, *Pax Indica*.

less and less meaningful in today's world, when India thinks of global governance, it must also think of its domestic implications. The ultimate purpose of any country's foreign policy is to promote the security and well-being of its own citizens. India wants a world that gives us the conditions of peace and security that will permit us to grow and flourish, safe from foreign depredations but open to external opportunities. This is the perspective from which India approaches global governance.

At the same time there is a consensus in our country that India should seek to continue to contribute to international security and prosperity, to a well-ordered and equitable world, and to democratic, sustainable development for all. These objectives now need to be pursued while taking into account twenty-first-century realities: the end of the Cold War, the dawning of the Information Age (also known as the Digital Age), the ease of worldwide travel and widespread migration, the blurring of national boundaries by movements, networks and forces transcending state frontiers, the advent of Islamist terrorism as a pan-global force, the irresistible rise of China as an incipient superpower while retaining its political authoritarianism, the global consciousness of 'soft power', and the end to the prospect of military conflict between any two of the major nation states.

Emerging powers like India are crucial actors in the world's efforts to address a matrix of challenges—several interconnected socio-economic and environmental issues that pose a threat not just to the concept of nation states, but to humanity—because they have had to engage with them constantly. We live in a world, after all, of poverty and inequality, malnutrition and epidemic disease, in which, as of mid-2018, the number of people displaced from their homes was seventy million—higher than the number of casualties in World War II.[14]

And yet, we must acknowledge that the legitimacy and universality of the institutions of the postwar era were underwritten by America,

---

[14]Adrian Edwards, 'Global forced displacement tops 70 million', UNHCR, 19 June 2019, https://www.unhcr.org/news/stories/2019/6/5d08b6614/global-forced-displacement-tops-70-million.html.

the sole superpower of the late twentieth century. The international liberal order, as it is popularly known, was designed and crafted by the Atlantic countries, first to cement their political and commercial interests, and later as a bulwark against communism as practised by the Soviet system. Global governance was designed to be flexible and open; it was based on multilateral institutions which promoted democracy and free markets. The idea and its execution were compelling: innovation flourished, new frontiers of human rights were established and for a time it seemed like peace would be the status quo. It was, as some believed in the heady post-cold war days, 'the end of history'.[15]

The twenty-first century, however, is different: The paradigms that allowed the world to grow following World War II are now besieged by numerous challenges. Inequality, identity and technology have intersected in an ugly manner. Globalization, once believed to be the panacea for the world's problems, seems to be turning on itself; and its principal tools—the internet, technology and capital—have been embraced by those that seek to disrupt the status quo. Revisionist powers like China are threatening to undermine a system that was fashioned without their consent. The Global Financial Crisis (GFC) of 2008 and American fatigue in engaging with multiple conflicts around the world are leading to a new phase in global relations. The Bretton Woods Institutions are now struggling to respond to new actors and voices. The old institutions, systems and actors, and the new challengers are unable to agree on the political economy of a new global order, resulting in the weakening of multilateral institutions. Simultaneously, states are now trying to create new forums to manage global affairs; there is a proliferation of new groupings and clubs such as the Group of Twenty (G20), Brazil, Russia, India, China and South Africa (BRICS), India Brazil South Africa Forum (IBSA), Shanghai Cooperation Organisation (SCO), Bay of Bengal Initiative for Multi-Sectoral Co-operation (BIMSTEC) among others, which

---

[15]Francis Fukuyama, 'The End of History?', *National Interest*, Summer 1989, pp. 3–18, https://www.embl.de/aboutus/science_society/discussion/discussion_2006/ref1-22june06.pdf.

aim to supplement, complement and sometimes even undermine established structures.

A CRISIS OF LEGITIMACY

Today, a crisis of legitimacy has plagued international institutions and relations as old powers are unable or unwilling to cede power to new actors.

As we have noted, following the end of World War II, the United Nations emerged as the single most important institution in the realm of global governance. Its efficacy in largely preventing wars and improving human development conditions, as well as setting the global agenda in whole new areas of transformation—from ending racial discrimination to safeguarding the environment—deserves much credit. The Millennium Development Goals (MDGs) adopted in 2000 were a good example of both the UN's convening power and its ability to persuade governments to focus on realizable outcomes. In recent years, the percentage of underweight children less than five years old in developing countries fell from 28 per cent in 1990 to 17 per cent in 2013,[16] the number of children who died before their fifth birthday fell from 12.7 million in 1990 to 6.3 million in 2013 and the number of women who died from pregnancy or childbirth fell from 532,000 in 1990 to more than 300,000 in 2015,[17] the number of people who died from HIV fell by 43 per cent between 2003 and 2015, malaria deaths fell 48 per cent between 2000 and 2015[18] and the global middle classes are exploding, from 1.8 billion in 2010 to an expected 3.2 billion in 2020.[19]

True power in the UN rests with the Permanent Members of the Security Council—a select club of five nations which largely represent the victors of World War II: the US, UK, France, Russia and China. Within the ambit of this organization, the impunity that these states enjoy in determining the agenda globally is enormous, and

---

[16]Figures taken from Ian Bremmer, 'Who Can Run the UN?', *Time*, 21 July 2016.
[17]Id.
[18]Id.
[19]Mario Pezzini, 'An emerging middle class', *OECD Observer*, 2012.

also inconsistent with the rapidly changing economic, political and demographic developments that mark the new century. This power structure has shaped the politics of the United Nations ever since its conception. During the Cold War, most disagreements in the UN centred on the world's division into two broad camps—the Soviet and the American. Following the collapse of the USSR in 1991, however, the inheritors of the liberal world order—the US, UK and France— collectively exercised a dominance in decision-making that had far-reaching consequences and involved very limited accountability. The sanctions imposed against Iraq in response to the Kuwait invasion in 1990 were an early indication of the new power realities; while the US and its allies carried out several indiscriminate bombing campaigns in Iraq, notably in 1991, 1998 and 2003, the sanctions which were imposed limited Iraqis' access to food and essential medicines. The ensuing humanitarian disaster was so extreme and long-lasting that some high-ranking UN officials resigned, claiming that the UN itself was complicit in war crimes.

These power politics are reflected within the decision-making process of the UN as well, reflecting the dominance of the veto power enjoyed by the Permanent Members (also known as the Permanent Five, Big Five, or P5). In 2006, when the race for the UN secretary general was on between Ban Ki-moon and Shashi Tharoor, all it took for the latter to withdraw was a negative vote from the US, effectively rendering meaningless the desires of every other member nation.[20] The US is far from being the only country to use the UN to achieve its own interests. Russia has used its veto power several times to prevent international condemnation of its aggressive geopolitical actions across the world, most recently in Syria, and China continued to needle India for years by preventing the designation of Masood Azhar as a terrorist (finally relenting in mid-2019). These events have slowly given credence to the perception that liberal internationalism was but a facade, intended to mask

---

[20]Saurabh Shukla, 'UN top job: Why India's candidate Shashi Tharoor had to drop out of the race,' *India Today*, 16 October 2006.

the reality that true power in state relations was still a function of military might.

The United Nations is far from being the only forum where these power politics play out. Another cause of consternation amongst nations is the hypocrisy of the developed countries in the area of multilateral trade. The birth of the WTO in Uruguay was meant to signal a new dispensation in which labour, capital and goods could traverse the globe freely. And yet, at a time when the world's developing and least developed countries continue to be scarred by food insecurity and diseases, it is these very institutions that prevent them from developing national policies to effectively address them. Take, for example, the question of patents and access to medicine; the Universal Declaration of Human Rights declares that, 'Everyone has the right to a standard of living adequate for the health and well-being of himself and of his family...' By implication, this must mean that everyone has a right to access affordable medicine and healthcare. However, the mercantilist economies in the developed world have different ambitions. While lifesaving drugs are developed in the Western world, their accessibility is significantly constrained by the current pharmaceutical patent system, globally exported through implementation of the World Trade Organization's Agreement on Trade-Related Aspects of Intellectual Property Rights Agreement (TRIPS), and the financial means required to obtain them.

A major consequence of the patent protection awarded under TRIPS was the high price of medicines, making them inaccessible to the average person, especially in developing and low-income countries. Attempts to remedy this were made in the 2001 Doha Development Round, which sought to better define the boundaries of compulsory licensing, which would allow states to prioritize public health over patent terms. The Doha Declaration identified the need to resolve the conundrum for countries lacking domestic manufacturing capabilities yet desperately needing medications for epidemics such as AIDS. Reaching consensus on this, however, created great debate among TRIPS council members. The US led an effort to restrict the Doha Declaration to certain diseases, namely, AIDS, malaria, tuberculosis, and other infectious diseases creating epidemics. Further, the US worked to limit the number of countries that could benefit from the importation of generic medications. The impact of these developments is significant in terms of cost per patient in all countries. Take, for example, Sofosbuvir, a medicine that is part of a treatment for hepatitis C, which can cause a potentially lethal infection of the liver. While the production cost of Sofosbuvir is estimated to be $68–$136 for a course of treatment, the company that holds the patent sells it for up to $84,000.[21] The cancer drug Imatinib, sold under the brand name Gleevec, also demonstrates the huge differences between a monopoly price and a generic price. In India, the Supreme Court refused to grant a patent for this product— keeping the prices affordable for millions of Indians. In South Africa, however, an individual may pay over $3,227 per patient per month for the same medicine.[22] In the US, the price of Gleevec has nearly tripled since its introduction in 2001; it cost $146,000 in 2017.[23]

The attempts to stall the adverse impact of climate change tell a similar story. Today, industrialized countries owe their prosperity to their previous pattern of industrial growth without regard to environmental consequences—they are responsible for more than a century of historical emissions, which have accumulated in the atmosphere since the start of the Industrial Revolution—and a high level of current emissions. The greenhouse gas emissions of one US citizen were equal to those of nineteen Indians or Sri Lankans, thirty Pakistanis, seventeen Maldivians, 107 Bangladeshis, 134 Bhutanese, or 269 Nepalis in 1996.[24] Two decades later, things do not seem to have improved much; estimates suggest that the poorest half of the global population—around 3.5 billion people—are responsible

---

[21]Rupali Mukherjee, 'Gilead's $1,000 pill gets patent in India', *Times of India*, 10 May 2016.
[22]E. T. Hoen, 'A Victory for Global Public Health in the Indian Supreme Court, in JPHP, 2013, pp. 370–73.
[23]Wang Zichen, 'Spotlight: Novartis freezes drug prices, but its Gleevec already unaffordable', *Xinhuanet*, 20 July 2018.
[24]Anil Agarwal, 'Climate Change: A Challenge to India's Economy', New Delhi: Centre for Science and Environment, accessed 15 June 2019, https://cdn.cseindia.org/userfiles/cse_briefing.pdf.

for only around 10 per cent of total global emissions attributed to individual consumption, yet live overwhelmingly in the countries which are most vulnerable to climate change.

India is probably most emblematic of these contradictions; the average Indian's coal consumption is around 20 per cent that of the average US citizen, and 34 per cent that of the average Organisation for Economic Co-operation and Development (OECD) citizen. And yet, in international negotiations, India finds itself caught in a shrill and binary debate pitching growth against climate. The debate itself stems from the inability or unwillingness of the established industrial powers to cede 'carbon space'—the amount of carbon dioxide-equivalent emissions that can be released into the Earth's atmosphere without triggering dangerous climate change.[25] Not only do developed nations refuse to take into account their historic role in aggravating climate change, they continue to actively resist policies in developing countries which may help them cope with the effects through the multilateral order they exercise power over. A case in point is the US–India solar panel dispute where the provision of domestic procurement in India's solar policy was successfully challenged before the WTO.[26] Taken together with China's flood of cheap panels, this case has effectively retarded India's ability to generate a domestic policy for renewable solar power.

These examples help explain the waning level of conviction in the legitimacy of these institutions—a reflection of their inability to represent a more diverse cross section of interests. Most nations now feel that these institutions have only represented the interests of a few developed countries at the expense of their own growth.

A CRISIS OF REPRESENTATION
This lack of legitimacy is directly related to the crisis of

---

[25] Vivan Sharan, 'The false debate on India's energy consumption', ORF, 10 November 2015.
[26] Recently, India won a similar case against the US as well. See D. Ravi Kanth, 'India wins solar case against US at WTO', *Livemint*, 27 June 2019. This is indicative of how developing countries are also developing the capacity to navigate multilateral rules. Most developing states continue to lack this ability.

representation that plagues these institutions. According to the Asian Development Bank (ADB), the Asian share of global gross domestic product (GDP) will double from 26 per cent in 2011 to 52 per cent in 2050, meaning that the majority of all economic activity on Earth will occur in Asia.[27] If history has any lessons to teach us, it is that international power shifts risk begetting conflict and change in the nature of representation. Today's power structures reflect twentieth-century power politics, in which the US occupies the driver's seat. While Russia and China represent two non-Western countries on the Security Council (though Russia, as a white European country, is still arguably part of the Global North), there is no representation from Africa, Latin America or rising Asian powers like India and Japan. The inequality of representation in multilateral institutions is reflected in the unchallenged and apparently permanent leadership of the World Bank and the International Monetary Fund (IMF) by nationals of the US and the EU, chosen by their governments rather than by the broader membership of these organizations. After a long-fought battle, voting quotas were adjusted slightly in 2016 to give China a larger say along with minor increases for other BRICS countries. However, these changes also adversely affected some African and South American nations, which saw their voting power decline. Further, while the increase in quotas might reflect some acceptance amongst the transatlantic powers about the growing influence of emerging powers, the US treasury continues to hold veto power over these institutions, regularly using them for geopolitical purposes.

And we really will need to see reform; the G20 Summit in Pittsburgh in September 2009 agreed in principle a systemic redesign of the international financial structure, and in some ways that was what legitimized it in the eyes of many of us as the premier forum for international economic cooperation. The G20 was seen as a meaningful platform for North–South dialogue, because the South is not completely outweighed by the North in the composition of the G20.

---

[27]'Asia 2050: Realizing the Asian Century', Asian Development Bank, August 2011.

The Pittsburgh Summit 2009 took a concrete decision to reform the Bretton Woods Institutions. The intention was clear: to pursue regulatory reform but also to dilute the disproportionate power wielded by the old 'developed' economies of the Western world at a time when the 'emerging' economies had not yet emerged. Voting share targets were in fact agreed in Pittsburgh—to shift 5 per cent of the IMF quota share and 3 per cent of the World Bank's voting power from the developed world to the developing and transition economies. However, this actually falls short of what India, along with Brazil, Russia and China, have called for; the BRIC countries have demanded 7 per cent of the IMF quota share, and 6 per cent of the World Bank's.[28] Nonetheless, they accepted the Pittsburgh outcome as an acceptable first step towards the longer-term objective of broad parity between the developed countries and the developing/transition economies. But after the Pittsburgh decision in 2008, delays in the US Senate ratification process meant that it was only in December 2015 that a modest change was finally effected. If it takes seven years for a first step, it does not augur well for the major change that is eventually sought.[29]

A backlash against the lack of representation in international institutions has been growing for several years now. The Bandung Conference in 1955 and Brioni meeting in 1956, which led to the birth of the Non-Aligned Movement in Belgrade in 1961, was instrumental in shaping a collective determination that countries which had recently emerged from the shackles of colonialism would not get drawn into a conflict in which they had no interest. A parallel process during this time was the emergence of the G77 in 1964 at the United Nations Conference on Trade and Development led by countries like China and India, both of whom sought to

---

[28]'Thierry Soret, 'Governance Arrangements for Global Economic Challenges: Where Do we Stand? A Political Science Perspective', A UNDP/ODS Working Paper, New York: Office of Development Studies, UNDP, 2009.

[29]IMF, 'Press Release: IMF Managing Director Christine Lagarde Welcomes U.S. Congressional Approval of the 2010 Quota and Governance Reforms', 18 December 2015, accessed 15 June 2019, https://www.imf.org/en/News/Articles/2015/09/14/01/49/pr15573.

lead a coalition of countries who felt that their concerns were not adequately represented at the UN and aspired to create a more equal and fair global economic and trade order centred on development.

Towards the beginning of the twenty-first century, as economic power drifted towards India and China, their dissatisfaction was now severe and stark and certainly more vocal. This dramatic shift was perhaps most accurately captured by the Goldman Sachs economist Jim O'Neill, who bluntly argued that the size of these emerging economies raised important questions about their lack of representation in global governance. Robert Zoellick, former president of the World Bank, spoke almost prophetically when he said that, 'If 1989 saw the end of the "Second World" with Communism's demise, then 2009 saw the end of what was known as the "Third World."[30] We are now in a new, fast-evolving multipolar world economy—in which some developing countries are emerging as economic powers; others are moving towards becoming additional poles of growth; and some are struggling to attain their potential within this new system.'

States are now acutely aware of this reality and are seeking to create new forums to manage the world. There is a proliferation of new groupings and clubs such as G20, BRICS, IBSA, SCO, among others, which aim to rewrite the rules of global governance. The major emerging powers are no longer willing to put up with this lack of representation.

These powers are increasingly throwing their weight around in international institutions in order to alter the balance of power in these established multilateral structures. During the Doha trade rounds in 2001, developing countries stalled trade negotiations as they felt that the pressure from industrialized western countries to liberalize their markets in agriculture, services and patents would put their own development trajectories at risk. Similarly, China, which has emerged as the world's most powerful revisionist force, has gone

---

[30]Robert B. Zoellick, 'The End of the Third World?: Modernizing Multilateralism for a Multipolar World', Washington DC: Woodrow Wilson International Center for Scholars, 14 April 2010, accessed 15 June 2019, https://www.wilsoncenter.org/sites/default/files/Zoellick.pdf.

about setting up new institutions such as the SCO and the Asian Infrastructure Investment Bank (AIIB) as alternatives to the World Bank and other Western-led multilateral institutions. India has joined China in establishing the BRICS New Development Bank (NDB). Successive economic crises, beginning with the Asian Financial Crisis in 1998[31], have produced a backlash against global economic institutions like the IMF and against states like America and Britain, which were viewed by the Asian region as the prime culprits of the crises and the subsequent austerity policies that crippled their economies.

The so-called Bretton Woods Institutions—the World Bank and the IMF, set up in the New Hampshire town of that name by the Allied Powers of World War II in 1944—have long rested on a cosy deal within the Western world, under which the former would always be headed by an American and the latter by a West European. The twelve managing directors of the IMF since then have all been Europeans (five from France, two from Sweden, and one each from Belgium, Germany, Netherlands, Spain and most recently from Bulgaria). All eleven presidents of the World Bank, needless to say, have been American.

America's continued dominance may well reflect its status as a genuine economic superpower, but Europe's is a reflection of arrangements that have long been questionable. The fact is that Europeans have dominated the IMF's Executive Board, the body responsible for the organization's day-to-day management. Despite accounting for barely 20 per cent of global GDP in purchasing power parity (PPP) terms, the member states of the European Union collectively account for 31 per cent of the votes on the IMF Board, and in practice cast up to 36 per cent of the votes[32] (since there are only twenty-four directors, smaller countries entrust their voting

---

[31]Michael Carson and John Clark, 'Asian Financial Crisis: July 1997–December 1998', Federal Reserve History, 22 November 2013, accessed 15 June 2019, https://www.federalreservehistory.org/essays/asian_financial_crisis.

[32]David Woodward, *IMF Voting Reform: Need, Opportunity and Options*, G-24 Discussion Paper Series, No. 49, New York and Geneva: December 2007, https://unctad.org/en/docs/gdsmdpbg2420077_en.pdf.

rights to the bigger ones—thus Italy casts the votes of Greece, Albania, Timor Leste, and Malta, and the Netherlands votes on behalf of a group that includes Israel, Armenia, and the Ukraine.) This 36 per cent vote share gives the EU countries an undue advantage in the race to get the 50.1 per cent needed to elect an IMF head.

The irony is that Europe is a borrower from the IMF. Instead of the insolvency of European countries like Greece, Spain or Ireland leading to a reduction in the EU's voting weight on the Board, the problems of Europe were cynically used to justify the appointment as the managing director of Christine Lagarde, from France, in 2011. Lagarde's successor, the Bulgarian Kristalina Georgieva, was the EU nominee and was appointed despite the fact that there were recommendations from Asia and elsewhere. Yet, it is precisely because of Europe's financial problems, Europeans argue, that a European is needed to head the IMF to deal effectively with them. (Wolfgang Münchau in the *Financial Times* explained that an IMF boss 'will have to bang heads together in meetings of European finance ministers, and will have to converse effectively with some notoriously difficult heads of government and state.')[33] Oddly, the same argument was never used when the 'Asian flu' was being dealt with by a European IMF director, Michel Camdessus, who was clearly unfamiliar with the mores of the continent. Had Asia's economic troubles in the late 1990s led New Delhi to call for an Asian IMF head, we would have been laughed out of court. The acronym IMF, it used to be said by shamefaced Third Worlders, stands for 'Insolvents Must Fawn'. With a European in charge, this may have to be amended to 'Insolvents May Flourish'.

When Lagarde was appointed the new chief of an institution supposedly controlled by 189 member nations, her appointment discriminated against 90 per cent of the world's population. As the Venezuelan commentator Moisés Naím trenchantly wrote, before the decision was taken: 'In its daily work, the IMF demands that the governments that seek its financial assistance adopt market principles

---

[33]Wolfgang Münchau, 'The IMF needs another European Head', *Financial Times*, 16 May 2011.

of efficiency, transparency and meritocracy in exchange for its help. Yet that same institution selects its leader through a process completely at odds with those values.'[34]

The 2008 financial crisis was another important event, which prompted greater demands for representation in these institutions from developing countries (who saw the financial policies of the north Atlantic countries as the primary cause for global economic fluctuations). It certainly seems incontestable that the recent global financial crisis showed that the surveillance of risk by international institutions and early warning mechanisms are needed for all countries. In other words, it is important that, in the context of global governance, the developing countries should have a voice in overseeing the global financial performance of all nations, rather than it simply being a case of the rich supervising the economic delinquency of the poor. The IMF remains, in the words of India's former chief economic advisor, Arvind Subramaniam, 'an important multilateral institution that remains basically non-universal in its legitimacy, deficient in wisdom and objectivity, and unduly politicised.'[35] The dominance of a handful of small industrialized Western countries in the international financial institutions looks increasingly anomalous in a world where economic dynamism has shifted irresistibly from the West to the East. We have clearly reached a point where there is need for a system redesign of global governance in the macro-economic arena, to ensure that all countries can participate in a manner commensurate with their capacity. The slow pace of reforms that would grant these economies a larger vote and quota shares in the IMF and World Bank has inevitably produced a search for outside options, specifically new multilateral development banks.

Similarly, at the Rio Earth Summit in 1992, when the UN Framework Convention on Climate Change (UNFCCC) was being negotiated, several developing countries successfully banded together

---

[34]Moises Naim, 'In the IMF succession battle, a stench of colonialism', *Washington Post*, 20 May 2011.
[35]'Arvind Subramanian: The IMF–Keynes' non-candidate', *Business Standard*, 20 January 2013.

to argue for principles like that of 'common but differentiated responsibility' (which would recognize the historic role developed countries played in aggravating climate change). This pattern of cooperation continued through several rounds of meetings, allowing developing countries to set favourable terms in the context of financing, capacity building and emission cut targets; for example, when ozone standards were being strengthened in the mid-1990s, developing countries together argued that tighter controls should be contingent on increased financing.[36]

The legitimacy crisis of the global regulatory framework thus entails a risk that the established structures could be hamstrung, or indeed replaced, by North–South differences or by other competing regional arrangements.

Interestingly, globalization and the spread of liberal values have themselves allowed rising powers to threaten the dominant position of a few countries. Following World War II, the idea of sovereign equality came to signify the equal representation of states in international norm-making. This one idea of multipolarity has come to represent an important element of institutional legitimacy for international governance. The first BRIC Summit in June 2009 expressed support for 'a more democratic and just multipolar world order'.[37] Successive BRICS communiqués have continued to strike this chord, as have declarations by the Non-Aligned Movement. In 2010, even the US was beginning to confront this reality. Former US Secretary of State Hillary Clinton observed during an official visit to New Zealand that, 'we see shifting of power to a more multipolar world as opposed to the Cold War model of a bipolar world'[38]

Even as international institutions reformed slowly, new informal groupings were cropping up, revealing that there was growing

---

[36]Edward A. Parson, *Protecting the Ozone Layer: Science and Strategy*, Oxford: Oxford University Press, 2003.
[37]Vladimir Radyuhin, 'Changing order', *Frontline*, Vol. 26, Issue 14, 04–17 July 2009.
[38]Hillary Clinton, 'Remarks at Christchurch Town Hall Meeting with Students and Civic Leaders,' U.S. Department of State, 5 November 2010, accessed 15 June 2019, https://2009-2017.state.gov/secretary/20092013clinton/rm/2010/11/150450.htm.

recognition amongst developed countries that new economic power centres in a globalized economy necessitated that global financial woes could only be tackled collectively. The birth of the G20 was an important landmark—soon after the global financial crisis of 1997–99, the membership of the Financial Stability Board (FSB), Basel Committee and other key standard-setting bodies was reviewed and expanded to include all G20 countries, with developing countries represented for the first time.

However, this crisis of representation does not manifest only in institutions run by the victors of World War II. As the world we know becomes increasingly multipolar and fragmented, no clear twenty-first century template has emerged on how to handle these challenges. Asia itself is highly fragmented, with several powers vying for influence—India, Japan, China, Indonesia are all locked into a simmering competition over who shapes the norms and rules of the region and its subregions. Leadership over new Asian institutions such as the BRICS NDB, the AIIB or regional connectivity projects like the BRI are increasingly being dominated by a rising China, which sees very little space for multipolarity within Asia even as it demands it in old institutions and within the old order.

Emerging powers are not simply confronting outdated models of global governance but are engaged in a complex relationship with the global economy which transcends boundaries and is characterized by overlapping roles and the influence of old and new institutions and actors. The rise of transnational corporations (TNCs) and civil society organizations, for example, has far reaching implications for the global order. How institutions address the demands brings us to the next crisis, that of the collective.

THE CRISIS OF THE COLLECTIVE

The very same institutions which underwrote the spread of globalization also created the space for power and authority to be diffused to a variety of non-state actors. Richard N. Haass, president of the Council on Foreign Relations (CFR), states that 'the principal characteristic of twenty-first century international relations is turning out to be nonpolarity: a world dominated not by one or two or even several states but rather by dozens of actors possessing and exercising various kinds of power.'[39]

This non-delegated fragmentation of state authority can come in different forms. Regionalism is the most evident; the formation of ASEAN or the SCO represent new institutions created along geographic lines. However, the emergence of new stakeholders, cutting across geographic boundaries, is a more complex phenomenon. This includes the rise of non-state actors: private actors such as transnational corporations, non-governmental organizations and terrorist groups such as Al-Qaeda and the Islamic State (ISIS). This diffusion of power is not necessarily undesirable or inefficient; to a large extent it has the potential to address some of the governance deficits prevalent in the current international order. However, it is unclear if new powers have the appetite to put forward a comprehensive international agenda uniquely distinct from the incumbents', considering that many of them are still 'rising' and have a host of complex domestic governance challenges back at home. What we have then is a dangerous situation; where no one power can claim legitimacy over an international order and a host of rising and quasi powers who do not see it within their capacity or interests to do so.

Rising powers such as India, Brazil, Indonesia and China seek to challenge some aspects of the global architectures in order to accommodate their own rise. These powers by their own claims 'were not present' when the current international architecture was set up. Today, various inter-regional groupings have charted their own governance agenda—such as the G20 and more prominently the BRICS and the ASEAN. Increasingly, the financial requirements of Asian countries for economic growth are being delivered by Asian institutions. Take, for example, the Chiang Mai Initiative (CMI), an alternative source of financial support created by the Association of Southeast Asian Nations Plus Three (ASEAN+3), which was organized with the support of China and Japan.

---

[39]Richard N. Haass, 'The Age of Nonpolarity', *Foreign Affairs*, May/June 2008.

While regionalism is one new collective implicating the global order, another strong trend is noticeable: sub-national actors now inhabit what can only be known as a Westphalia-plus world order where technology and globalization itself are catalysing and creating organizations and subnational actors like cities, which work with or against nation states within global governance architectures.

While the global political economy in the twentieth century was premised on the exercise of sovereignty by Westphalian nation states, today it is driven by market forces determined by private transnational corporations. As the epicentre of governance shifts away from state-led models, such TNCs have a greater say in how global issues are discussed and resolved. Increasingly they are also determining the scope and direction of domestic policy.

The 2,000 largest companies in 2019 accounted for more than $40 trillion in revenues and upwards of $186 trillion in global assets.[40] These firms employed ninety million people worldwide. If Walmart were a country, it would be the twenty-fourth largest by GDP.[41] A majority of these TNCs continue to reside in developed countries: nearly 75 per cent of the Fortune Global 500 list are based out of G7 countries.[42] According to *The Economist*, multinational corporations (MNCs) account for 2 per cent of global employment, but own or orchestrate the supply chains that account for 50 per cent of world trade, 40 per cent of the value of the West's stock markets, and the majority of the world's intellectual property.[43]

Ultimately, this implies that TNCs from developed countries have a larger say in issues of global governance when compared to their counterparts in developing countries. Their ability to set norms and standards ultimately implies that developing countries become importers of norms as opposed to having an equal say in how they

---

[40]Jonathan Ponciano and Sarah Hansen, 'The World's Largest Public Companies 2019: Global 2000 By The Numbers', *Forbes*, 15 May 2019.
[41]Ruqayyah Moynihan and Fernando Belinchón, '25 giant companies that are bigger than entire countries', *Business Insider*, 25 July 2018.
[42]Luca Ventura, 'World's Largest Companies 2019', *Global Finance*, 29 August 2019.
[43]'The retreat of the global company', *The Economist*, 28 January 2017.

are conceived. Furthermore, the transnational tax avoidance strategies of TNCs have made it increasingly difficult for all countries to collect tax from them, and in particular developing countries whose tax administrations generally have lower capacities than those of the developed countries.[44]

The global mobility of capital has created political dynamics that significantly retard the ability of nations to tailor their policy options. Governments are forced to compete in a manner that attracts the most generous quantities of foreign investment and capital to their countries and therefore choose policies which favour transnational corporations and investors. This has made it difficult for governments to pursue autonomous macroeconomic policies in areas such as fiscal policy, tax rates, exchange rates and labour laws.

A second major process in the twenty-first century is the rapid pace of urbanization. The dawn of the Industrial Revolution meant that technology, innovation and capital were creating new forms of economic potential that were ripe for exploitation. To benefit from these trends, millions of people began migrating towards urban centres to seek new economic opportunities and social mobility. In the 1800s an insignificant portion of the world population lived in cities; by the 1950s that figure had risen to 30 per cent and estimates suggest that by the 2050s almost two-thirds of the world's population will reside in cities.[45]

Urbanization has also created a demand for local governance which, in turn, is spurring international reorganization: there is increasing realization that if democracy is to remain a bottom-up process, cities and other municipal actors will have to emerge at the forefront of shaping urban norms and rules. This realization was reflected in the World Cities Summit Mayors' Forum in 2016, which saw some 110 mayors and city leaders representing 103 cities from sixty-three countries and regions from around the world

---

[44]John Myers, 'Which countries are worst affected by tax avoidance?', WEF, 12 April 2017.
[45]Sam Meredith, 'Two-thirds of Global Population Will Live in Cities by 2050, UN says', *CNBC*, 17 May 2018.

discussing liveable and sustainable city challenges and integrated urban solutions.[46] Other initiatives such as the Global Parliament of Mayors also reflect the increasing desire of local governments to engage globally in order to meet the demands and challenges that urban lifestyles pose. The focus on climate change and resilience is probably among the most significant departures cities make from their national policies.

Yet the rise of these 'global cities' can exacerbate inequality within nation states. Many of these cities are surrounded by economically distressed rural communities, often leading to competing value systems and objectives. During Brexit, for example, almost all of London voted to stay within the EU, while most rural populations voted against. Similarly, during the American presidential elections, many large cities such as New York were strong votaries of increased globalization and migration, while many in the Rust Belt states felt economic and social anxiety as a result of these processes and voted to reject 'Davos Man'[47], the epithet often used to describe representatives of the new global elite. Telecommunications, strong transport systems and a ruthless division of labour have created financial capitals like London and Mumbai which are somewhat disembodied from their national systems. Often, it can seem like the fate of these megacities are intertwined with each other rather than with other areas within their own home countries.

A third trend is the emergence of radical non-state actors such as the ISIS. Misguided Western intervention in the Middle East, highlighted most spectacularly by the US invasion of Iraq in 2003, led to a collapse of state power in several of these regions. The collapse of these regimes has given rise to an even more terrifying transnational organization—the ISIS, which is a fitting, and unsettling, example of what can follow the collapse of state

---

[46]'World Cities Summit Aligns Focus on Urban and Social Innovations, and Public-Private Partnerships to Build Resilient Cities, Urban Redevelopment Authority, Singapore,' Urban Redevelopment Authority, 15 July 2016.
[47]Samuel Huntington, 'Dead Souls: The Denationalization of the American Elite', *National Interest*, 1 March 2004.

power. ISIS is a non-state actor that places modern technology in the service of a radical and anti-modern agenda. ISIS is perhaps the first terrorist organization which has adapted furiously to the internet. Social media has become a key tool for ISIS in spreading its propaganda and enhancing its recruitment. In less than a few years, ISIS has extended its dominion over vast swathes of territory in Iraq and Syria. Despite international coalitions severely degrading its progress, the ideological attraction of its message continues unabated. Disenfranchised youth from across the world have been influenced to yearn for the revival of a Muslim caliphate and the end to a nation-state order that the great powers invented and imposed. The organization revels in media attention and glorifies the terror it imposes on Western states. Today, the appeal of an Islamic caliphate has taken root in many parts of the world, from the suburbs of Paris, to the rural backwaters of the Philippines and even in Kashmir. ISIS continues to threaten the core values of globalization and represents the most powerful counter ideological force to Western-led liberalism.

As transborder challenges, such as terrorism, climate change, extreme poverty, financial crisis, nuclear non-proliferation and food crises proliferate, civil society organizations have become a key stakeholder in determining global norms. According to the Yearbook of International Organizations, the number of international NGOs increased from 6,000 in 1990 to more than 50,000 in 2006, reaching 65,000 in 2013.[48] In fact, India is reported to have nearly 3.3 million registered NGOs.[49] Coalitions of domestic and transnational civil society actors have played significant roles in promoting human and labour rights, environmental standards and other social concerns within countries where political institutions limit or even repress

---

[48] *Child Outlook: A policy briefing on global trends and their implications for children,* June 2014, UNICEF, https://www.unicef.org/publications/files/Child_Outook_June_2014_Special_Edition_12June2014.pdf.
[49] 'Civic Freedom Monitor: India', International Center for Not-for-Profit Law, 20 February 2019, accessed 16 June 2019, http://www.icnl.org/research/monitor/india.html.

activities in support of those aims. Human Rights Watch, for example, originated in the effort to monitor the implementation of the human rights provisions of the 1975 Helsinki Accords within the Soviet Bloc. Some non-state actors today have even hijacked the global agenda for the provision of public goods. For example, the Bill & Melinda Gates Foundation arguably has more sway over public health policies than the WHO. Even in India, think tanks such as the Centre for Internet & Society and Internet Democracy Project, have had an influential role to play in the new multi-stakeholder norms for internet governance including for reforms at the ICANN and the recent transition to IANA.

Technology will also continue to be a great disrupter, if not the most important driver of change and disorder in the twenty-first century. As companies such as Google, Alibaba and Facebook sit on mountains of data and have more information at their disposal than most governments, they will employ this information to improve their understanding of human motivations and desires. These companies will be able to influence behaviour on a much larger scale than nation states. These technologies will also test the capacity of international regimes to manage them. No state can afford to ignore technology as a force in the lives of its citizens. The new era is characterized by greater individual autonomy, stemming from a combination of more education, relatively greater wealth, and technologically-driven capabilities. Consider, for example, the wide and varied grassroots-driven protests in the Middle East, Latin America, North America, and East Asia, just in the past few years, which were facilitated by technology, from satellite television to WhatsApp messages. These new technologies will also empower individuals to a greater extent than ever before in history. They will allow preferences of political leadership to be challenged, often precluding desired state outcomes. The extent of this diffusion is a hopeful development, insofar as it allows democratic pressure for good governance. However, a word of caution is in order. The state is now able to use these same technologies with great sophistication in some cases and brutal power in others to enhance its own reach and capacity.

Having said this, it is also clear that emerging technologies are at the centre of a global contest for leadership and dominance. Consider the US diplomatic campaign against Huawei; the world's superpower is singling out a private firm that is a world leader in 5G communications in the belief that it is central to China's high technology ambitions and works covertly for the Chinese government. China is no different; its 'Made in China 2025' policy aims to dominate the supply chains of technologies ranging from industrial robotics to electric vehicles. This is not a phenomenon that is unique only to China or the US: there is a visible zero-sum competition for control over technologies in every part of the world. Mercantilism and nationalism are defining state policy in this area even as global governance processes and norms are failing to curtail harmful uses of emerging technologies. As these technologies continue to get more sophisticated, and more central to strategic state interests, there is a lingering question over the capacity of global institutions, norms or processes to govern them.

Indeed, countries and communities all realize that technology allows them a chance to shape their destinies, discover who they are, establish what they prefer and assist them to aspire to a new or revived state of being of their choosing. Robotics and artificial intelligence (AI) are both easing lives and threatening occupations. The heady mix of advancement in bioscience, material science and data science is hurtling us all towards a new age where the questions we may have to engage with are simply unfathomable from where we stand at present. Ethics, social sciences and larger debates on morality and values will have to undergo serious reconsideration if society is going to keep up with science.

THE CRISIS OF IDENTITY

Nevertheless, as power over politics and economics drifts away from the old notions of the nation states, social cohesion within them sometimes also comes under duress, which leads us to the crisis of identity, where the homogenization supposedly unleashed by globalization is, in fact, achieving the reverse and exacerbating identity divides leading to a fractured world, arguably more unmanageable than ever before.

The promise of a more equal world seems unfulfilled, both within countries and between them. Economic growth has benefited status quo actors and traditional power structures, leaving vast swathes of humanity disaffected and disillusioned. This disillusionment has created an immense breeding ground for groups that would use identity to create radical and subnational movements, often to serve violent needs. An extreme fringe of the Muslim community in Europe, the Buddhists in Myanmar, and Shia-Sunni postures in the Middle East: all of these are using this difference to either inflict violence on the 'other' or to motivate violence against those seen as irreconcilable enemies.

The spread of finance and trade across borders has not only created a world which is more economically integrated, but also one that is socially integrated. Modern communication systems like the internet, mobile and social media have united communities across the world like never before. While this might have appeared to be the precursor to a more liberal world, these technologies appear to be producing contradictory outcomes; audiences are also more fragmented than before; and this fragmentation of national boundaries is propelling nationalist fervour as individual citizens are increasingly voicing their frustrations online and challenging the state's authority from the bottom up. Many would argue that illiberal forces, nationalist and subnationalist movements, and partisan politics are beginning to threaten the democratic ethos developed over the past seven decades. In sheer numbers, more countries have adopted democracy as their principal political system than ever before. But there is also little doubt that there has been a political capture of democratic systems within these countries by those who do not feel constrained by democratic norms.

It was thought that globalization and the spread of the international liberal order would lead to a certain convergence of values globally and result in the creation of a cosmopolitan community, which identified broadly with the rest of the world and had greater confidence in institutions of global governance such as the United

Nations. These hopes were in for a rude shock when 52 per cent of the British voting population chose to exit the EU, the watershed for global and interconnected communities. There are two major causes that this backlash against globalization can be attributed to—the first is rising economic insecurity as the collapse of manufacturing industry and global flows of capital, labour and goods led to the erosion of organized labour. Austerity policies in the European countries led to shrinking social security and ultimately these insecurities have allowed populist politicians to fuel an anti-establishment and xenophobic narrative against those they perceive to be the 'other'. The second is that the spread of 'liberal values' was rejected by an older generation who felt that their identity was declining and that immigrants and non-Christians were fuelling a displacement of norms and values which they cherished. These processes however should not be seen as mutually exclusive; instead they continuously interact, creating a feedback loop which causes anger and resentment. While a new global elite has undoubtedly emerged with global interests transcending identities, in certain countries, including India, globalization has accentuated identity divides.

Today economic indicators and access to modern services and provisions are skewed to the advantage of certain communities and regions and has resulted in the 'haves' having a lot a more and the 'have-nots' having little hope to change their lot. Sample some of the numbers from Oxfam. Since 2015, the richest 1 per cent has owned more wealth than the rest of the planet.[50] 'Eight men now own the same amount of wealth as the poorest half of the world. Over the next twenty years, 500 people will hand over $2.1 trillion to their heirs—a sum larger than the GDP of India, a country of 1.3 billion people. The incomes of the poorest 10 per cent of people increased by less than $3 a year between 1988 and 2011, while the incomes of the richest 1 per cent increased 182 times as much. An FTSE 100

---

[50]Deborah Hardoon, 'An Economy for the 99%', Oxfam Briefing paper, Oxford: Oxfam International, 26 January 2017, accessed 15 June 2019, https://www.oxfam.org/en/research/economy-99.

CEO earns as much in a year as 10,000 people working in garment factories in Bangladesh. In the US, over the last thirty years, the growth in the incomes of the bottom 50 per cent has been zero, whereas incomes of the top 1 per cent have grown 300 per cent.[51]

The heyday of globalization lasted less than three decades from 1980. The 2008 financial crisis seems to have been a turning point. The pre-2008 years were generally full of optimism, confidence that the poor were becoming richer, millions of people were rising out of poverty every year, democracy and freedom were inevitable even in the worst dictatorships, and that the world itself had transformed into one 'global village'. It felt like a sort of historic golden age had begun, and there was every reason to be seduced by this narrative when the going was good. Francis Fukuyama published his famous 'End of History' thesis, arguing that in the grand global struggle about the future of human political and economic organization, the forces of democracy and liberal capitalism had won a definitive victory. His book, *The End of History and the Last Man*, epitomized the hubris and confidence of that era.

But the Great Recession of 2007–09 changed all that. The economic crisis led many to question who the real winners and losers from globalization were. Since 2008, wage growth has been weak, but returns for the wealthy continue to be robust: in the UK, wages have grown only by 13 per cent since 2008 but the stock market is up by 115 per cent.[52] Credit Suisse does an annual study of inequality in forty-six major economies around the world; before 2007, it found wealth inequality was on the rise in twelve of them; today wealth inequality is growing sharply in thirty-five of the forty-six states.[53]

The poor and the unemployed in the developed world began to feel that they had no stake in the globalized system, and demanded to know why their governments' policies benefited people in faraway

---

[51]Id.

[52]Ruchir Sharma, 'Globalisation as we know it is over—and Brexit is the biggest sign yet', *The Guardian*, 28 July 2016.

[53]Shashi Tharoor, 'The Two Backlashes Against Globalization', *Project Syndicate*, 12 October 2017.

lands like China and India with what used to be *their* jobs. They wanted to go back to the security of older, more familiar economic ways, in which each generation assumed they would earn more and live better than their parents did.

That isn't feasible, but populist political responses were inevitable. The responses from leaders have been increasing political denunciation of global trade, hostility—even violence—towards foreigners, and imposition of austerity measures, which also tend to hurt the poor more. This in turn exacerbates the problem.

The result: we are witnessing two kinds of backlashes against globalization. While they overlap in some cases, they also are discrete in their prevalence. If what we have described so far is anti-economic globalization, there is also what one can call anti-cultural globalization, whose proponents seek the comforts of traditional identity and resist the homogenization of preferences and behaviours that are either a consequence of globalization itself or ride on it. The rise and success of Trump, along with Marine Le Pen in France, Norbert Hofer in Austria, Viktor Orbán in Hungary, AfD in Germany, Recep Tayyib Erdog̃an in Turkey, and in certain ways Narendra Modi in India, also exemplify a global backlash against cosmopolitanism, multiculturalism and secularism as proffered by the Atlantic order. This denunciation of the global order and its manifestations is shaped around cultural rootedness, religious or ethnic identity and nationalist authenticity. It is, in terms popularized by the philosopher David Goodheart, a battle between the 'anywheres'—those comfortable anywhere in the world, with no restrictive sense of local allegiance—and the 'somewheres', people rooted in a place, a culture, a religion and a specific way of life.

Identity is a real factor in the 'cultural backlash': Trump's 'Make America Great Again' was also code for 'Make America White Again'. (But it's not going to happen: the demographic reality is that, by 2032, a majority of the American labour force will be non-white.)[54]

---

[54]Valerie Wilson, 'People of color will be a majority of the American working class in 2032: What this means for the effort to grow wages and reduce inequality', Economic Foreign Policy Institute, 9 June 2016.

There is undeniable nostalgia for a slower, less unfamiliar universe, but it may well prove to be the dying kick of a fading generation.

Trump is often seen as a uniquely American phenomenon, but he is in many ways part of a broader global revolt by nationalists and traditionalists against a liberal capitalist elite. But the resentment and rejection he tapped emerges from both the traditional left and the right. In the US, we have seen, on the left, the Occupy Wall Street (OWS) movement of those young people claiming to represent the excluded 99 per cent, and the insurgency of Bernie Sanders. But there has also been, on the right, the revolt of the unemployed, bitter, increasingly xenophobic and in many cases racist (as Unite the Right, a white supremacist rally held in August 2017 in Charlottesville, has shown) white blue-collar voters who propelled Trump into the White House. The defeat of Hillary Clinton was in large part because she was seen as being part of a globalized elite linked to Wall Street—as epitomized by her well-paid speeches at Goldman Sachs.

Outside America, such sentiments were most strikingly manifest in the Brexit vote in Britain against the European Union. British working-class resentment of cosmopolitanism was compounded by their distaste for the large numbers of non-English-speaking immigrants from other parts of the EU. Add to this the fact that the total population of billionaires in the world has increased to 2,153, provoking class resentment by this concentration of wealth in the hands of a few.[55] Ninety-five[56] of them live in London alone, and if Brexit was a vote from which London stood aside by voting 'stay', in a way it was also the rest of the UK voting against London and its elite by preferring to leave.

Yet these two kinds of backlash do not always overlap. Erdoğan and Modi, like Xi, in China, are still globalizers, so while they desire nationalist rootedness, economically they want to be Davos Man, not reject him. Beneath both overlapping trends lies the spectre of economic uncertainty. Protectionist barriers have begun to go up

---

[55]'Billionaires: The Richest People in the World', *Forbes*, 5 March 2019.
[56]'Rich List 2019: The richest people in London', *Sunday Times*, 12 May 2019.

in those very nations that had for years advocated the free flow of goods, labour, and capital—an irony that would have been funny had it not smelt a great deal like hypocrisy.

The backlash against globalization is not limited to economics alone. An annual report published by the European and World Values Survey between 1981 and 2012 reveals that hostility towards immigrants and those of other religions has been increasing as nationalism and a sense of pride in one's culture remain embedded in the value systems of most individuals.[57] These sentiments have also corresponded to a loss of faith in the value and purpose of international organizations, including the EU, UN, IMF, and the World Bank. These attitudes serve to highlight the inherent tension between national democratic sovereignty and elite-led efforts at global integration. The constraints imposed on public opinion by international norms have led to a deficit in democracy, leaving people increasingly frustrated with their own governments.

Of course a primary criticism of studies in inequality has been the myopic focus that they have had on Western societies. Most of the global poor reside in developing countries and least developed countries like those on the African continent. Identity, race and religion in these countries play an important factor in determining how they interact with the processes of globalization. It is possible to link inequality in many countries to specific patterns of integration into the world economy as socially included groups who wield power over domestic institutions reap the benefits of globalization. In India, social identities such as caste and gender indirectly determine the place of an individual in the modern Indian economy.

India was in the news recently when the annual Human Development Report revealed it was one of the most unequal societies in the world. According to Credit Suisse, the richest 1 per cent of India's population own 73 per cent of the country's wealth

---

[57]R. Inglehart, C. Haerpfer, A. Moreno, C. Welzel, K. Kizilova, J. Diez-Medrano, M. Lagos, P. Norris, E. Ponarin, B. Puranen et al. (eds.), 'World Values Survey: Round Six', Madrid: JD Systems Institute, 2014, Country-Pooled Datafile Version: www.worldvaluessurvey.org/WVSDocumentationWV6.jsp.

whilst the poorer half own just 1 per cent.[58] As these identities interact with domestic institutions, they create patronage alliances and as globalization breaks down traditional communities, it alters an individual's understanding of 'self' defined by nationality, ethnicity and religion. Coupled with economic marginalization, it heightens an individual's sense of insecurity. Instead of creating a more unified and harmonious global community, we have a world more fractured across identity barriers than ever before.

The complex interaction between inequality and authoritarianism is playing out all across Asia as well. Despite the apparent spread of democratic governance in recent decades, according to Freedom House, most countries in the Asia Pacific are either not free or partially free. In Thailand, a military junta seized power through a coup in 2014, enacting a wide array of restrictive laws that prosecuted even minor criticism, forcing through a constitution that guaranteed the military excessive power over civilian affairs. In Myanmar, despite the recent transition to democracy, Rohingya Muslims continue to face serious persecution, causing a migration crisis in South Asia. Rodrigo Duterte has ended the Philippines' long dalliance with the US and is pursuing closer ties with China, while employing extra-legal means to deal with drug peddlers and criminals, often prosecuting civil society organizations as well. In China, Xi Jinping continues to consolidate his rule, jailing critics and dissidents and enacting severe restrictions on internet access and freedom of assembly. Authorities in both Malaysia and the Maldives cracked down on demonstrators protesting allegations that top politicians had embezzled vast amounts of money from state coffers. In India, the ruling Bharatiya Janata Party (BJP) has faced criticism on its inability to stop violence against minorities, mainly Muslims, and Dalits.

Taken together, technology and identity have created a new dynamic. New communities are now formed on digital networks; and assimilation, which was earlier through physical proximity, is now

---

[58]'Income Inequality gets worse; India's top 1% bag 73% of the country's wealth, says Oxfam', *Business Today*, 30 January 2019.

almost entirely online. This aggregation on the internet creates new spaces for exclusions, divisions and differences between individuals who might otherwise be neighbours. Never before has the assimilation of two cultures been more difficult. Social media has allowed new actors and voices to take part in debate and discussion; yet these discussions are increasingly polarized, egged on by opaque algorithms, and deliberations are now vitriolic and crass. Identity and technology are also slowly becoming tools of conflict.

During Russia's campaign in Ukraine and Crimea, these two factors came together to exacerbate social tensions. A report by the NATO StratCom on 'Russia's information campaign in the Ukraine'[59] highlights some important factors that shaped Russian strategy. The first was to frame broad messages such as 'brother nations', common history, the Orthodox religion and common culture, which have been used to encourage the inhabitants of East and South Ukraine to think about a joint future destiny with Russia. The second is employing state media to manipulate video and photographs; Russian state TV produced material to bolster the various narratives we have mentioned. TV channels such as Russia Today (RT) and Sputnik are designed with the specific objective of disseminating Russian viewpoints to a foreign audience. The third is manipulating opinion on social media. With an army of trolls at its disposal, Russia used Twitter as a means to disseminate its official narrative.

Meanwhile, one does not have to accept the Huntingtonian theory of the 'clash of civilisations' to acknowledge that the acceptance of pluralism across the globe is profoundly challenged by the new assertion of older, totalizing identities, most visibly Islam. Due to globalization and the insecurities it bred, observers like Huntington felt that Muslims would contest and clash with the non-Islamic world. The theory suggests that Islam operates as a collective agent with a predisposition towards violence as a consequence of its anathema

---

[59]'Analysis of Russia's Information Campaign against Ukraine', NATO StratCom Centre of Excellence, 2014, accessed 15 June 2019, https://www.stratcomcoe.org/analysis-russias-information-campaign-against-ukraine.

to global pluralism. This is a highly contestable idea since resistance to global pluralism clearly infects many cultures professing various religions. As economic modernization and social change separate people from their local identities, the strength of a nation state to represent its people also weakens. This longing for identity is exploited by 'fundamentalist actors' who seek to provide context and meaning to individual lives. These civilizational conflicts are visible even under the aegis of nation states; the India-Pakistan dispute, for example, is fundamentally about the two countries' differing perceptions of the role of religion as a determinant of nationhood. China similarly employs its rhetoric of '100 years of humiliation' as a symbol of disaffection for Western civilizations which have inhibited it from occupying its true place in the world.

THE CRISIS OF SOVEREIGNTY

Finally, we have the crisis of sovereignty. Ever since the Treaty of Westphalia was signed in the seventeenth century, the concepts of statehood and sovereignty were tightly intertwined. Sovereignty has become the touchstone upon which the legitimacy and authority of statehood resides. Sovereignty has become the organizing principle of today's world order, giving states political and economic meaning. The principles of this system—territorial integrity and non-intervention—reflected an understanding that states were the smallest political unit in international relations. Ever since its origin in Europe, the Westphalian system has expanded across the world. The forces of decolonization and independence in Asia and Africa rallied around state sovereignty as a principle for legitimizing their call for independent statehood. While the norm of territorial integrity has often been ignored and subverted, it still remains the guiding force for global governance today.

Today, however, we are witnessing the decline of the nation state. The processes of globalization have eroded the traditional power that a state had over its boundaries. Globalization has created a complex political network increasingly disconnected from the objectives of the state. The proliferation of international organizations, civil society, supranational organizations have challenged the power of the state to be the sole arbiter of policy. Similarly, the function of the state in providing public goods is also increasingly being eroded as public-private partnerships flourish and technology and capital create a new type of power centre, those who control data. Further, international institutions such as the United Nations are increasingly developing normative frameworks for intruding on state sovereignty—witness, for instance, the debate surrounding the Responsibility to Protect (R2P), which allows humanitarian intervention to prevent atrocities (though it is often denounced as a moral fig leaf for more cynical or self-interested motives). Specialized regimes of public international law have intervened in areas that were considered the sole domain of the state, such as the environment, trade, human rights and finance. This trend has been complemented by the spread of supranational and intergovernmental organizations and transnational corporations, whose rules and authority are increasingly undermining this Westphalian model.

These complex undercurrents are further buffeted by contrasting opinions of the limits of sovereignty and its place in global governance. On the one hand, nations that are emerging from colonial administration and from relative insignificance are reclaiming sovereignty and, on the other hand, developed nations are seeking to aggregate themselves and global institutions for greater influence and weight. Some developed countries, notably the US, remain wedded to their sovereignty, however, while some developing ones see the merit in collectivity. The BRICS and the US have strong notions of sovereignty, while the EU and Africa seek to aggregate the collective to garner greater weight and voice in crucial debates on trade, climate and other specific issues. These two contesting vectors are reshaping the very notion of sovereignty and defeating the effort to shape global governance forums.

In its efforts to be recognized as a 'global player', the European Union has repeatedly declared its commitment to 'effective multilateralism', claiming that its abundant internal experience has made it 'instinctively multilateral' on the global scene. The European

Security Strategy strongly underlines the importance that the UN should have in the multilateral system, and a large number of statements and European Council conclusions confirm this priority given to strengthening the UN. A 2003 statement says that 'Europe's attachment to multilateralism—and to the United Nations, as a pivot of the multilateral system—will help determine whether, and how, the institutional architecture established in the years after World War II can continue to serve as the bedrock of the international system.'[60] Similarly, Article 10 A of the Treaty of Lisbon reads: 'It [the EU] shall promote multilateral solutions to common problems, in particular in the framework of the United Nations.' The EU is perhaps the most successful model of pooled sovereignty and, despite the shock of Brexit and nationalist movements occupying its political space, the integration project continues to remain strong.

Following the collapse of the Soviet Union and finding its external security guaranteed by the US under the aegis of NATO, Europe was consumed with the process of nation-building for much of the later part of the twentieth century. The EU is so far the only supranational organization which is premised on nations pooling their sovereignty in order to replace power politics with institutional norms and rules. The European Parliament, the Court of Justice of the European Union (CJEU) and other such organizations today make laws and rules that have permeated into the national systems of most EU countries. It is this confidence in multilateral institutions which has also shaped the EU's conversations about global governance. Its concern about the effects of climate change produced the Kyoto Protocol and its belief in international justice allowed it to gestate the idea of an international criminal court. The EU even sought to strengthen the nuclear non-proliferation regime through its ratification of the Comprehensive Test Ban Treaty (CTBT). These initiatives prompted Robert Kagan to famously characterize Europe

---

[60]'The European Union and the United Nations: The choice of multilateralism', Communication from the Commission to the Council and the European Parliament, COM/2003/0526 final, 2003, accessed 15 June 2019, https://eur-lex.europa.eu/LexUriServ/LexUriServ.do?uri=CELEX:52003DC0526:EN:HTML.

as being 'from Venus' (since America was 'from Mars') and as 'moving beyond power into a self-contained world of laws and rules and transnational negotiation and cooperation'.[61]

This commitment to multilateralism, however, requires certain concessions to state supremacy. The majority of the planet's greatest contemporary challenges in such diverse fields as peace-building and peacekeeping, development, human rights, environment or public health are by their very nature collective action problems. However, not all nations are comfortable with an arrangement that cedes authority over their resources, especially military resources, to supranational institutions. Even during their infancy, nations which escaped the clutches of colonialism were instinctively opposed to efforts which would subvert their sovereignty. For example, at the Bandung Conference in 1955, Nehru portrayed NATO as 'one of the most powerful protectors of colonialism'. He felt that collective defence pacts were a threat to the territorial integrity and dignity of postcolonial states, finding it 'intolerable...that the great countries of Asia and Africa should come out of bondage into freedom only to degrade themselves or humiliate themselves'[62] by joining such pacts. Similarly, efforts by the UN to limit the principle of state supremacy were often viewed with suspicion by most post-colonial states. At the UN debate over R2P, Egypt on behalf of the Non-Aligned Movement noted that 'mixed feelings and thoughts on implementing R2P still persist. There are concerns about the possible abuse of R2P by expanding its application to situations that fall beyond the four areas defined in the 2005 World Summit Document, misusing it to legitimize unilateral coercive measures or intervention in the internal affairs of States.'[63]

---

[61]Robert Kagan, 'Of Paradise and Power', *New York Times*, 30 March 2003.
[62]Luis Eslava, Michael Fakhri, and Vasuki Nesiah, (eds.), *Bandung, Global History, and International Law: Critical Pasts and Pending Futures*, Cambridge: Cambridge University Press, 2017, pp. 59-60.
[63]'Statement by H. E. Ambassador Maged A. Abdelaziz, the Permanent Representative on behalf of the Non Aligned Movement', New York, Permanent Mission of the Arab Republic of Egypt to the United States, 23 July 2009, accessed 15 June 2019, http://www.globalr2p.org/media/files/egypt-2009-r2p-debate.pdf.

Viewed from this perspective, most Asian states have found it difficult to premise regional integration on the 'pooling' of sovereignty as espoused by European nations. ASEAN, for example, has strongly upheld the principle of sovereignty; its economic integration has been premised on reinforcing sovereignty, as opposed to eroding it. This is why it is often hesitant to intervene during humanitarian crises in other Southeast Asian states; by refusing to criticize the military junta in Myanmar, ASEAN chose to call for constructive engagement, as opposed to the EU, which condemned the regime. The Organization of African Unity (OAU), which was created to address some of the post-independence concerns on political and economic stability, similarly refuses to jeopardize national sovereignty in its pronouncements and actions. The African Union (AU) as a supranational institution is largely toothless in terms of enforcing norms or rules upon its constituents and instead acts as leverage during trade talks or climate change negotiations. The BRICS grouping, which was created as an institutional bulwark against Western hegemony in international institutions, also represents a core group of nations that are strongly wedded to their sovereignty.

The greatest resistance to effective global governance comes from the United States itself. After creating several multilateral institutions following the end of World War II, largely to institutionalize its own hegemony, it is not truly prepared to see its room for unilateral action restricted. This history of American unilateralism is a long one, rooted in the notion of 'American exceptionalism'. Its refusal to ratify the Comprehensive Test Ban Treaty, rejection of the Mine Ban Treaty and reluctance to ratify the Treaty of Rome establishing the International Criminal Court (ICC), all confirm that the US has always sought to protect its own sovereign decision-making power. The war on Iraq in 2003 was probably the pinnacle of American unilateralism. Despite strong opposition from the international community, its own allies in Europe and a veto from the United Nations Security Council, America's success in prosecuting the war only reaffirmed its belief in the power of its own technical and military supremacy and its hesitations in subordinating these to consultation with the international community. President Donald Trump's withdrawal from the Paris Agreement to combat climate change is only the latest example of America's unwillingness to engage in multilateral processes that do not suit its interests.

In conclusion, with these five crises characterizing global governance today, it is imperative that the world find new ways to navigate current failures in governance processes. The ideals, norms and institutions which formed the basis of the international order are now outdated. The very system that was designed to deliver untold wealth has concentrated it in the hands of a few. The very system that sought to prevent conflict is now besieged by new powers and actors who had no say in its formation. The very technologies that promised to bring communities together seem to be tearing them apart; in a world that was destined to share 'common values' and evolve a 'common humanity', the difference in the value of human life based on colour, culture, country and community has never been more apparent.

The liberal order, which was designed to be adaptable to a changing world, is now constrained by the rigidity and inflexibility of old power structures. Today's problems are no longer multilateral: they affect individuals, communities and businesses in every nook and cranny of the world. As this complex twenty-first-century landscape evolves, governance will arguably need to be recast and repackaged in creative ways to respond to changing circumstances. New security threats will necessitate innovative responses; new trading and investment regimes will merit a revision of the existing multilateral system; the changing climate will challenge traditional alliances in the international sphere; the development needs of billions will result in an unprecedented race for resources; and new technological platforms will mould, indeed 'code', the fabric of political and social interactions.

To address and solve these issues, 'Re-forming', rather than reforming, global governance is the need of the day.

CHAPTER 2

WARRING FOR PEACE, POWER AND BOUNTIES

The United Nations was seen by visionaries like former US President Franklin Delano Roosevelt as the keystone of the arch of international peace and security. We have noted earlier his historic speech to the US Congress after the Yalta Conference, in which he stated that the UN would be the alternative to the various sorts of political and military arrangements that had led to war in the past. It is worth reiterating the words of his successor, President Harry Truman, that we quoted in the introduction: 'You have created a great instrument for peace and security and human progress in the world,' he declared to the assembled signatories of the UN Charter in San Francisco on 26 June 1945. '...If we seek to use it selfishly— for the advantage of any one nation or any small group of nations— we shall be equally guilty of that betrayal.'[1]

That was then, of course, and this—seventy-four years later—is now. How many of today's critics of the United Nations would recognize the voice of an American president in Truman's speech that historic day? Our book will argue that they would see it as well-meaning, but ultimately naïve. The central challenge is perhaps the very institutional architecture of the UN, which places the responsibility for international peace and security on the five Permanent Members of the Security Council and makes their

---

[1] Harry Truman, 'Addressses at Final Plenary Session of United Nations Conference on International Organization', United States Department of State Bulletin, 26 June 1945, accessed 15 June 2019, http://www.ibiblio.org/pha/policy/1945/1945-06-26b. html.

decisions binding on the rest. The end result is that the victors of World War II retain a monopoly over violence and conflict. The UN, at its finest hours during the Cold War, merely tempered what Gilbert Achcar calls the 'clash of barbarisms'.[2] While Achcar used this phrase to describe the state of being between the violent evangelism of the US under the Bush administration and the radicalism of Bin Laden's Al-Qaeda, it is also an accurate formulation of the many kinds of simmering conflicts that we see today. These are not necessarily always a 'clash' as Achcar would describe them; they are, however, 'exertions' of assorted barbarisms.

The thawing of the Cold War freeze and the evolution of power relationships among the five Permanent Members of the Security Council have created the environment in which the world will be making its choices about the management of international conflict.[3] The end of the Soviet Union loosened the straitjacket within which many potential conflicts had been confined. Many erupted amid the disinclination of the big powers to intervene; during the Cold War, both sides had sought to prevent conflicts arising that might engage their interests. Today, the stakes are lower; Somalia is not seen as threatening to the world order as Stalingrad, American withdrawal from Afghanistan or Syria would at worst not be as painful as defeat in Vietnam, and Sarajevo, 1992, for all its emotional impact, did not carry the globe-threatening resonance of Sarajevo, 1914. In this climate, warring factions, unfettered by bondage to one superpower or another, pursue their ambitions without regard to an outside world that clearly cannot summon the will or the resources to intercede decisively. A post-ideological world stokes its frenzies in the flames of nationalism, ethnicity, and tribal triumphalism. Old injustices and older enmities are revived and intensified; history becomes a whip with which to flail those who are inclined to compromise. Few rules are observed in

---

[2]Gilbert Achcar, *The Clash of Barbarisms: September 11 and the Making of the New World Disorder*, New York: Monthly Review Press, 2002.
[3]Shashi Tharoor, 'The Future of Peacekeeping', in D. Pocock and J. Whitman (eds.), *After Rwanda: The Coordination of United Nations Humanitarian Assistance*, London: Macmillan Press Ltd, 1996, p. 21.

these wars, fewer still in the tenuous moments of peace that punctuate them. The techniques of a calmer era, peacekeeping included, seem inadequate to the moment.

The 2003 invasion of Iraq was certainly a turning point, and in many ways a precursor to the behaviour of other powers in the twenty-first century. The military intervention in Iraq was initially sought to be couched in the language of humanitarianism by its proponents—a moment to exhibit the relevance of the contested Right to Protect doctrine. But this was hotly rejected by the votaries of R2P, who argued that the war was squarely anchored in Washington's geopolitical interests rather than in any real concern for suffering Iraqi civilians. R2P suddenly came to life again, though, with the aerial military intervention by NATO forces in Libya in 2011. Since the UN Security Council resolution that authorized the NATO action permitted countries to use 'all necessary measures' to stop the assaults by Muammar Gaddafi's forces on Libyans rising up against his oppressive regime, the bombardments were described as humanitarian in intent, aimed at saving Libyan lives. The idea was supposed to be to level the playing field so that the contending parties could negotiate a peaceful settlement, as had happened in Egypt and Tunisia. This was meant to be a war for peace.

It didn't work out that way. The Western air forces did not simply stop their action once they had neutralized Gaddafi's attacks on rebel-held Benghazi. They went on pounding ground targets, causing considerable civilian casualties. An attack on Gaddafi's compound, which killed one of his children and three of his grandchildren, suggests that the objective had moved well beyond the imposition of a 'no-flight zone' to protect civilians on the ground to getting rid of Gaddafi himself—in effect, regime change. Exactly as it eventually transpired.

Over a decade after American interventions in Iraq, Russia would invade Ukraine in clear violation of international law and the UN framework. If Iraq characterized the barbarism of the West and that of the Islamic world, the annexation of Crimea and continued military interventions in Ukraine were a clash between an ever-expanding military bloc (NATO) and a disgruntled former superpower resentful of its declining geopolitical influence. As John Mearsheimer would argue: 'the Ukraine Crisis is the West's Fault'.[4] The end of the Cold War and of the subsequent era of American unipolarity, many would have assumed, would lead to a gradual slide into irrelevance for NATO. Instead, the bloc kept expanding eastwards—in many ways, it can be argued, forcing Moscow's hand in East Europe and the Middle East. Only a few years after the events in Crimea, China would go on to ignore the ruling of an international tribunal regarding its expansive claims in the South China Sea. The final decision, which would find that China had violated the United Nations Convention on the Law of the Sea (UNCLOS), was pointedly ignored in China. Only days after the verdict, Beijing would release a White Paper which doubled down on China's 'historic rights in the South China Sea'. The then US President, Barack Obama, meanwhile, authorized the US navy to sail through disputed waters to reaffirm the country's 'commitment to a regional order where international rules and norms...are upheld'.[5] Again, in the South China Sea, we see a particular kind of clash— that of hypocrisies. China's, first and foremost, for believing that it possesses a sovereign right over the waterways that touch upon the shores of several other claimants. And the US, for assuming that it possesses the right to enforce international rules and norms that it has not ratified itself (the US is not, for all its bluster, a signatory to the UNCLOS).

These are, of course, some of the most geopolitically consequential conflicts that the UN has failed to mitigate. And its failures aren't limited to them. The UN faces criticism across the world for overstretch in its peace and security efforts (and irrelevance in others, from Libya to Syria to Iran). Nevertheless, each of these incidents make clear that there exists a certain class of states that are immune to the

---

[4] John J. Mearsheimer, 'Why the Ukraine Crisis is the West's Fault: The Liberal Delusions That Provoked Putin', *Foreign Affairs*, 18 August 2014.
[5] Remarks by President Obama at U.S.-ASEAN Press Conference, The White House, 16 February 2016, accessed 15 June 2019, https://obamawhitehouse.archives.gov/the-press-office/2016/02/16/remarks-president-obama-us-asean-press-conference.

limitations of the rules-based system—those that can ignore the UN at will. This is not to say that the United Nations is not a relevant organization to these powers. Indeed, whenever possible, the UN becomes a convenient forum to exercise perverse state interests.

The US has, of course, ranked amongst the worst offenders, given its role as superpower for the past three decades. Even today, there is a strong community in Washington that abhors multilateral constraints on the exercise of state power. The notion has gained ground, particularly in the wake of Robert Kagan's *Of Paradise and Power*, that the elemental issue in world affairs is the incompatibility of the American and 'European' diagnoses of our contemporary geopolitical condition. In this view, the US sees a Hobbesian world, rife with menace and disorder, that requires the imposition of order and stability by a Leviathan; whereas the Europeans imagine a Kantian world, to be organized along amicable liberal principles, presumably while speaking French the whole time. In the real world, a Hobbesian Leviathan could not possibly function if he were to be tied down by a system of rules designed to serve smaller states: he would be a Gulliver restrained by, in the late Charles Krauthammer's words, the 'myriad strings' of the Lilliputians 'that diminish his overweening power'.[6] Hence the answer lies in disregarding the United Nations and, as Professor Michael J. Glennon[7] argued, restoring might to its rightful place in world affairs.

The second President George Bush and latterly President Trump seem to be following this prescription. America, however, is far from the only, or the worst, such actor. Take Syria, for example—or more specifically, how Russia managed diplomacy over Syria at the United Nations. Since the start of the conflict in 2011, Russia has used its position as a Permanent Member to block numerous Security Council resolutions condemning large-scale human rights violations to protect the legitimacy of the brutal Assad regime. Moscow makes

---

[6]Charles Krauthammer, 'The Unipolar Moment Revisited', *National Interest*, No. 70, 2002, pp. 5–18, accessed 15 June 2019, JSTOR, www.jstor.org/stable/42897438.
[7]Michael J. Glennon, 'Why the Security Council Failed', *Foreign Affairs*, May/June 2003.

no pretence that it sees the UN as anything more than a tool, making many references to the US's own behaviour in seeking political cover for interventions in areas like Kosovo or Libya, for example. Beijing has learnt the same lessons. For years now, it has attempted to undermine the United Nations human rights regime—arguably one of the most important pillars of the organization. In 2018, China, a large-scale human rights violator, successfully introduced a resolution at the Human Rights Council that downplayed individual rights to emphasize the role of the state and development processes in creating socio-economic rights.[8] Later, during a 2019 review of rights records by the council, Beijing sent out letters to the ambassadors of several countries warning that participating in or co-sponsoring a panel that was reviewing China's practices in Xinjiang would damage bilateral economic relations. And with so many developing states dependent on Beijing's largesse under the Belt and Road Initiative, this thinly veiled warning would have been hard to ignore. Most surprisingly perhaps, China successfully convinced nearly thirty-seven countries on the council, many of them Islamic states, to issue a joint letter supporting China's activities in Xinjiang as necessary to maintain law and order.[9] This is not merely evidence of how the UN can be co-opted to serve state interests, but how these perverse efforts may well strike at the very heart of the UN's raison d'etre.

The question of peace and security goes well beyond how larger powers have ignored the United Nations when they see fit. There is also the question of how interventions have and haven't taken place. Even well-meaning interventions, sometimes sanctioned by the UN, and other times made irrespective of UN decision-making, have often been prompted by the geopolitical interests of a few states. In Panama, the Gulf War, in Kosovo or in Haiti, the US, either

---

[8]'Win-Win Cooperation for the Common Cause of Human Rights', Permanent Mission of the People's Republic of China to the United Nations Office at Geneva and Other International Organizations in Switzerland, 1 March 2018, accessed 15 June 2019, http://www.china-un.ch/eng/hom/t1538784.htm.
[9]Tom Miles, 'Saudi Arabia and Russia among 37 states backing China's Xinjiang policy', Reuters, 15 July 2019.

acting alone, or in consonance with its NATO allies, intervened to ostensibly protect humanitarian interests. However, not all events have prompted equally strong responses. While the politics of selective interventionism has, more often than not, led to more devastation than was sought to be addressed, UN inaction has produced equally adverse results. In April 1995, this question was brought into sharp relief by events in Burundi. The then United Nations Secretary-General, Boutros Boutros-Ghali, spent weeks urging governments to take preventive action; though some steps were taken by the Security Council, notably through the dispatch of a mission to take stock of the situation and the issuance of a presidential statement calling for restraint, they did not prove enough to prevent a looming tragedy. Similar examples occurred in other crises. Where powerful nations did not see their interests directly engaged, efforts were not pursued with seriousness, resources and certainly not with troops. If conflict does occur despite the best efforts of the diplomats and peacemakers, it is vital that it be nipped in the bud before it does the kind of damage that the world witnessed with horrified impotence during the Rwanda genocide in 1994. Had the United Nations's General Roméo Dallaire had 5,000 reinforcements within days of the shooting down of the presidential aircraft that unleashed the carnage in Rwanda, he might have been able to save more than 500,000 lives; but none were forthcoming, and when the Security Council finally approved an enhancement of his force, Dallaire had to wait more than three months for governments to make troops available to the United Nations. These dynamics were at play again most recently in the aftermath of the Arab Spring—where the Security Council authorized military intervention in Libya, but not in Syria. In Libya, the UN acted rapidly—authorizing military force and referring the case to the International Criminal Tribunal. The people of Syria, as we all know, have suffered from great power conflict, a brutal regime and the inaction of the international community.

It is not as if the international community was not aware of this dichotomous approach. When the US was agitating its case for Kosovo in the United Nations, diplomats from the G77 pointed out the US was asking for the deployment of significant UN resources in Europe despite opposing 'nation-building' exercises in other parts of the world, especially Africa. Indeed, the US was only able to mobilize support for Kosovo, limited as it was, after agreeing to a provision that emphasized that 'all future and existing peacekeeping missions shall be given equal and non-discriminatory treatment in respect of financial and administrative arrangements.'[10] As for why the United Nations and the international community were slow to act, it is not a stretch to suggest that these conflicts were seen as irrelevant to the interests of great powers. In other words, the political and economic costs of mobilizing a response were seen as greater than allowing millions to perish under dictatorial circumstances. The fact remains that selective interventionism, whether by the UN, the US, Russia or other great powers, has consistently undermined the legitimacy of the international order. There is a long history behind such behaviour—all of which now act as precedents for those who would rather ignore the limitations the UN imposes on the international community or subvert the organization to suit their own interests.

And, finally, there is the question of peacekeeping itself. Who actually provides the peacekeepers? The fact is that countries from Asia, Africa and Latin America provide the overwhelming number of peacekeeping forces—more than 90 per cent. This leads to a situation where the conflicts are often embroiled in great power struggles, with both the victims and the UN peacekeepers primarily being from the countries or regions that are, broadly speaking, most afflicted by the violence. This state of affairs stems primarily from the United Nations rules. While the UN mandates financial contributions from each country, contributions to the peacekeeping forces depend on the decision of member states. Therefore, while the US, China, Japan, Russia and France may rank amongst the highest financial contributors, countries like Ethiopia, India, Pakistan, Bangladesh and

---

[10]'Assembly authorizes secretary-general to enter into commitments not exceeding $200 million to finance UN mission in Kosovo', Press Release, GA/9579, 28 July 1999, accessed 15 June 2019, https://www.un.org/press/en/1999/19990728.ga9579.html.

Rwanda rank amongst the largest providers of troops. Even so, most contributors to the UN peacekeeping forces often complain about delays in payments and inefficiencies in equipment and logistical support required to carry out effective peacekeeping operations. India has routinely agitated this case at the UN, demanding timely and adequate compensation for its peacekeeping expenses.

The problem is all the more ironic when seen against the comparative costs of other military activities—two days of 'Operation Desert Storm', for instance, would have paid for all of the United Nations peacekeeping operations that calendar year (1991)—and even against the kinds of military expenditures national governments are usually willing to contemplate out of their defence budgets. An instructive indication of this came in 1993 when NATO planners, asked to prepare for a possible operation to implement a peace settlement in Bosnia and Herzegovina, estimated its annual cost at $8.3 billion—by ironic coincidence the exact figure, at that point, of the United Nations cumulative expenditure on all peacekeeping operations since 1948. If peacekeeping is to have a future, governments will have to overcome the syndrome under which legislators are always willing to pay for war, but not for peace. The General Assembly routinely exhorts member states to pay their assessed contributions for peacekeeping operations 'on time and in full', but in practice only a handful of states send in their contributions within the stipulated thirty days after the issuance of a letter of assessment (which itself comes at the end of a lengthy process of budget preparation and review by two different governmental bodies, and a vote by the General Assembly).[11] For the most part the experience has been that, three months after assessments are levied, barely 50 per cent of the required funds have come in.

The result is to tie the operational hands of the United Nations—which frequently has to deal with commercial contractors, and in some cases government providers, who want cash 'up front' before providing goods and services to peacekeeping operations—and,

[11] Shashi Tharoor, 'The Future of Peacekeeping', p. 21.

equally troubling, limits the ability of the Secretariat to reimburse troop-contributing countries. In the case of developing countries, this can cause serious hardship, particularly since governments with hard-currency problems tend to await United Nations reimbursement before paying their troops. The resulting problems of morale in mixed missions like the United Nations Protection Force (UNPROFOR), where soldiers subsisting on the United Nations allowance of $1.25 a day served side by side with Western troops earning hardship bonuses in addition to their much higher regular salaries, have contributed to serious operational difficulties on the ground. Even more discouraging are the recent developments in the US Congress, which has already mandated a unilateral reduction of the US peacekeeping contribution and has even considered legislation which would 'offset' the costs of national military efforts against UN dues, which would thereby have eliminated, for all practical purposes, US financial support for United Nations peacekeeping if this had become law. It did not, but with President Trump's well-known disdain for the world body, there is no telling what he might yet do.

While Western states are gradually withdrawing from responsibilities that they once monopolized jealously, it is increasingly clear that China has picked up on this model. Beijing is now the second largest provider of peacekeeping finance amongst the P5 countries, and rapidly ramping up the number of peacekeeping missions it participates in. In 2015, China pledged to create a force of nearly 8,000 peacekeepers along with a $1 billion grant to be disbursed over a ten-year period. This is not wholly an altruistic endeavour. There are three reasons that China has ramped up its support for UN peacekeeping operations. First, at the simplest level, China is expanding its role in global governance institutions in an attempt to establish itself as a responsible power. It has realized that the withdrawal of Western powers from these processes will create a vacuum it can exploit. Second, as China's economic interests expand along the Belt and Road Initiative, its multimillion dollar geo-economic thrust, lending its military officials to peacekeeping operations in these countries, allows it the ability to gain influence with the member states it has invested in. And, finally, China sees an opportunity to influence human rights regimes in investing money and troops towards peacekeeping operations. Already, it has run a comprehensive campaign to decrease funding to human rights oversight mechanisms during peacekeeping and NGO and civil society participation during operations. It has similarly been less inclined to subscribe to the 'liberal' proposition for development, convincing states to adopt a state-led model for development.

Each of these examples—of the larger powers disregarding the UN, of leveraging it to suit their interests, and of relegating conflicts to others when they have no stake in them—makes clear that the UN's core agenda, of peace and security, is just as susceptible to Darwinian interests as the other interests it seeks to serve. Having said that, we must also acknowledge that the UN has never been, and will never be, a perfect body. It has acted unwisely at times, and failed to act at others. There is no shortage of examples of the UN's setbacks. In the summer of 2006, protestors in Beirut smashed and tried to set fire to the UN office there in the wake of the summer war between Israel and Hezbollah. But in Israel, the UN was being attacked as the home of anti-Israeli opinion. In 2003, just after the Iraq war, a Pew poll taken in twenty countries after the fall of Baghdad showed that the UN had suffered a great deal of collateral damage over Iraq. The UN's standing had gone down in all twenty countries. The UN's credibility was down in the US because it did not support the US administration on the war, and in nineteen other countries because it did not prevent the war. So once again, the UN, as usual, got hit from both sides of the debate.

But the United Nations, at its best and its worst, is a mirror of the world: it reflects not just our divisions and disagreements but also our hopes and convictions. Even those countries that once felt insulated from external dangers—by wealth or strength or distance—now fully realize that the safety of people everywhere depends not only on local security forces, but also on guarding against terrorism; warding off the global spread of pollution, of diseases, of illegal drugs and of weapons of mass destruction; and on promoting human rights, democracy and development, and on eradicating poverty and illiteracy. Maintaining international peace and security is fundamental to global governance, and that requires international institutions that ensure global stability.

As the great second secretary-general of the UN, Dag Hammarskjöld, put it, the United Nations was not created to take mankind to heaven, but to save humanity from hell. And, to an extent, it has. We must not forget that the UN has achieved an enormous amount in its seventy-four years.[12] Most important of all, it prevented the Cold War from turning hot—first, by providing a roof under which the two superpower adversaries could meet and engage, and second, by mounting peacekeeping operations that ensured that local and regional conflicts were contained and did not ignite a superpower clash that could have sparked off a global conflagration. Over the years, more than 190 UN-assisted peace settlements have ended regional conflicts. And in the past twenty years, more civil wars have ended through mediation than in the previous two centuries combined, in large part because the UN provided leadership, opportunities for negotiation, strategic coordination and the resources to implement peace agreements. More than 350 international treaties have been negotiated at the UN, setting an international framework that reduces the prospect for conflict among sovereign states. The UN has built global norms that are universally accepted in areas as diverse as decolonization and disarmament, development and democratization.

However, its ability now to maintain peace and order in the international system is at risk not because it does not enjoy an impressive track record of peacekeeping, but because its legitimacy as an institution is under strain. This is so because the countries that are to guarantee international security are the ones that are least interested in upholding it beyond a point. This state of affairs is all the more disappointing given that the UN is now a repository of institutional knowledge on maintaining international security.

---

[12]Extracted from 'The women's foreign policy group presents Shashi Tharoor under UNSG "The future of UN"', Shashi Tharoor Official Website, 3 May 2006, accessed 15 June 2019, http://shashitharoor.in/writings_essays_details/118.

It has drawn together the human capital, academic knowledge, technical expertise, political will and international reach to deliver peace, security and development around the world—especially in regions or conflicts where great powers were not implicated. The operations that brought Namibia to independence, that transformed the society and politics of Cambodia and El Salvador, that restored hope in Mozambique, were all multidimensional efforts that demonstrated the ability of the UN to maintain international peace and security. The techniques involved worked; the world cannot do without them.

Early in 1995 the *New York Times* turned its magisterial gaze upon the future of United Nations peacekeeping, an activity that had come in for considerable criticism in the American media over the preceding two years. 'Rethinking and retrenchment are in order... There should be a shift back toward more limited objectives like policing cease-fires,' it declared. 'U.N. peace-keeping does what it can do very well. It makes no sense to continue eroding its credibility by asking it to do what it cannot.'[13]

This somewhat startling advocacy of a return to traditional verities gave pause to many UN officials who had been engaged in the practice of peacekeeping during its tumultuous history. Was the *Times* right, and if so, were we to contemplate a future of retreating headlong into the past?

At one level, there was something oddly comforting about the thought of seeking safety in well-worn practices; resting on old laurels is a good deal easier than wresting new ones. Yes, 'traditional peace-keeping' is something the United Nations has done well and continues to know how to do. The UN's least problematic operations are always those where the parties agree to end their conflicts and only need the UN's help to keep their word, where the risks are low, the tasks assigned to the peacekeepers are those that are basic bread-and-butter skills for any army in the world, and the shoestring resources available to the United Nations are adequate for the job at hand. In these situations, the United Nations can bring a wealth of

---

[13]'The Future of U.N. Peacekeeping', editorial, *New York Times*, 8 January 1995.

experience and precedent to bear in the successful conduct of such peacekeeping operations. Many of those in this business would like nothing more than to say: 'Give us the buffer zones in Cyprus or Kuwait, the elections in Cambodia or Mozambique, the package-deals in Namibia or El Salvador, and we'll deliver you an effective, efficient, success-story, on time and under budget.' All professionals— and United Nations peacekeepers are no exception—are always happy to be asked to do what they can do best.

Sadly, however, this attractive formula has one thing wrong with it: It's a good answer, but only to part of the question. Traditional peacekeeping is all very well if the only security crises confronting the world are those which are ripe for the peacekeeping treatment. But classical, consensual peacekeeping does not respond fully to the nature of the world we live in and the challenges the new world disorder poses to the international community.[14] If the nature of United Nations peacekeeping has acquired a certain elasticity in recent years, it is precisely because circumstances have led the world to make demands on the military capacity of the United Nations which vastly exceed anything the organization was called upon to do a generation ago. We will not be able to face the twenty-first century by remaining firmly rooted in the twentieth.

In admitting, understandably, that the UN cannot afford to become part of the problem as it did by taking sides in Somalia; in acknowledging that the world cannot easily find troop contributing countries willing to commit forces to halt genocide, as the UN had hoped it might in Rwanda; in accepting that the UN can protect humanitarian aid deliveries, but that it cannot force them through, as it discovered in Bosnia; in conceding all this, the UN does not need also to abandon the functions of policing the local

---

[14]For analyses of these contemporary challenges, see James N. Rosenau, *Turbulence in World Politics: A Theory of Change and Continuity*, Princeton: Princeton University Press, 1990; Lawrence Freedman, 'Order and Disorder in the New World', *Foreign Affairs* 71 (1991–92), pp. 20–37; Thomas G. Weiss, 'UN Responses in the Former Yugoslavia: Moral and Operational Choices', *Ethics and International Affairs*, 1994, Volume 8, pp. 13–14; and *Survival* 35, Spring 1993, special issue on 'Ethnic Conflict and International Security'.

police, of protecting ethnic minorities, of upholding human rights standards, of running free and fair elections, of supervising mistrusted local administrations, of creating conditions conducive to political accommodation and national reconciliation, all of which it has done in recent years with success—and all of which take us beyond the *New York Times'* prescription.[15]

The fact remains, however, that these functions were never the organization's primary purpose. Rather it was to create and maintain the conditions that would allow international peace. And the barriers to these efforts are numerous. The more difficult problems relate to situations in which agreements are non-existent or short-lived; where the United Nations does not enjoy the formal consent or the practical cooperation of the parties amidst whom it is deployed; and when the nature of the ongoing conflict obliges us to confront searching questions about the need to use force in order to be effective, with the concomitant risk that doing so will jeopardize the United Nations' impartiality and thus the very effectiveness it is trying to attain; and perhaps most importantly, when the largest powers allow Darwinian instincts to guide their behaviour, refusing to constrain themselves to the norms that are expected of the international community.[16]

Of course, even with these daunting challenges, abstention is not really an option.[17] For most of the crises that thrust themselves on the United Nations' agenda, indifference is impossible. This is not just a moral matter, though the suffering caused by these conflicts—in many of which the infliction of agony on innocent civilians is a direct aim, rather than a by-product, of war—remains an affront to the world's conscience. In a world of instant satellite communications, with television images of suffering broadcast as they occur, few democratic governments are immune to the public clamour to 'do something'. For a couple of years in the 1990s, the international community, pressed to respond and unready with

---

[15]Shashi Tharoor, 'The Future of Peacekeeping'.

[16]Id.

[17]Shashi Tharoor, 'The Changing Face of Peace-Keeping and Peace Enforcement', *Fordham International Law Journal*, Vol. 19, Issue 2, 1995.

an alternative international security mechanism, found in United Nations peacekeeping the 'something' it could 'do'. Peacekeepers took unprecedented risks, made foreseeable mistakes, suffered an intolerable level of casualties; governments, accountable politically for the safety of their soldiers, cut their losses and proved unwilling to risk additional ones. In the process, we have all learned what peacekeeping cannot do; and yet we cannot afford to do nothing. The challenge of the future is to define that 'something' in terms of what is doable—in other words, to identify how the United Nations can be enabled to respond to future Somalias and Rwandas while retaining the support of member states.

Nevertheless, what to do, and who should do it, remains a strand of inquiry that the Security Council has in recent years refused to even acknowledge. This is despite the fact that past attempts at imposition have often gone awry, as the years of chaos in Iraq after the American military triumph in 2003 demonstrated.[18] War creates casualties. Often these exceed the beneficiaries; it has only been a few decades since an American general so fatuously declared in Vietnam that 'it was necessary to destroy the village in order to save it'. If you want peace, you must prepare for war—only in order not to have to go to war. Once you do, peace is no longer possible; the logic of war renders the very idea absurd, as we saw every day in Libya. The French philosopher Blaise Pascal remarked, centuries ago, that 'he who would act the angel, acts the beast'. To pretend that angels must do beastly things for angelic purposes is either naïve, or cynical, or both. When the war ended in Libya, amidst all the smoke and the rubble lay one more discredited notion, that of going to war in the name of peace.

And as we will continue to argue in successive chapters, international security was merely a function of the converging or competing interests of a select group of nations. In 1993, member states of the United Nations attempted to challenge this status quo, leading to the establishment of an 'Open-Ended Working Group on

---

[18]Shashi Tharoor, 'War for Peace', *Forbes*, 30 May 2011.

the Question of Equitable Representation on and Increase in the Membership of the Security Council and Other Matters related to the Security Council'. The creation of this group was considered an extraordinary concession by the P5, who jealously guarded their privileged position in the United Nations. Fourteen years of heated conversations, debates, discussions later, the most tangible outcome of these proceedings has been to attain the status of 'Intergovernmental Negotiations' in 2007. More uncharitably, the group is often referred to as the 'Never-Ending Shirking Group'.

◆

In 2000, Senator Jesse Helms, then chairman of the powerful United States Senate Committee on Foreign Relations, visited the United Nations and offered a harsh message: 'A United Nations that seeks to impose its presumed authority on the American people, without their consent, begs for confrontation and—I want to be candid with you—eventual U.S. withdrawal.'[19] This forceful, yet honest, assertion of American priorities is a transparent testament to how major powers in the Security Council understand the United Nations. Remember that the senator was saying this on behalf of a nation that has entrusted itself with the responsibility of maintaining collective security in the international system. Indeed, it is not difficult to understand why leaders from the developing world have consistently questioned the legitimacy of the United Nations Security Council.

And these criticisms have acquired much more salience today. The world has evolved significantly towards greater global governance since the end of World War II. And yet, as we have noted, the global governance structures of today still reflect the realities of 1945 and not of 2020. As we look around the world of 2019, we cannot but fail to note the increase in the number of major powers across the world since the structures of the international system were put in place in 1945. It is an undeniable fact that the emerging powers

---

[19]Barbara Crossette, 'Helms, in Visit to U.N., Offers Harsh Message', *New York Times*, 21 January 2000.

have moved very much from the periphery to the centre of global discourse and global responsibility, and they have now a legitimate and an increasingly voluble desire to share power and responsibility in the global system. So, too, do the so-called 'social forces'—NGOs, civil society movements, multi-national corporations, and transnational terrorist organizations—which have become impossible to ignore in any discussion of global governance, but a detailed examination of which lies outside the scope of the book

India, for one, feels very strongly that there is a clear need for an expansion of the Security Council in both categories—permanent and non-permanent. During her tenure as India's External Affairs Minister, the late Sushma Swaraj offered a harsh criticism of the United Nations ability to guarantee collective security. At the United Nations General Assembly (UNGA), she thundered that the UN has 'failed to effectively address the new challenges to international peace and security... When we ask ourselves whether we have been able to prevent conflicts taking place in several parts of the world, the answer is "no",' she said. 'If we ask whether we were able to find permanent solution to these conflicts, the answer is "no". If we ask whether we were able to show the path of peace to a world which is going on the way of violence, the answer is "no".[20] For a country like India to make these claims is a damning condemnation of the legitimacy of the United Nations. More so because India is, despite all it has had to endure, a strong votary of the United Nations. It has consistently called for reform through the institution rather than undermine it from without. Indeed, India sees the Security Council as part of a broader process of renewing the United Nations, not because it has failed but because it has succeeded often enough to be worth reforming.

And there are good reasons for India's assessment. The global nature of the determining forces of today's world are contending and even contradictory: on the one hand, are the forces of convergence,

---

[20]'UN fails to address new challenges to peace, security: India', Press Trust of India, 2 October 2015.

the increasing knitting together of the world through globalization, modern communications and trade, and on the other, are the opposite forces of disruption, religious polarization, notions of the clash of civilizations, and terrorism.[21] We have to recognize both the positive and negative forces of the world today, and from it, a consciousness of the increasing mutual interdependence that characterizes our age. It is clear that global governance rests on the realization that security is not indeed just about threats from enemy states or hostile powers, but that there are common phenomena that cut across borders and affect us all. Nor can they be solved by any one country or any one group of countries, which make them unavoidably the shared responsibility of humankind.

There is an obvious list of such problems: terrorism itself, the proliferation of weapons of mass destruction, the degradation of our common environment, climate change, persistent poverty and haunting hunger, human rights and human wrongs, mass illiteracy and massive displacement. There are financial and economic crises (because the financial contagion becomes a virus that spreads from one country to others), the risk of trade protectionism, refugee movements, drug trafficking. And we must not overlook the threat of epidemic disease as exemplified in the recent past by SARS, AIDS, swine flu, Ebolo, Zika and Nipah.

At a time when these multiple global challenges continue to cascade, and during a time when great power transitions are straining the utility of multilateralism, the United Nations has failed to reform its most important and criticized institution: the Security Council. And these imperatives aquire further urgency given that there is now more conflict and contest in the international system; around the world, nationalism and self interest have replaced internationalism and multilateralism as the defining political mood. These tendencies are making themselves felt on international trade, migration and

---

[21]'Address by Minister of State for External Affairs, Dr. Shashi Tharoor on India's Role in the Emerging World Order', Indian Council of World Affairs, Sapru House, New Delhi: Indian Council of World Affairs, 26 March 2010, accessed 15 June 2019, https://icwa.in/mospeech.html.

international security. The UN, as an institution and as a value system, appears increasingly less relevant to managing the world. Despite these extraordinary imperatives, the only time the United Nations Security Council entertained reform seriously enough to enact it was in 1965, when the number of non-permanent seats was increased from six to ten. It is beyond obvious that the United Nations has failed to enable mechanisms that would allow for its own institutional evolution.

We are in a situation where the P5 are unrestricted in their ability to influence peace and security around the world. Often, their petty squabbles about words and phrases in documents and resolutions spill over into the real world with disastrous consequences for those that are the subjects of these debates. Consider Yemen, for example, where a Saudi-backed coalition has widely been held responsible for causing a humanitarian crisis. Nevertheless, the United States opposed British efforts to condemn such military action in the United Nations, worrying that the language was overly critical of the Saudi regime. Similarly, the US was adamant that the UN mission in Congo be scaled back as a condition for American support, a position that caused considerable anguish in France, which has vested interests in the former colony. The US has even attempted to pass resolutions in the UN demanding fresh elections in Venezuela, given the Trump administration's tensions with President Nicolás Maduro. China, meanwhile, continues to veto any UN debates on the human rights situation in North Korea; it has time and again blocked UN attempts to condemn the ethnic cleansing of the Rohingya from Myanmar; and consistently (until June 2019, when it finally relented) prevented the designation of Jaish-e-Mohammed's Mazood Azhar as a terrorist in order to annoy India. Russia, of course, has not behaved any better: consistently protecting the Syrian regime as well as a host of African dictators that Moscow is cultivating as part of its efforts to engage with the continent more comprehensively.

It is increasingly clear that a reform package that incorporates both Security Council and Bretton Woods reforms could transform global governance, whereas failure to reform could doom it. The international system—as constructed following World War II—will be almost unrecognizable by 2030 owing to the rise of emerging powers, a transformed global economy, a real transfer of relative wealth and economic power from the West, or the North, to other countries in the Global South, and the growing influence of non-state actors, including terrorists, multinational corporations and criminal networks. Water, on which demand is projected to outstrip easily available supplies over the next decade or so, will gain prominence on the international agenda. In the next two decades, this new international system will be coping with the issues of ageing populations in the developed world; increasing energy, food, and water constraints; and worries about climate change and migration. Global changes, including India's own transformation, will mean that resource issues— including energy, food, and water—will become potential security issues and sources of cross-border conflict.

Human security requires a world in which sovereign states can come together to share burdens, address common problems and seize common opportunities. How can such security be ensured? Clearly, there is an ineluctable link to the emerging concept of global governance. Human security cannot be the pursuit of any one nation, however rich or powerful it might be. It manifestly requires international cooperation within global bodies, as well as action by international and inter-state organizations such as the United Nations itself (including through the operations of specialized agencies working on health, children, labour standards, etc., and the negotiation, conclusion and application of international treaties and conventions). What about the old-fashioned idea of security in the military sense? That is no exception: the UN conducts peacekeeping missions, and so do regional organizations like ECOWAS in West Africa and NATO in Europe, often (but not always) acting under a mandate from the world body. These are all examples of collective military action in a global-governance context, and they involve nation states ceding some degree of control over the deployment of their national defence and security forces to supranational institutions. Even a non-UN authorized mission like that of the International

Security Assistance Force (ISAF) in Afghanistan involves contributions from several countries, all in the name of a higher global good.

Scholars, diplomats, and government leaders all differ in their recommendations for these challenges. Some argue that if the UN is indeed in crisis, the way forward is to strengthen the United Nations' administrative tools for operation. After all, very few organizations possess the type of global influence or reach that the United Nations does. Sceptics, on the other hand, will argue that the United Nations is an institution that has far passed its retirement date. This is a view that has gained traction both in the communities that once participated in the ideation of the UN, and those who have suffered most at its hand. In March 2003, as the debates were raging in the Security Council over Iraq, a BBC interviewer rather glibly asked Shashi Tharoor, 'So how does the UN feel about being seen as the "i" word—irrelevant?' He was about to go on when Tharoor interrupted him. 'As far as we're concerned,' he retorted, 'the "i" word is "indispensable".'[22]

Today, it is likely caught between these two descriptions. It is certainly not indispensable, at least in the realm of international security, considering that the largest powers have often dispensed with its tenets and rules. Nor is it irrelevant, given that, for better or for worse, it remains the only global institution vested with the responsibility of maintaining peace. It is more accurate to argue today that the United Nations is 'intransigent'. It is an ageing institution, created for a different time and unable or unwilling today to react to new realities and circumstances.

Faced with multiple and interrelated pressures to reform and adapt, it has stubbornly failed to do so—held hostage by the priorities and preferences of a few. And unless this monopoly ends, the UN will gradually drift further away from its purpose—it will be an institution that is too big and complex to abandon, but too old and slow, and unrepresentative of today's world, to matter.

---

[22]Shashi Tharoor, 'Indispensable, not irrelevant', *The Hindu*, 16 March 2003.

CHAPTER 3

SUSTAINED DEBATE OVER
SUSTAINABLE DEVELOPMENT

There are two strands that are central to global governance that have been debated at length and it is worth exploring them in some detail. These debates are the discourse on development and the discourse on internet governance. The discourse on sustainable development was a product of twentieth century politics and the internet was born at the turn of the century. The climate, and Earth's resources more generally, are ordinarily thought of as the global commons. They are outside the sovereign jurisdiction of any one state. Cyberspace, meanwhile, is certainly global in reach and effect. However, it remains the product of state infrastructure, planning and innovation. As these next two chapters will make clear, this difference would affect the manner in which power was entrenched and exercised over these mediums.

In this chapter, we will discuss global arrangements to achieve sustainable development and combat climate change. There are two crucial elements to this debate. The first, is the institutional order itself. The narratives and debates that shaped institutional responses to climate change were themselves biased from the start—placing the burden on developing countries despite the fact that communities in the developed world, which had itself developed with scant regard for the environment, remained the largest consumers of energy and producers of waste. Unsurprisingly then, the institutions that were at the forefront of this issue were guided by vested interests and incorrect assumptions. The second element is the outcomes themselves. Again, we will see that despite some convergence on the quality of life, there remains significant inequity in the development pathways of developing and developed nations. The consequences of this failure cannot be understated: with millions of individuals still struggling to access clean energy and safe habitat, 'survival of the fittest' will continue to remain a way of life.

COLONIALISM'S CLIMATE

Today we are living in an era of epochal change in relation to the planet's climate. Unfettered industrialization and unsustainable patterns of consumption have contributed to rising temperatures and large-scale environmental degradation. At the same time, inequality and poverty continue to remain the mainstay of ordinary life. Access to water, health, sanitation, food and, shelter continues to evade those who need it the most. Even worse is that these two trends are tied in the most toxic manner. In 2017, Hurricane Harvey made landfall along the coast of Texas and Hurricane Irma made landfall along Florida, causing devastation to property and life, effectively bringing the states to a standstill. In 2019, floods in Assam, Bihar, Nepal and Bangladesh displaced nearly four million individuals and caused over a hundred deaths.

Efforts to mitigate the adverse impacts of climate change have been fitfully conducted for over three decades now and the imperatives that need balancing are not minor. On the one hand, ever-increasing carbon emissions and unsustainable resource consumption are straining the world's ecological systems, to the point that they will no longer be able to sustain life. On the other, millions of poor in the most underdeveloped parts of the world struggle to meet their daily needs for shelter, water, food, and energy. To meet these demands, countries around the world will inevitably burden the world's resources further. Since there are no easy technical fixes for climate change, and measures to absorb greenhouse gases (such as reforestation) are relatively limited compared with the projected scale of emissions, the only effective way of reducing the build-up of greenhouse gas concentrations is to reduce emissions.

For the Global South, the hypocrisy of the developed world is unbearably evident. Having already achieved high standards of living by far exceeding their fair share of carbon emissions, not only have developed countries refused to reform their political and economic governance models which created and perpetuated this injustice, they have increasingly sought to shift the burden of mitigating climate change onto developing countries. The simple truth is that even if developed countries managed to decelerate their emissions soon, the remaining carbon space left for the Global South would be minimal. It is this lack of carbon space that the Global North fails to acknowledge and that invigorates the Southern narrative around equity. The fact is that the only proven roadmap for development involves accelerating energy services and the most cost-effective manner to do so is by increasing carbon emissions.

The story of development and industrialization in the North is an old one, but deserves to be retold in the context of climate change and inequality. Prior to the year 1500, there was very little difference between the Atlantic powers and the rest of the world in terms of development and progress. However, following the invasion of Latin America, the African slave trade, and the colonization of Asia, the progress and wealth of Western nations was premised almost entirely on resource extraction from the rest of the world. Contrary to the popular narrative of the West bringing technology and civilization to the rest, research has revealed that nations which were colonized by the Europeans are far worse off today. Wherever Europeans settled in small numbers, they set up 'extractive institutions' which were systematically designed to drain resources, wealth and, labour from their colonies. Invariably, these extractive institutions appropriated the mass of the Global South's natural resources in order to fuel European industrialization and expansion, which is truly where the saga of environmental degradation begins. Cecil Rhodes summed up the philosophy behind this conquest well: 'We must find new lands from which we can easily obtain raw materials and...exploit the cheap slave labour...from the natives...the colonies would also provide a dumping ground for the surplus goods produced in our factories.'[1]

---

[1]'Rhodes Less Trampled', *Weekly Standard*, 24 November 2017.

The scale of colonialism was staggering. At its height in 1922, the British empire covered more than a quarter of the planet's land area.[2] For Europeans, empire became a way of life. An enormous amount of goods and resources were extracted from the colonies to be consumed in the North. Under British rule, for example, Indian farmers were forced to cultivate 'cash crops' such as indigo and tobacco which degraded farmland, rendering them unfit for cultivation.[3]

The British weren't concerned with the well-being of their subjects either. Indeed, the economic policies of the British Raj, in the midst of severe droughts, produced famines that claimed the lives of over thirteen million Indians between 1876 and 1902 alone, and possibly thirty million overall.[4] Before the British arrived, India generated 27 per cent of global GDP in 1700, and by the time they left, India's share had been cut to just 3 per cent. Meanwhile, Europeans increased their share of global GDP from 20 per cent to 60 per cent during the colonial period.[5] The fact is that Europe didn't develop the colonies, the colonies developed Europe.

The Spanish colonization of Latin America tells a similar tale. In the sixteenth century, Spanish settlers established a vast empire premised on wars against the indigenous populations of central and southern America. Many of these people were herded into environmentally destructive settlement patterns and forced labour, often to extract valuable minerals like silver and gold which formed the basis of Spanish conquest in the rest of the world. The Spanish arrival also disrupted indigenous ways of life and ecological systems by introducing European diseases like smallpox, measles and influenza.

---

[2]Adam Taylor, 'Map: The rise and fall of the British Empire', *Washington Post*, 8 September 2015.

[3]Richard Grove, 'Climatic Fears: Colonialism and the History of Environmentalism', *Harvard International Review*, Vol. 23, No. 4, Winter 2002, pp. 50–55.

[4]Joseph McQuade, 'Colonialism was a disaster and the facts prove it', *The Conversation*, 27 September 2017; Shashi Tharoor, *An Era of Darkness: The British Empire in India*, New Delhi: Aleph Book Company, 2016.

[5]Jason Hickel, 'Enough of aid—let's talk reparations', *The Guardian*, 27 November 2015.

Some population modelling suggests that the population of the Americas declined from approximately 61 million in 1492 to 5.6 million in 1650.[6]

Not only was colonialism responsible for environmental damage, the institutions it left behind were often the primary cause of structural inequality and oppression. In sixteenth-century Brazil, the Portuguese were engaged in sugar exports which were premised on the 'latifundio', which was a large estate with a single landlord, monoculture and slave labour.[7] The entire sugar cane industry in Brazil, therefore, was built on extreme social inequality, where economic and political power was concentrated in a small, repressive elite class. Similarly, in Mexico, the Spanish elite institutionalized the infamous 'encomienda' which legally entitled them to the fruits of indigenous labour. In Peru, the 'mita' system obligated the indigenous male populace to work in agriculture and gold mining.[8] On top of all this, colonial rulers employed exploitative tax systems which unjustly burdened colonial populations in order to generate state revenue.

Ultimately, even in the post-colonial era, the effects of such extractive institutions and export-led policies ensnared the Third World in a continuous cycle of deprivation and poverty. The scramble for Africa is perhaps the best example of this. Throughout the 1800s, the colonial powers carved up the continent into arbitrary colonies, protectorates and free trade areas. The slave trade generated from this endeavour was staggering; millions of Africans were shipped off to different parts of the world, especially to the Americas to fuel colonial expansion. Ultimately, an impoverished continent was left behind—scarred by environmental damage, ethnic conflict and dictatorships. In fact, some estimates suggest that if the slave trade had not occurred, 72 per cent of the average income gap between

---

[6]Alexander Koch et al., 'Earth system impacts of the European arrival and Great Dying in the Americas after 1492', *Quaternary Science Review*, Vol. 207, 2019, pp. 13-36.

[7]Warren Dean, 'Latifundia and Land Policy in Nineteenth-Century Brazil', *Hispanic American Historical Review*, Vol. 51, No. 4, 1971, pp. 606–25.

[8]Melissa Dell, 'The Persistent Effects of Peru's Mining Militia', *Econometrica*, Vol. 78, No. 6, 2010, pp.1863–1903.

Africa and the rest of the world would not exist today, and 99 per cent of the income gap between Africa and other developing countries would not exist.[9] The economic effects of this enterprise were obvious: In 1750 the 'Third World' (as it would come to be known), including Africa, Asia and Latin America, produced some 70 to 76 per cent of the world's goods and services; by 1913, that number had fallen to around 7 to 8 per cent.[10]

As European colonialism in Asia and Africa began to collapse through the 1950s, states across the Global South began to determine their own economic policies. Refusing to simply be exporters of raw materials, but largely lacking significant capital accumulation (which had mostly been drained to the metropolitan countries), they sought to industrialize on their own terms using nationalization, import substitution, subsidies, and tariffs to achieve this. Not only did developing countries begin achieving high growth rates, they also began reaching out to each other to form alliance networks. In Bandung, they grouped together to reject neo-colonialism, and the Non-Aligned Movement was formed to oppose interventions from both sides of the Cold War divide. Eventually, this movement came to include a vast number of countries from the Global South, culminating in the formation of the Group of 77 (G77), who were successful in passing a non-binding declaration for the New International Economic Order (NIEO), which enshrined their right to determine their own economic policies and exploit their natural resources.

Leaders of the newly independent states recognized that they had to control their own resources in order to survive and prosper, and so they used their power in the UN General Assembly to contest what they perceived as unbalanced legal rules. Thus, the 1960 UN Declaration on the Granting of Independence to Colonial Countries and Peoples affirmed that 'peoples may...freely dispose of

---

[9]Nathan Nunn, 'The Historical Origins of Africa's Underdevelopment', *Vox EU*, 8 December 2007.
[10]Shiraz Dossa, 'Slicing up "Development": Colonialism, Political Theory and Ethics', *Third World Quarterly*, Vol. 28, No. 5, 2007, pp. 887–99.

their natural wealth and resources'[11] and a 1962 resolution declared that the 'right of peoples and nations to permanent sovereignty over their natural wealth...must be exercised in the interest of their national development and the well-being of the people...concerned.'[12]

However, the resolution also provided that 'appropriate compensation' was to be paid 'in accordance with the rules in force in the State taking such measures...and in accordance with international law'—the latter phrase having been insisted upon by the United States and Britain. Unlike the colonial era, where Northern intervention was predicated on the 'civilized' west conquering the 'Orient', the post-World War era would see this discourse shift marginally, with the 'industrialized North' developing the 'poor South'. From the start 'development' has always been a justification for the international intervention of the North in matters of the South. From this point on, the paradigm of progress was measured in strictly Western economic terms. It was as if the extent to which the former colonial powers had relied on the exploitation of the resources and labour of the colonized states was forgotten.

Decolonization was not truly a reconciliatory process. The West systematically rejected any discourse which highlighted the extent to which its former colonies had been exploited and undermined—which is why, even today, the Western perception of the problems that plague the developing world is that they are largely due to authoritarian and/or corrupt regimes, inequalities, poverty, and brutal ethnic and tribal conflict. The former colonies were now simply 'backward' or underdeveloped states who were again in need of Western intervention.

The Western states were clever in their recognition of the Third World's sovereignty. The leases, contracts and, concessions

---

[11]Declaration on the Granting of Independence to Colonial Countries and Peoples Adopted by General Assembly resolution 1514 (XV) of 14 December 1960, accessed 19 June 2019, https://www.un.org/en/decolonization/declaration.shtml.

[12]Permanent Sovereignty over Natural Resources by the General Assembly resolution 1803 (XVII), New York, 14 December 1962, http://legal.un.org/avl/ha/ga_1803/ga_1803.html.

entered into before independence were assiduously protected. The 1941 Atlantic Charter, proclaimed by President Franklin Delano Roosevelt and British Prime Minister Winston Churchill, described a world order in which all states would have equal access 'to the trade, and to the raw materials of the world'. In doing so they sought to somehow characterize the resources of the Third World as belonging to humanity as a whole, enmeshed in an international order which authorizes the expropriation of resources. (At Churchill's insistence, India was specifically excluded from those states to whom the Charter's principles would apply. He argued that this Charter should primarily apply to those countries freed from Nazi rule, and not those still governed by the British crown.)

This goal of 'development' was taken up with great vigour by the institutions of the Atlantic system. Consider a United Nations text bemoaning the plight of the Global South:

> There is a sense in which rapid economic progress is impossible without painful adjustments. Ancient philosophies have to be scrapped; old social institutions have to disintegrate; bonds of caste, creed and race have to burst; and large numbers of persons who cannot keep up with progress have to have their expectations of a comfortable life frustrated. Very few communities are willing to pay the full price of economic progress.[13]

In today's world, this report would have been seen as arrogant and indicative of the West's racism and ethnocentrism. At the time however, it exemplified the growing ambition of the developed world to radically restructure 'underdeveloped societies'. Despite their noble intentions, it very soon became apparent that the development discourse was but a veil behind which American and European economic development was premised. While the North

---

[13]Laurence W. Witt, 'Measures for the Economic Development of Underdeveloped Countries', New York: United Nations, 1951, pp. v, 108, *American Journal of Agricultural Economics*, Vol. 33, Issue 4, Part 1, November 1951, pp. 585—87.

plundered the world's resources, the Global South bore the brunt of adverse environmental consequences based on the large-scale burning of fossil fuels such as coal and oil, heralding a phase of industrialization which brought the planet's ecosystem to the verge of collapse. Consider, for example, the findings of the UN Millennium Ecosystem Assessment (MEA) in 2005, which concluded that economic activity during the previous fifty years produced more severe degradation of the planet's ecosystems than in any prior period in human history.[14] While the Global North benefited from value creation and wealth produced by the expropriation of Southern mineral resources, the developing world was mired in poverty and inequality. As we have noted, even today, the per capita carbon footprint of the world's most industrialized states far outstrips those of the South.

As if historical debasement weren't enough, the 1980s hastened economic collapse and heightened inequality in the South. After the demise of the so-called 'New International Economic Order' and the establishment of the 'Washington Consensus' in favour of liberal capitalism dominated by the West, the debt restructuring and market liberalization programmes imposed on several Latin American, African, and Asian states led to the uncontrolled proliferation of privatization and deregulation in developing country markets. While some of these export-led manufacturing policies did successfully reinvigorate many of these economies, what went unnoticed then was the widespread inequality and environmental degradation that the export of raw materials led to. In addition, these policies bankrupted millions of small-scale farmers in these developing countries by pitting them directly against the subsidized agricultural markets in the North. These economic policies, which were forced upon the developing world by the IMF and the World Bank, both West-dominated institutions, only exacerbated the environmental degradation of the South and worsened economic and social inequality. The elimination of social

---

[14]'Ecosystems and Human Well-being: Synthesis', *Millennium Ecosystem Assessment*, Washington DC: Island Press, 2005.

safety and the general misery of the poor resulted in food riots (known sardonically in some places as 'IMF riots') in many Southern countries. On top of this, private companies and industries descended on these weak states in order to mine resources, and left behind polluted rivers, air and soil. In effect, the South became the dumping ground for waste, while value from these resources was created in the North.

Lest the Western world pretend that these hazards were the unintended side effects of globalization, it is worth reading an internal memo prepared by Lawrence Summers, then chief economist for the World Bank in 1991. Summers himself had been a strong backer of structural adjustment policies. He wrote in an internal memo:

> ...Just between you and me, shouldn't the World Bank be encouraging more migration of dirty industries to the LDCs [less developed countries]?... The economic logic behind dumping a load of toxic waste in the lowest wage country is impeccable, and we should face up to that... Under-populated countries in Africa are vastly under-polluted; their air quality is probably vastly inefficiently low compared to Los Angeles or Mexico City... The concern over an agent that causes a one in a million change in the odds of prostate cancer is obviously going to be much higher in a country where people survive to get prostate cancer than in a country where under-five mortality is 200 per thousand.[15]

The terminology of 'developed' and underdeveloped itself arrived at a time when the Global North was intent on convincing the Third World about the necessity of Northern intervention in governments and markets; and 'under-development' came to signify an apparently causeless and a historical state of things. Dominating the knowledge paradigms has always been an integral part of North–South relations. Earlier, religious and racial doctrines were used to justify colonialism. Today, globalization and market-led development are used to justify a

---

[15]Basil Enwegbara, 'Toxic Colonialism', *The Tech*, Vol. 121, Issue 16, 6 April 2001.

new form of control.

In the Global North, citizens have come to associate wealth and prosperity with large households, even larger vehicles, air-conditioned environments, carbon intensive food processing and much more. Much of their lifestyles have come about as a result of resources, material and industry taken from the South. However, most of the countries which have exported the raw materials to supplement Northern lifestyles have not transitioned into middle income economies. In fact, almost 80 per cent of these countries have per capita income below the global average, and since 1995, more than half of these countries have failed to match the average global growth rate.[16]

Despite all this, the North sees the environment in biological terms, as a natural phenomenon which needs to be tackled collectively, with responsibility borne equally. As we will see later in this chapter, developed nations believed that developing states had to meaningfully participate in climate change negotiations and bear the costs of mitigation and adaptation. However, out of the seven billion people that inhabit our planet, around two billion still lack access to essential medicines, 840 billion have no electricity, and 820 million are chronically undernourished.[17] The richest 14 per cent of the world's population have a mean life expectancy of eighty-four, while the poorest 34 per cent of households live for only thirty-six years on average.[18] Undeniably, the individuals who find themselves on the starker side of these statistics reside in developing and underdeveloped states and it is these figures that shape the Southern discourse on climate change and development. It is difficult to preach development

---

[16]Richard Dobbs et al., 'Reverse the curse: Maximizing the potential of resource-driven economies', McKinsey Global Institute, December 2013, accessed 15 June 2019, https://www.mckinsey.com/~/media/McKinsey/Industries/Metals%20 and%20Mining/Our%20Insights/Reverse%20the%20curse%20Maximizing%20 the%20potential%20of%20resource%20driven%20economies/MGI_Reverse_the_ curse_Full_report.ashx.

[17]James Ellsmoor, 'Global Population Without Access To Electricity Drops By 400 Million Since 2010', *Forbes*, 23 May 2019 and FAO, IFAD, UNICEF, WFP and WHO, *The State of Food Security and Nutrition in the World 2019. Safeguarding against economic slowdowns and downturns*. Rome: FAO, 2019.

[18]Samir Saran, 'Putting life first', *The Hindu*, 3 August 2015.

restraint to a poor-country resident who cannot even dream of what every Westerner takes for granted, that one can flick a switch on the wall and have one's room bathed with light.

The South believes that equity and climate justice must play a key role in any climate change governance architecture. They are keenly aware that any bargain in which equity does not adequately account for the historical role that industrialized nations have played in exacerbating environmental degradation is patently unfair. They also understand that domestic compulsions make it impossible to sacrifice traditional development models in favour of those the North might perceive to be environmentally friendly.

The truth is that the global order as we know it today is built upon the legacy of conquest and colonization by the West. The narrative of development which has taken root over the past few decades is also a part of the same legacy. The West has arrived at its present levels of socio-economic development through a historical process which was premised on colonialism, exploitation and enslavement. It would be amiss to say that poverty and underdevelopment in the South is accidental. It is instead a continued part of that same historical process which has led to the dominance of the Western states in the present world order.

SUSTAINABLE DEVELOPMENT AND A CHRONOLOGY OF HYPOCRISY

If anyone truly believed that the wave of independence movements in the twentieth century would end the climate colonialism of the West, a history of the sustainable development and climate change discourse would prove them wrong. In place of their ostensibly backward economic models, the West sought to reaffirm the fundamental primacy of consumption and extraction of raw materials, redefining the hierarchies of man and nature.

One of the earliest attempts at understanding the relationship between economic growth and the environment took place at a seminal UN conference on the environment in Stockholm in 1972. The conference itself was originally prompted by Sweden's desire to see the environment on the global agenda. However, the road to Stockholm was not particularly straightforward. The conference stemmed from the largely Northern concern about the deterioration of the physical environment. Developing countries were not particularly keen on participating as it did not truly address their concerns.

In part, this was because the 1970s were also a time when developing countries were beginning to find their voice in institutions of global governance. By organizing themselves into G77, they succeeded in making the UNGA adopt the establishment of the New International Economic Order, which sought to reverse the injustice perpetrated on colonized nations, recognizing their right to sovereignty over their natural resources, improving access to developed markets and increasing transfer of technology and finance. That the North rejected both the premise and the intent of the NIEO was a different matter altogether; clearly no such order could be achieved without the acquiescence, at the very least, of the North.

The negotiations at Stockholm were no different. Developing countries approached the conference with scepticism, claiming it was an ill-disguised plot to restrict their economic development while the rich countries enlarged their gluttonous consumption of the planet's resources. The demand from the developing world that their development be addressed as well was most emphatically highlighted in General Assembly Resolution 2849 (XXVI) of 20 December 1971. The G77, who were successful in injecting this position into the Stockholm preparatory committee, blamed environmental degradation entirely on the developed countries and called on them to clean up the environment and pay for damage in developing countries as well. The vehemence of these demands took the developed world by surprise and threatened to derail the negotiations as the developed world was unwilling to accept this position, much less give any significant amount of funding. Thanks to the persistence of the developing world, it was at Stockholm in 1972 that the linkages between the environment and development were first explored. The conference represented one of the earliest acknowledgements that a business-as-usual approach to economic growth would devastate the environment as we knew it.

The ideological and political rhetoric was so high that it led the *New York Times* to observe that: 'Among the unexpected developments was the bluntness with which the newer nations taxed the advanced countries with prime responsibility for global environmental deterioration, and with an obligation accordingly to make reparations to the "third world" in various forms, from technical assistance in pollution control to special consideration in world trade.'[19]

However, the West was quick to turn this narrative around. It is unlikely that many in the West will remember that one of the first countries to actively participate in climate change negotiations was India. At the UN Conference on Human Environment held in Stockholm in 1972, the then Indian Prime Minister Indira Gandhi, who was one of only two heads of government present, stated:

> We do not wish to impoverish the environment any further, [but] we cannot forget the grim poverty of large numbers of people… When they themselves feel deprived how can we urge the preservation of animals? How can we speak to those who live…in slums about keeping our oceans, rivers and the air clean when their own lives are contaminated at the source? Environment cannot be improved in conditions of poverty…[20]

Indira Gandhi's message was a powerful wake-up call for the world. If economic growth and social mobility were premised on 'unsustainable' development, then how could India, which even today continues to host some of the poorest people in the world, fail to meet their needs? Around fifteen years after Indira Gandhi's famous speech, the World Commission on Environment and Development

---

[19]Gladwin Hill, 'Sense of Accomplishment Buoys Delegates Leaving Ecology Talks', *New York Times*, 18 June 1972.
[20]Indira Gandhi, 'Address to the United Nations Conference on the Human Environment', Stockholm, 14 June 1972, accessed 15 June 2019, http://lasulawsenvironmental.blogspot.com/2012/07/indira-gandhis-speech-at-stockholm.html.

(WECD) gathered to release a report which would set the tone for development and climate change discourse for years to come. The Brundtland Report, as the WECD came to be known, by itself did well to recognize the disastrous impact of mankind's gluttony for energy, and to recognize that we would have to find a model of development which served the needs of the present and those of the future. Hence, the idea of 'sustainable development' was born.

Perhaps less famous, but just as important, is another key hypothesis developed by the WECD about poverty, claiming that it was 'a major cause and effect of global environmental problems'. Sample these words: '…But poverty itself pollutes the environment, creating environmental stress in a different way. Those who are poor and hungry will often destroy their immediate environment in order to survive: They will cut down forests; their livestock will overgraze grasslands; they will overuse marginal land; and in growing numbers they will crowd into congested cities. The cumulative effect of these changes is so far-reaching as to make poverty itself a major global scourge.'[21]

The force of this narrative caught on globally, especially by dominant institutions of global governance. As the United Nations Human Development Report (HDR) phrased it in 1990, 'poverty is one of the greatest threats to the environment'.[22] Again, the correlation was stressed in a IMF survey in 1993, 'Poverty and the environment are linked in that the poor are more likely to resort to activities that can degrade the environment.'[23] In fact, in 1992, *The Economist* published a report titled 'The question Rio forgets', (the reference was to the Rio Conference that took place two decades after the Stockholm one) insisting that population growth was the most critical aspect which needed to be addressed when it came to global warming

---

[21]'Our Common Future', Report of the World Commission on Environment and Development, 1983, https://sustainabledevelopment.un.org/content/documents/5987our-common-future.pdf.

[22]'Human Development Report 1990', Published for the United Nations Development Programme by Oxford University Press, New York, 1990.

[23]'Seminar Explores Links Between Macro Policy and the Environment', *IMF Survey*, 14 June 1993, pp. 177 and 187.

and climate change, writing that 'much of the damage that could result from climate change in the next century is occurring right now, and it has nothing to do with carbon dioxide...the root cause of this damage is a combination of population growth and poverty in the Third World.'[24]

That poverty was the proximate cause of climate change was so well-entrenched in Western elite opinions that none of them ever paused to question if this was true or ask themselves why it was that with less than 20 per cent of the population, developed countries had produced more than 70 per cent of historical emissions since 1850 up until 2011?[25] This self-serving paradigm—that population and poverty are the major cause of climate change—shaped the sustainable development discourse for a few decades. What economists, scientists and governments failed to acknowledge then was that environmental stress was primarily caused by the consumption-led economic order of the Global North.

While maintaining that poverty was the root cause of environmental damage, the tone set at Stockholm did not truly deter the Global North from ending their exploitative environmental practices. For example, as the clamour for better regulation of industrial waste grew in Europe and America, these countries resorted to the cheapest practice available—shipping it to the Third World. From 1989 to March 1994, it was estimated that the OECD countries exported over two million tons of toxic and hazardous waste to the developing world.[26] More often than not, these countries had no technology to manage this waste, and the environmental and social costs of such practices were staggering. Although the Basel Convention (on the Control of Transboundary Movements of Hazardous Wastes and Their Disposal) ultimately prohibited the transhipment of many forms of toxic waste, the practice of exporting waste to the Third

---

[24]'The Question Rio Forgets', *The Economist*, 30 May 1992.
[25]'Developed Countries are Responsible for 79 Percent of Historical Carbon Emissions', Centre for Global Development, 18 August 2015.
[26]'Database of Known Hazardous Waste Exports from OECD to non-OECD countries 1989-March 1994', Amsterdam: Greenpeace International, 1994.

World continued unabated for several years.

By the end of it all, not only had the developing countries failed to assert the adverse role of the West in aggravating environmental degradation, they found themselves at the receiving end of the very same countries' criticism on account of their booming populations.

To be fair, however, the events at Stockholm did ultimately catalyse a larger conversation on the impact of unsustainable growth and climate change. In 1988, the UNGA explicitly identified climate change as 'a common concern of mankind'. At the same time the International Panel on Climate Change (IPCC) was formed which would regularly assess the impact of human activity on climate change. The IPCC First Assessment Report (FAR) was released in 1990, which warned that, in spite of some degree of numerical uncertainty, human activity was leading to increased atmospheric concentrations of atmospheric carbon dioxide and rising average temperatures. Many of these developments were hastened by the visible effects of climate change and environmental degradation. The discovery of a hole in the ozone layer over the Antarctic, and chemical and nuclear disasters in Bhopal and Chernobyl, all served to rouse community efforts to confront climate change.

After Stockholm, the next major climate change and sustainable development initiative was to be held in Rio in 1992. In the intervening decades, environmental issues had reached the centre stage of the global political agenda. Despite the force of scientific evidence and community demands, the United States continued to be the main stumbling block to these efforts. Much scepticism in relation to the science of climate change continued to emanate from the United States. It is worth pointing out that at this time the average per capita emission of fossil carbon dioxide from developing countries was barely one-tenth of the OECD average; and per capita emissions from regions such as the Indian subcontinent and Africa were around one-twentieth of those of the US.[27] In the run-up to Rio, the rift

---

[27]Matthew Paterson and Michael Grubb, 'The International Politics of Climate Change', *International Affairs*, Royal Institute of International Affairs, Vol. 68, No. 2,

between the Global North and the South had reached a tipping point. So intense was the debate that civil society organizations from both sides were engaged in a war of evidence: the Washington-based World Resources Institute (WRI) had presented a report on projected emissions, highlighting the negative role developing countries would be playing in the near future. This report was vehemently attacked by the New Delhi-based Centre for Science and Environment (CSE) as a 'politically-motivated' attempt to 'blame developing countries for climate change and perpetuate the current global inequality in the use of the earth's environment and its resources.'[28]

Unlike Stockholm, the euphoria of the developing world in negotiating better terms for themselves in global governance issues was fading. It was clear from the start that the developed world would not restructure the relationship between the Global North and the South. Using their entrenched positions in institutions of global governance, the United States and its allies argued that international law could not treat developing countries more favourably than developed ones (as the New International Economic Order demanded). They maintained that a non-binding UN resolution could not alter customary law and that they were still entitled to compensation for any foreign property which was expropriated. Conveniently they forgot that much of this 'foreign property' was obtained through colonial conquest.

The developed world was also quick to develop new international laws which would undermine attempts by recently independent states to exercise sovereignty over their natural resources. For example, when disputes began to arise with respect to oil contracts with the Arab states in the early 1970s, international tribunals devised new legal norms based on 'general principles of law' (primarily taken from Western legal systems) which privileged Western transnational corporations over the domestic laws of the oil producing states.[29] By the early

---

April 1992, pp. 293–310.

[28]Ibid.

[29]Charles N. Brower and Jeremy K. Sharpe, 'International Arbitration and the Islamic World: The Third Phase', *American Journal of International Law*, Vol. 97, No. 3, July 2003, pp. 643–56.

1980s, it had become clear that the development promised to the newly independent states had not materialized and the industrialized states had successfully blocked any meaningful structural changes in the global economy that would have narrowed the gap between the Global South and the Global North.

No wonder the enthusiasm with which the developing world negotiated for the NIEO was now waning. In its place, free-market liberalization and deregulation of industry had become the mainstay of global economic governance as part of the 'Washington Consensus'. This consensus was most effectively shaped by the World Bank and the IMF which demanded 'structural adjustment policies' from the Global South to manage their burgeoning external debt. The conditions attached to these policies were simple—liberalize markets, deregulate finance and reduce the role of the state. In essence, the IMF and the World Bank wanted the developing world to be more accountable to external capital and foreign creditors than they were to their own domestic constituents.

By pushing countries to increase their foreign exchange to service their foreign debt, structural adjustment programmes also forced them to exploit their resources. In Ghana, for example, the government was forced to intensify commercial forestry, which accelerated the depletion of its forest cover by up to 75 per cent.[30] Similarly, in Chile, close to 40,000 hectares of forest were felled and replaced with non-native plantations for cellulose and wood products, leading to soil erosion and the displacement of indigenous populations. In addition, the costs of servicing external debt in the late 1980s had already far exceeded any export earnings of the countries of Latin America, Africa and, Asia. As a result, much of the finance which was mobilized at home was transferred abroad, instead of being invested for development initiatives. The wide-ranging structural adjustment policies had also led to a freewheeling phase of trade liberalization, accompanied by constraints in government spending on basic social

---

[30]Bill Rau, Shea Cunningham and Walden Bello, *Dark Victory: The United States and Global Poverty*, London: Food First Books, 1994.

services like health, education and other environmental programmes. At the time, these policies led to a collapse in state capacity and widespread poverty and hunger in many developing states.

Against this backdrop, the United Nations Conference on Environment and Development (UNCED) also known as the Rio Summit was held in June 1992 in Rio to mark the twentieth anniversary of the Stockholm conference. The Rio Earth Summit was one of the largest of its kind, and representatives from 178 countries and over 100 heads of state or government gathered to sign a new environmental treaty which culminated in Agenda 21, the Rio Declaration on the Environment and Development.[31] The declaration outlined the goals of sustainable development. It stated, 'Human beings...are entitled to a healthy and productive life in harmony with nature,' and that 'environmental protection shall constitute an integral part of the development process and cannot be considered in isolation from it.' States were enjoined to 'cooperate in the essential task of eradicating poverty' and to 'cooperate in a spirit of global partnership to conserve, protect and restore the health and integrity of the Earth's ecosystem.'

However, the conference could not truly defuse the polarization between the Global North and South. Not only were the differences between them sharp in the negotiation of the terms of the treaty, but were visible in every meeting and at every venue. In fact, the divide was so stark that negotiators wanted to find a venue with a design that did not seat delegates on opposing sides. Finally, when a room which contained a perfectly round table was found, 'the "Group of 77" immediately insisted that exactly one half of the circle be occupied by representatives of developing countries, while all other delegations were to sit along the other half, with the chairman... seated at the intersection.'[32]

---

[31] Agenda 21, United Nations Conference on Environment & Development, Rio de Janerio, Brazil, 3 to 14 June 1992, accessed 15 June 2019, https://sustainabledevelopment.un.org/content/documents/Agenda21.pdf.
[32] Peter H. Sand, 'International Environmental Law After Rio', 4 EJIL, 1993, pp. 377–89.

That the conference itself was called 'Environment and Development' was no coincidence. Like in Stockholm, developing countries had made it clear that unless their right to exploit resources to improve living standards domestically was squarely on the agenda, there was very little purpose in the conference. However, while the South might have succeeded in introducing the narrative of development into the conference, it was the Global North, especially the United States, which failed to truly achieve any meaningful headway in mitigating climate change. While many European nations were keen to adopt binding commitments and timetables, the United States was vehemently opposed to any such deal. In fact, President H. W. Bush was willing to throw away the conference by not attending it if any binding commitments or timetables were set, declaring that 'the American way of life is not up for negotiation'.[33] Unfortunately for the rest of the world, the American way of life implied that in the 1990s, with a mere 5 per cent of the world's population, it was the world's single largest carbon dioxide emitter, accounting for 24 per cent of the planet's fossil carbon dioxide emissions.[34]

Among the participating nations, the United States was also the only country unwilling to recognize the adverse impact of the West's unsustainable consumption lifestyle on the world. Instead it continued to peddle the old narrative of poverty and overpopulation being the primary causes of pollution and environmental degradation. This disagreement led to long, heated debates at the PrepComs, and then at UNCED, where the United States agreed to withdraw its objections when the text was amended to address 'unsustainable lifestyles in developed countries' less directly.[35]

Not only would the United States oppose any reference to unsustainable lifestyles, it would oppose the inclusion of a 'right to

---

[33]Thalif Deen, 'US Lifestyle is Not up for Negotiation', *IPS*, 1 May 2012.

[34]'Question and Answers about Global Warming and Abrupt Climate Change', Worldwatch Institute, accessed 15 June 2019, http://www.worldwatch.org/node/3949.

[35]'A Summary of the Proceedings of the United Nations Conference on Environment and Development 3–14 June 1992', *Earth Summit Bulletin*, Island Press and International Institute for Sustainable Development, Vol. 2, No. 13, 16 June 1992.

develop' for the developing world.[36] Southern countries pressed for the inclusion of the principle that 'the right to development is an inalienable human right' and asserted that 'all peoples have an equal right in matters relating to reasonable living standards'. The United States refused to consider such language because it assumed that the developing countries would use it to demand more financial assistance from the developed ones. Development, insisted the United States, could only be a goal, shared by all nations of the world and not a right. Developing countries, however, feared that sustainability would become the new conditionality on financial assistance. They believed that sustainable development was another ploy by Northern countries to stall their development, a duty that did not apply to the Global North, which was already developed.

For these reasons, financing was another key debate during the preparations for the Rio Earth Summit. When asked to approximate the financial requirements of cutting emissions, the UNCED secretary-general, Canadian oil and mineral businessman, Maurice Strong, estimated that the amount would total $625 billion per year.[37] The UN recommended that developed countries would have to contribute at least $125 billion of this amount in the form of aids and grants to help developing countries raise this money. Still recovering from debt servicing and the adverse balance of trade, many in the South wanted to ensure that the financing for the United Nations Framework Convention on Climate Change (UNFCCC) would be 'additional to existing flows of Official Development Assistance', which were pegged at 0.7 per cent of the gross national product (GNP) of developed states. Most developed countries, including Japan, the United States, Germany, Canada and Australia, were not prepared to provide this assurance and despite the fact that the words ultimately found themselves inserted into the text, efforts to define 'new and additional' were set aside.[38]

---

[36]Id.

[37]Stanton S. Miller, 'The Road From Rio', *Environment, Science and Technology*, Vol. 26, No. 9, 1992, pp. 1710–13.

[38]Lavanya Rajamani, 'The Making and Unmaking of the Copenhagen Accord',

There was a fierce debate on how this money would be administered as well. While the developing countries had adopted the 'Beijing Declaration', which called for the creation of a common 'Green Fund', the developed countries ultimately had their way insofar as the Global Environment Facility (GEF) of the World Bank was made the nodal agency. Unfortunately, this did little to give the developing world a larger say in how donors would disburse the money which was raised, considering that the developed world maintained a vice-like grip on the Bretton Woods Institutions. Despite the vehemence with which the developing world opposed this move, considering that they viewed these very same institutions as being in thrall to the countries responsible for their poverty, the fact that America and Europe had their way, only goes to show how far these institutions were propped up instead by the might and resources of a handful of countries.

Perhaps the most enduring legacy of the Rio conference, and a major win for the developing world, was the differentiation of countries on the basis of their historical responsibility, specifically into Annex-I and Annex-II states, with the former bearing the brunt of the responsibilities, incorporating the hotly contested formula of Common but Differentiated Responsibilities (CBDR) for climate change. While the UNFCC was critical in putting into place several such key principles, it is worth nothing that the United States only ratified the treaty after issuing a statement to the effect that, 'The U.S. does not accept any interpretation of Principle Seven (CBDR) that would imply a recognition or acceptance by the United States of any international obligations or liabilities, or any diminution in the responsibilities of developing countries.'[39] In effect, America was saying that while it 'recognized' the historic role that developed countries had played in aggravating environmental degradation, they would not accept any binding commitments to change. Unfortunately, the

---

International & Comparative Law Quarterly, Vol. 59, Issue. 3, pp. 824–43.
[39]'Report of the United Nations Conference On Environment And Development', United Nations General Assembly, June 1992.

United States had its way in this respect and no definite timelines or emissions targets were set.

The Rio conference gives us an opportunity to truly examine the meaning of sustainable development. Despite the enduring legacy of colonialism, and the failed policies of structural adjustment, the developed world was continuously unwilling to alter its own ways of life, instead choosing to bargain either for a softer deal or one in which the developing countries would agree to a greater share of the burden.

The conference itself took place when many in the Global South were still recovering from the adverse impacts of the neo-liberal policies of the IMF and the World Bank. Despite the noticeable shortcomings of trade liberalization, the then managing director of the IMF Michel Camdessus argued that it would lead to greater investment in less-polluting technologies and the increase in efficiency would automatically serve to conserve natural resources. This was a questionable claim. It would truly be naïve, or disingenuous, to believe that colonialism was done and dusted with in the late twentieth century. While sovereign states could now exercise control over territory, large multinational corporations still had a vice-like grip over their resources. Consider, for example, the trend of the 'maquiladora' system in Mexico, a term applied to the practices of foreign companies that established factories in Mexico for the sole purpose of exporting their products to that company's country of origin.[40] In the 1990s almost 75 per cent of these foreign companies were American and the industrial waste produced by these maquiladoras was at the time indiscriminately dumped in Mexico, accounting for several health hazards such as birth defects and miscarriages. While the Mexicans might have felt grateful that the US had generated jobs in their country by establishing factories there, the bottom line was that the US had not merely got the goods produced less expensively by lower-wage workers, but it had effectively exported the waste and

---

[40]Emilio Godoy, 'Mexico: Maquiladora Factories Manufacture Toxic Pollutants', *IPS*, 23 August 2011.

environmental hazards the production of those goods might have generated in the US.

The Niger Delta is another such example. While the area itself is one of the world's most important coastal marine ecosystems, it is also the location of massive oil deposits, whose extraction for decades by multinational corporations have generated an estimated $600 billion in profit since the 1960s.[41] Despite this, the Niger Delta is one the poorest areas in the world, mired in conflict and unemployment; a few dominant players such as Shell, ExxonMobil, Chevron-Texaco accounted for an estimated 99 per cent of the crude oil production. A history of these companies reveals that oil spills and inefficient waste management by them caused widespread environmental degradation in the delta. One of the most egregious disasters in the 1980s caused more than 8.4 million US gallons of oil to be discharged into the Atlantic Ocean from a Texaco facility, leading to several pollution-related deaths and loss of marine biodiversity in the area.[42]

Despite this, efforts by developing states to reign in the profligacy of TNCs came up short. The United Nations Centre on Transnational Corporations (UNCTC), which was then a part of the UNCTAD, had developed a series of recommendations for inclusion in the final summit declaration, which outlined environmental regulations for business. However, corporate lobby groups such as the International Chamber of Commerce (ICC) were extremely active in preventing the inclusion of any such recommendation in the final document. Under American pressure, the then UN secretary-general, Boutros Boutros-Ghali, shut down the Centre itself.[43] In fact, American diplomats had actively lobbied to kill any consensus on the document and its recommendations. Ultimately, all recommendations in relation

---

[41]'Counting the Cost: Corporations and human rights abuses in the Niger Delta', *Platform*, 2011.

[42]'The Price of Oil: Corporate Responsibility and Human Rights Violations in Nigeria's Oil Producing Communities', Human Rights Watch, 1999.

[43]Mark Tran, 'New man faces same old problems of UN reform', *The Guardian*, 10 October 2006.

to a code of conduct for corporate behaviour were removed from the agenda and the then secretary-general of the Earth Summit, Maurice Strong, invited a new corporate lobby group, the World Business Council for Sustainable Development (WBCSD), to write the recommendations on industry and sustainable development themselves. Ultimately, the document itself only contained pablum on how business could improve sustainable development, without any genuine commitment to ameliorating the problems the developing countries had faced.

Ultimately, the real success of the Rio Earth Summit was in galvanizing the public—both in the North and in the South— to the realities of environmental degradation and (to some extent) to its linkages with development. At Rio, governments around the world began to realize that a 'business as usual' scenario was simply insufficient to deal with the complex challenges of climate change and that economic and political architectures would have to recalibrate their approach to tackle this. Boutros-Ghali, in a closing speech, spoke glowingly of the 'spirit of Rio' that emerged during the summit: 'It is no longer enough for man to love his neighbour, he must now love the world. Beyond man's covenant with God and his social contract with his fellow men, we now need an ethical contract with nature and the Earth... The Earth has a soul. To restore it is the essence of Rio.'[44]

While the conference at Rio helped drive home the point that the developing world could not duplicate the growth model of the industrialized world, it did little to alter the major paradigms of consumption-driven economic growth. Post the Rio conference, it became extremely evident that the developed world had failed to meet their financing requirements or achieve any significant reductions in their emissions reduction. In 1997, when the UNGA held a special session to review the progress made in meeting the Rio agenda, it found that only four countries—Denmark, Sweden,

---

[44]United Nations Conference on Environment and Development; UNCED, June 1992.

Norway, and the Netherlands—had met their 0.7 per cent of GNP target. Collectively, the OECD countries had in fact *reduced* their official development assistance (ODA) to 0.22 per cent of GNP in 1997, falling from 0.33 in 1992.[45]

The story with respect to emissions was no different. By 1996, greenhouse emissions in the United States were 8.3 per cent above 1990 and continuing to rise steadily.[46] Despite the fact that the Europeans were the most adamant amongst the developed world to set binding emissions targets and timetables, their own accomplishments fell woefully short of their rhetoric. By 1996, it was clear that, of the world's major industrial powers, only three would have cut their emissions to under the 1990 level in the year 2000—and none of them would succeed because of a reorientation in their economic policies. Russia succeeded because the collapse of the Soviet Union had slowed down the pace of industrial activity. Germany reached its targets because many of the coal plants it had inherited from erstwhile East Germany were shut down. And Britain cut subsidies to its own polluting industries.[47] But nowhere, in any of the large economies, was there any sign of a serious and purposeful effort to reduce carbon dioxide emissions for environmental reasons.

The period after the Rio Earth Summit also marked the most intense phase of globalization and it only took two years for the rhetoric of Rio to fade away into the reality of Marrakech with the signing into force of a new treaty establishing the World Trade Organization (WTO) in place of the General Agreement on Tariffs and Trade (GATT). With it, the dominant economic view of free markets and trade liberalization was firmly embedded into world politics. The WTO itself was premised on high growth rates and improvements in national incomes, which would necessarily require resource extraction, effectively throwing out any potential gains Rio

---

[45]'Aid Targets Slipping Out of Reach?', OECD, 2007.
[46]J. W. Anderson, 'Climate Change, Clinton and Kyoto,' Resources for the Future, November 1997.
[47]Id., 'The Kyoto Protocol on Climate Change: Background, Unresolved Issues and Next Steps', Washington DC: Resources for the Future, 1997.

might have made. Most developing nations were now engaged in a race to the bottom to attract private foreign investment, generally lowering labour costs and reducing environmental compliance obligations. To be fair, Rio had already accepted this dominant economic model. Agenda 21, for example, had recommended 'promoting sustainable development through trade liberalization and making trade and environment mutually supportive'. Governments were therefore expected to take into account 'the results of the Uruguay Round' and 'to promote an open, non-discriminatory and equitable multilateral trading system'.

It is worth noting that it is this very same trade system that allows Northern countries to maintain their economic hegemony. In the 1990s, the developed states were particularly protectionist in many of the sectors in which the developing countries were better placed to compete, such as agriculture and textiles. In fact, the UNCTAD estimated that they could have exported $700 billion more a year by 2005 if rich countries did more to open their markets.[48]

Despite their grandstanding at Rio, it also became clear that the Bretton Woods Institutions were instrumental in aggravating climate change. Between 1992 and 2002, the World Bank invested nearly $22 billion in oil, coal and gas industries, compared to the pitiful $1 billion in renewable energy projects. In fact, nine out of ten beneficiaries of energy sector lending via the World Bank were TNCs hailing from countries which were members of the G7, including General Electric, ExxonMobil, Chevron-Texaco, Amec Foster Wheeler, AES Corporation, Enron and others. The World Bank suggested in 2002 that a single multinational corporation, Shell, had contributed more greenhouse gas emissions (through burning gas as part of oil extraction in Nigeria) than all other sources of greenhouse gases in sub-Saharan Africa combined. By some estimates, only 122 major TNCs were responsible for almost 80 per cent of all carbon dioxide in 1999.[49]

---

[48]'Trade and Development Report', UNCTAD, 1999.
[49]'Kingpins of Carbon: How Fossil Fuel Producers Contribute to Global Warming', Natural Resources Defense Council, the Union of Concerned Scientists and the US Public Interest Research Group Education Fund, Washington DC, July 1999.

Clearly then, despite the celebratory rhetoric at Rio, very little real progress had been made in mitigating climate change or in eradicating poverty. Even before the ink had dried on the Rio outcome documents, developing countries were pushing for binding emissions targets. However, developed countries, led by the United States, were also attempting to reduce the implications of 'common but differentiated responsibility', demanding greater participation from developing countries in mitigating the global burden. This served US foreign policy interests well, as it helped divide the G77 on the key issues. For example, after Argentina and South Korea agreed to 'voluntary commitments', the US parroted this development as examples of developing countries who actually wanted to see the Kyoto protocol succeed.

Despite America's insistent position that developing countries must also contribute to mitigation efforts, the Kyoto Protocol ultimately managed to conclude with those parties listed in Annex-I of the Protocol committing themselves to reduce their overall emissions of six greenhouse gases (GHGs) by at least 5 per cent below 1990 levels in the first commitment period between 2008 and 2012.

However, even before the protocol was officially adapted in Kyoto, the US Senate had unanimously passed the Byrd–Hagel Resolution, which stated that it is 'critical for the Parties to the Convention [...] to include limitations on Developing Country Parties' greenhouse gas emissions' and that the 'Senate strongly believes that the proposals under negotiation, because of the disparity of treatment between Annex I Parties and Developing Countries and the level of required emission reductions, could result in serious harm to the United States economy.'[50]

At the time, negotiators from the United States argued that Southern emissions would surpass Northern emissions in 2035. However, if put into perspective, this would imply that by 2035, 20 per cent of the world, constituting the Global North, would be

---

[50]Byrd–Hagel Resolution, 1st Session of the 105th Congress, S. Res. 98.

emitting just as much as 80 per cent of the world, the Global South.[51] In fact, as we have noted and are repeating here for emphasis, the CHG emissions of one US citizen were equal to those of nineteen Indians, thirty Pakistanis, seventeen Maldivians, nineteen Sri Lankans, 107 Bangladeshis, 134 Bhutanese, or 269 Nepalis.[52] Unfortunately, the sins of Rio were on full display once again at Kyoto. A review by the secretariat of the UNFCCC found that carbon dioxide emissions of all industrialized countries declined only by 1.3 per cent during 1990–2006. Moreover, this reduction was primarily due to the countries whose economies were in transition, specifically the erstwhile Soviet Union states. Excluding these countries, the emissions of Annex I states had actually increased by 14.5 per cent.[53]

The developed countries were also successful in negotiating for 'market based' solutions to climate change, which is why the Kyoto Protocol sanctioned 'emissions trading'. The term refers to market-driven transactions where high greenhouse-gas-emitting countries (which face high costs of curbing emissions) can trade their obligations with low-emitting countries. This mechanism originated in a proposal from Brazil to implement a Clean Development Fund, which was meant to incorporate the polluter- pays- principle—in effect it was a tax on failure to comply with the Kyoto commitments. However, the proposal was turned around at the end of the negotiation process at Kyoto into the 'Clean Development Mechanism' (CDM)—a mechanism through which developed countries could gain carbon credits for carbon offset activities. Clearly, this mechanism was just another way for the developed world to actually restructure their own economic models. It allowed richer countries the ability to continue polluting as long as they made some clean energy investments in developing countries.

[51]S. Basu, 'India will not accept emission reduction targets', *The Hindu*, 22 November 1997.
[52]Anil Agarwal, 'Climate Change: A Challenge to India's Economy', Occasional Paper, Centre for Science and Environment, 2011.
[53]Sunita Narain et al., 'Climate Change: Perspectives from India', UNDP, November 2009.

From the outset it was clear that the CDM was more of a commercial venture and did little to address the root cause of climate change. In terms of ecological effectiveness, CDM would ultimately prove to be a disaster. By subsidizing carbon-based energy technologies, it created further obstacles to the penetration of non-carbon-based energy technologies and could lock them out for several decades. Apart from this, it was almost impossible to verify the impact that these projects were having on improving sustainable development in developing countries. That the CDM was primarily a market venture and not an ecological measure is evident from the geographical scope of the projects undertaken. Over 75 per cent of registered CDM projects were in just four countries, with 48 per cent in China and 20 per cent in India. In contrast, the forty-eight 'least developed countries' account for just 1 per cent of projects and 0.6 per cent of credits issued, while sub-Saharan Africa (excluding South Africa) hosts 1 per cent of projects and accounts for 1.5 per cent of credits issued.[54] This spread was despite the fact that it was undoubtedly the least developed countries that needed the investment and technology the most.

Not only was it clear that the Kyoto Protocol was unlikely to address climate change in any meaningful way, the developed world also continued to remain blind to the extractive practices of their own industries. Africa perhaps is the best example of how the West fails to appreciate the colonial legacies of environmental degradation and poverty. In 2003, the *New York Times* published an article entitled 'Striking it poor: Oil as a curse', highlighting scholarly work which has consistently warned that for more than a decade developing countries whose economies are dependent on oil or other extracted materials continue to be affected by poverty, authoritarian governments and civil war.[55]

In the North, the mainstream arguments continued to attribute

---

[54]'The State of Play on the Clean Development Mechanism: Review of Barriers and Potential Ways Forward', United Nations Conference on Trade and Development, 2009.

[55]Daphne Eviatar, 'Striking it Poor: Oil as a Curse', *New York Times*, 7 June 2003.

this to 'bad governance' and lack of state capacity in poorer countries and their chronic tendency towards corruption. However, civil society and NGOs have almost consistently argued against the hypocrisy of this narrative. In 1999, Global Witness published a report titled 'A Crude Awakening', which highlighted the adverse role that multinational oil companies and commercial banking industries played in plundering resources and embezzling revenues from oil extraction in Angola.[56] This is a story that has played out in almost every mineral-rich country—war, poverty and environmental degradation have followed Western capital and corporations who systematically stymied government efforts to redistribute wealth generated from natural resources.

In fact, by the year 2000, it was clear that most resource-rich countries were clustered at the bottom of the UNDP Human Development Index and were clustered right at the top of the Transparency International Corruption Perception Index. By the World Bank's own estimates, countries with few natural resources grew at two to three times the rate of resource-rich countries between 1960 and 2000.[57]

Not only did Kyoto fail to appreciate the colonial legacies of underdevelopment in the developing world, the developed countries, especially the United States, continued contending that global warming and environmental degradation did not constitute an immediate threat to the United States and that the economic costs of complying with any commitments was too high. The scale of what some did not hesitate to dub 'ecological imperialism' was almost unbearable for several nations who were particularly vulnerable to climate change. While poorer countries were still paying their dues to the IMF, the richer countries refused to acknowledge even the existence of an ecological debt.

Around the same time, it is worth noting that absolute poverty, measured by the $1 a day standard laid down by the World Bank and the UN, dropped from 1.25 billion people in 1990 to 986 million in 2004.[58] However, it is also true that much of this decline is because of high economic growth in two countries, China and India. These successes notwithstanding, poverty was very much present in the world. In fact, in many countries, poverty continued to worsen. Between 1981 and 2001, the number of people living on less than $1 per day in sub-Saharan Africa doubled from 164 million to 313 million people.[59] In Latin America and the Caribbean, it climbed from thirty-six million to forty-nine million and the percentage of people living on less than $2 per day in Eastern Europe and Central Asia rose from 2 per cent in 1981 to 20 per cent in 2001, largely as a result of the collapse of communism in those regions.[60] At the same time inequality was at an all-time high. Between 1960 and 1991, the poorest 20 per cent of the world's people saw their share of global income decline from 2.3 per cent to 1.4 per cent. Meanwhile, the share of the richest 20 per cent rose from 70 per cent to 85 per cent. That doubled the ratio of the shares of the richest and the poorest—from 30:1 to 61:1.[61] It was also becoming increasingly clear that the world's poorest suffer the most when ecosystems are degraded. For example, in 1998, weather phenomena like El Niño and Hurricane Mitch killed thousands and displaced millions. Today, for the first time, environmental refugees outnumber political refugees.[62]

This was a significant factor in the UNGA's decision in 2000 to adopt its 'Millennium Declaration' that called upon member states

---

[58]'Population Living on Less Than $1 Per Day, 1981-2004', World Resources Institute.

[59]World Resources Institute (WRI) in collaboration with United Nations Development Programme, United Nations Environment Programme, and World Bank, 2005, 'World Resources 2005: The Wealth of the Poor—Managing Ecosystems to Fight Poverty', Washington DC: WRI, September 2005.

[60]Id.

[61]Jan Nederveen Pieterse, 'Global Inequality: Bringing Politics Back In', *Third World Quarterly*, Vol. 23, No. 6, December 2002, pp. 1023–104.

[62]Toula Drimnos, 'Governments are planning for climate-driven migration—in the worst way possible', *National Observer*, 14 May 2019.

to take actions at all levels in order to halve the proportion of the world's people whose income was less than $1 per day, who suffer from hunger, and who are without access to safe drinking water and basic sanitation, by the year 2015. However, these goals were hobbled from the start. For one thing, though agreement on them marked an important milestone in the global consensus on development, they are a declaration of intent rather than concrete policy. For another, they did not address the structural causes of poverty, specifically historical injustice and an unfair international trading regime. Goal 8, calling for the rich countries to transfer significant resources to the poor to help them attain these goals, has remained almost entirely unimplemented.

To be fair, the Millennium Development Goals were not simply a response to the understanding that millions of the poorest individuals continue to remain that way, but were also inspired by the recognition that several of the macroeconomic policies over the last few decades had failed. The Asian financial crisis in 1997 and the continued stagnation of economic growth in Africa had led to a deepening mistrust of international economic institutions and many people now viewed globalization as a force which privileged the interests of rich Western corporates over the needs of the poor in developing countries.

On this account, at best the MDGs might be understood as a declaratory complement to the international economic regime, at worst as yet another vehicle for advancing the will and preferences of influential states and their industries. For the Bretton Woods Institutions, the failure to develop or to reduce poverty is seen as a domestic challenge arising out of bad governance and corruption. All the while, they continue promoting private foreign investment and international trade, selectively disregarding the links between domestic economies and the fundamental structure of the international economy, which largely operate to the disadvantage of the countries they seek to assist. These structures then make a fundamental contribution to the inequality and underdevelopment of the developing world.

Despite the obvious disparities in the causes and impact of climate change, stark differences between the developed North and the impoverished South have marked international negotiations on climate change. Agreements like Kyoto and Rio have been overshadowed by the failure of the developed world to live up to their commitments on emissions and aid. In the years following Kyoto, the narrative that some developing countries were now equally responsible for the problem was gaining traction, particularly considering that China had overtaken the United States as the largest greenhouse gas emitter in 2007. While such absolute numbers are often confusing, they did pave the way for developed states to demand more action from developing countries.

China now produces the largest amount of overall national emissions, topping the United States. But this figure must be put in perspective; for one thing, China's population is four times larger than the United States, making its per capita emissions roughly 75 per cent less. Further, taken together, the developing countries accounted for around half of all emissions, which is still far below what would be considered equitable based on population sizes and levels of economic growth. It is also important to point out that much of the pollution in developing countries is almost directly attributable to exports meant for consumption in the developed world. Indeed, as Qin Gang, China's then foreign ministry spokesperson, said in June 2007, 'China is now the factory of the world. Developed countries have transferred a lot of manufacturing to China. What many Western consumers wear, live in, even eat, is made in China. Consequently, much of the emissions from industries in the Global North were exported [to China].'[63] It was estimated that in 2004, 23 per cent of global carbon dioxide emissions were traded internationally, primarily as exports from China and other emerging markets to consumers in developed countries.[64]

Not only were these statistics misleading, they also tend to

[63]Chris Buckley, 'China says exports fuel greenhouse gas emissions', Reuters, 21 June 2007.
[64]Steven J. Davis and Ken Caldeira, 'Consumption-based accounting of CO_2 emissions', PNAS, 23 March 2010.

ignore the fact that the industrialized countries had almost universally failed to deliver on their commitments to transfer technology, aid or knowhow. The poorest, in particular, have fewer resources, in finance, technology and existing infrastructure, to adapt to what lies ahead. Some studies estimate that for every 1°C rise in average global temperatures, average annual growth in poor countries could drop by 2 to 3 per cent, with an associated cost in human development and basic survival. Already, it is estimated that the fallout from climate change kills 300,000 people a year, including through the spread of disease and malnutrition, and seriously affects another 325 million. Four billion people are vulnerable in some fashion; 500 million are at extreme risk. Developing countries have 98 per cent of the affected people, 99 per cent of all deaths from weather disasters and they bear 90 per cent of the total economic losses.[65]

Against this backdrop, the fourth assessment report of the Intergovernmental Panel on Climate Change (IPCC) warned for the first time that global warming was unequivocal and accelerating, with global average temperatures rising by the largest and fastest margins in the history of the Earth. These changes will increase the severity of droughts, land degradation, desertification, the intensity of floods and more. Rising temperatures will also contribute to a rise in heat-related diseases such as malaria and lead to food insecurity as land continues to degrade. It is also increasingly certain that the poorest countries and the poorest within them will face the worst of the effects.

Despite the force of this evidence, the United States was at the forefront of demanding that a new climate change structure should be 'very different' from the Kyoto Protocol, rejecting the top-down approach favoured by the EU and developing countries. Under this approach, first, an overall mitigation target would be decided for industrialized countries, which would then be broken down to the individual countries according to their relative responsibility and

---

[65]'Human Impact Report: Climate Change—The Anatomy of a Silent Crisis', *Global Humanitarian Forum*, 2009.

capability. However, according to the US proposal, the international system would mainly be a collection of actions decided and implemented domestically. This proposal flew in the face of several years of negotiating history. Since the early 1990s, the developing countries had united under two unalterable positions—first, that they would not accept any responsibility for climate mitigation and, second, that the developed world must help the developing world with technology and finance if the rich expected the poor to play their part.

However, the period after Kyoto saw the developing world adopt a more realistic, and therefore more accommodative, approach. The 2009 United Nations Climate Change Conference, commonly known as the Copenhagen Summit, was meant to negotiate a new climate change deal following the end of the Kyoto protocol timelines, reflected in the unofficial slogan on the conference taken up by activists and civil society organizations: 'seal the deal'. However, outrage and scandal threatened to kill the process right at the start with the leak of the 'Danish text', a document produced by a select club of developed nations which proposed to hand effective control of climate change finance to the World Bank and abandon the Kyoto Protocol, which was the only legally binding treaty then in force and would also make finance for developing countries contingent on a range of reforms.[66]

As if this lack of representation wasn't enough, the Copenhagen Summit also became another avenue for the Global North to display its bullying tactics. Thanks to WikiLeaks, we also know that the United States employed bribery, blackmail and other unsavoury tactics to obtain the support of island states and other Latin American states which continued to oppose the deal.[67] According to the cables, US Undersecretary of State Maria Otero told the Ethiopian prime minister that unless his country signed the Copenhagen Accord, the prospect of US financial aid to Ethiopia would be halted. Similarly, Bolivia and Ecuador were punished for their opposition by having

[66]John Vidal, 'Copenhagen climate failure blamed on Danish Text', *The Guardian*, 31 May 2010.
[67]Damian Carrington, 'U.S. Manipulated climate accord in Copenhagen: WikiLeaks', *The Hindu*, 4 December 2010.

their US development aid cut. In another cable, EU negotiator Connie Hedegaard suggested to the United States that the Alliance of Small Island States (AOSIS) countries 'could be our best allies' given their need for financing.[68] Even worse was the fact that the the CIA, via the US State Department, sent a series of 'intelligence gathering directives' to its diplomats to gather intelligence on UN staff and senior diplomats. The directive instructed them to find evidence of circumventions that other states had made with respect to their obligations under the UN environmental treaties in order to undermine negotiating positions on grounds of inconsistency.

Ultimately, to save face, former US President Barack Obama managed to convince the leaders of Brazil, South Africa, India, and China to put forward voluntary, bottom-up pledges, representing a giant shift in the position of developing countries. China and India announced voluntary targets to reduce emissions intensity by 2020. Brazil announced actions to achieve a level of emissions in 2020 that would be at least 36 per cent lower than business-as-usual projections. South Africa announced a 34 per cent deviation below the business-as-usual scenario by 2020, with South Africa's emissions set to peak by 2025.[69] Despite the willingness of developing countries to commit themselves to emission reductions, the developed world continued to reduce their share of the burden. In fact, Executive Secretary of the UNFCCC Yvo de Boer pessimistically noted in his final press conference in Copenhagen that pledges by non–Annex I countries were at the upper end of their 'range' while Annex I countries were not even at the lower end of the range suggested by the IPCC.[70]

In addition, the AOSIS bloc asserted that a new protocol had to aim for limiting warming to no more than 1.5 °Celsius. Unfortunately, the developing countries found this so objectionable

[68]'US embassy cables: EU raises "creative accounting" with US over climate aid', *The Guardian*, 3 December 2010.

[69]Stephen Minas, 'FPC Briefing: BASIC positions-Major emerging economies in the UN climate change negotiations', Foreign Policy Centre, accessed 15 June 2019, https://fpc.org.uk/wp-content/uploads/2013/07/1560.pdf.

[70]Ole Kristian Fauchald et al., *Yearbook of International Environmental Law*, Vol. 20, New York: Oxford University Press, 2011, p. 276.

that they walked out en masse for half a day during the conference—setting the precedent to allow developed nations to abandon unmet commitments under the Kyoto Protocol, thereby throwing away the only functioning international accord on climate change.

Ultimately, Copenhagen was a failed summit and ended on a pessimistic note. In the final days of the negotiations, the physical access of civil society representatives to the conference premises was limited and negotiations moved into a 'Friends of the Chair' setting of about twenty-five countries, excluding the bulk of the 195 parties to the UNFCCC. The choice to negotiate in a closed setting was heavily criticized by a small group of parties (Venezuela, Bolivia, Cuba, Nicaragua, and Tuvalu), and led to a stand-off in the final plenary, in which the Copenhagen Accord was only 'taken note of' by the conference of the parties (COP).[71] The accord itself was a win for the developed countries, having successfully obtained commitments from major developing countries, effectively throwing the binding emissions of the Kyoto Protocol out of the window.

It was clear that a part of how climate change politics operates is via the representation of a particular set of interests—particularly the interests of the more powerful developed countries. In centring the debate around Western development norms, a kind of technocratic imperialism occurs which leaves out large parts of humanity from having any meaningful say in determining their future. The programmes initialized by the powerful Western states have for long ignored the history of colonialism, reducing the narrative instead to focus on 'poverty' as a problem capable of being alleviated through 'development' programmes. Rather than questioning the means or the ends of this development, failed strategies are time and again repeated, reinforcing the appearance that these are the only viable alternatives. To date, the climate change governance regime has stymied discussion of alternative approaches, in accordance with the interests of the Western powers.

---

[71]supra note, 38.

INSTRUMENTS OF POWER

If today's sustainable development and climate change discourse is dominated by a small club of industrialized countries, it is because they control the key elements which are necessary to frame an appropriate response to climate change and development: technology, finance and knowledge.

Technology has always been a priority for the Global South, especially after the independence of the former colonies, when they realized that the technological gap between them and the industrialized North would lead to uneven development. As late as 1900, when the United Kingdom had 72 to 80 per cent of the new technologies in industry (broadly those that enabled the first and second industrial revolutions), the Third World countries had only 4 to 9 per cent of these new technologies in their industrial systems.[72] In the 1950s, TNCs exploited this advantage and entered into largely one-sided contracts which guaranteed them access to resources such as land, water and labour while transferring very little technology overall.

In 1961, Brazil submitted a document which largely went unnoticed for several decades, highlighting the role intellectual property regimes had to play in development. The deliberations which the document set off ultimately culminated with the UNGA's adoption—by consensus—of Resolution 1713 (XVI), entitled 'the role of patents in the transfer of technology to under-developed countries'.[73] For the first time, the role of technology in addressing international economic concerns and the wider disparity in North–South relations was laid out. In the 1970s, when the developing world was struggling to implement the NIEO, one of its fundamental tenets involved 'access to the achievements of modern science and technology, and promoting the transfer of technology and the creation of indigenous technology.' However, the developed North never truly

---

[72]Elias H. Tuma, 'Technology Transfer and Economic Development: Lessons of History', *Journal of Developing Areas*, Vol. 21, No. 4, 1987, pp. 403–28.

[73]Ahmed Abdel Latif and Pedro Roffe, 'Fifty years later, the IP, technology transfer and development debate lives on', *ICTSD Bridges*, 23 November 2011.

accepted this premise, continuing to emphasize the importance of contractual relations and intellectual property. The Northern TNCs in fact went a step further, arguing that regulating technology would actually slow the pace of development in the developing world by reducing the incentives for corporations to invest.

Today, it is clear that if the dangers of climate change are to be mitigated, technology will have a large role to play. However, it is also clear that much of this technology continues to be concentrated in industrialized nations where markets, infrastructure, funding and robust education systems have created a virtuous cycle. If poorer countries are to transition into low carbon economies, it becomes essential that any climate change regime address this discrepancy in technological development. Much of the Global South is reliant on technologies developed in more industrialized nations, which are largely embroiled in complex domestic patent regimes. From the start, developing countries wanted a comprehensive mechanism to enable the transfer of clean technologies and were especially keen on employing government-to-government non-commercial exchanges. Developed nations, on the other hand, preferred market-based solutions which made monitoring extremely difficult.

However, despite the obvious benefits that new technologies can bring, the UNFCC has done little to clarify the mechanism of technology transfer in a manner that has clear legal and policy implications. Instead, it has settled for a rhetorical position that falls short of establishing definition in practice. The language on intellectual property rights (IPR) in Agenda 21 of the Rio Earth Summit did not come out of a vacuum. It stemmed from the experience of countries like India and South Korea, which faced immense barriers in obtaining technology to implement the Montreal Protocol on Substances that Deplete the Ozone Layer, 1987. At the same time, there are severe limitations inherent in Agenda 21. The document called on states to 'promote, facilitate and finance…the transfer of environmentally sound technologies and related know-how…on favourable terms, including on concessional and preferential terms'. Not surprisingly, however, no specific institutional or financial mechanism to support such an objective was proposed, nor were any timetables for action put forward. Already data from the Energy Information Administration (EIA) reveals that by 2035 carbon emissions of non-OECD countries will exceed those of the OECD member states by more than 100 per cent. However, technological innovation in environmentally sustainable technologies continues to be highly concentrated in the Global North, especially in the US, Germany and Japan, accounting for almost 60 per cent of all climate-related innovations.[74] Similarly, research reveals that most transfers of technology—up to 73 per cent—represents flows between developed nations, with only 22 per cent being exported to developing countries—even then, China accounted for most of these transfers.[75] Of course, the rise of China in the intervening period has certainly changed these benchmarks to some extent. Its investment in renewable technologies, especially in solar and wind, have led to the IEA calling it the 'undisputed' renewable growth leader.[76]

Unfortunately, despite the near monopolization of such technologies, industrialized countries have rejected Southern calls for non-commercial terms for technology transfer, arguing that such an arrangement would be incompatible with the protection of intellectual property rights. This is most likely because developed countries enjoy an enormous financial advantage from the royalties and fees on their patented technologies. The US, for example, had in excess of a $20 billion trade surplus in licence fees and royalties on industrial processes sold abroad in 1995. This saga has continued into the twenty-first century as well, with developing economies paying close to $45 billion as payments for intellectual property in 2002.[77]

So entrenched is the notion that intellectual property regimes aid technology transfer that industrialized nations refused to even consider the question of intellectual property and technology transfer

---

[74]Howe Zhuohao Wang, 'Only three countries lead 60 percent of global environmental technology innovations', *Yale Environment Review*, 11 November 2012.
[75]Id.
[76]Renewables 2017, International Energy Agency.
[77]World Development Indicators, World Bank, 2004.

when some developing countries, including India and China, asserted the need to address intellectual property issues within the discussions on technology. Despite evidence to the contrary, developed countries led by the Unites States argued that IPR catalysed innovation and did not constitute a barrier to technology transfer. The dynamics of these disputes were visible at the Copenhagen Summit, where the US successfully removed any mention of IPRs from the final document.

Ultimately, technology is only one facet of the control exercised by the Global North. Despite the fact that the need to adequately shore up finance to tackle climate change is well understood, the mechanisms, amounts and timetables continue to remain inadequate. The World Bank estimates that a two degree rise in global temperature could result in a permanent loss of GDP in South Asia of upto 5 per cent and an even more dramatic 38 per cent loss for coastal areas. Adapting to this temperature rise will cost between $70 to $100 billion per year between 2010 and 2050.[78] Additionally, climate mitigation policies in developing countries alone require $140 to $175 billion per year in the next twenty years. To support a low carbon transition, the world will need close to six trillion dollars year on year for the next two decades, with at least 60 per cent of this amount needed in developing countries.

Since the end of World War II, the developed world pledged aid under official development assistance programmes. However, from the very beginning there was a systemic flaw in the manner in which development aid is distributed. Throughout the 1950s, developing countries were insistent on the creation of a UN financial institution under which decisions would be made on the basis of sovereign equality. The rich countries, headed by the US, opposed the project, refusing to set up a financial body where decisions would be made in the UN. Following years of negotiations, the International Development Association (IDA) was set up as a compromise solution,

---

[78] *The Cost to Developing Countries of Adapting to Climate Change: New Methods and Estimates*, World Bank, 2010, accessed 15 June 2019, http://documents.worldbank. org/curated/en/667701468177537886/pdf/557260WP0EACC0Box0349464B01PU BLIC1.pdf.

which ultimately favoured the developed countries because the World Bank and the IMF were its principal agencies. Yet it remained bound by the World Bank's voting rules, which meant keeping it under the control of the main sponsors.

If the history of climate change negotiations reveals anything, it is that the developed world has almost always failed to live up to its financial obligations, especially in the area of climate change and sustainable development. Immediately after pledging to raise upto 0.7 per cent of the GNPs for developing countries in Rio under Agenda 21, Official Development Aid (ODA) actually fell from $62.4 billion in 1992 to $48.7 billion in 1997. In 2005, total aid from the twenty-two richest countries to the world's developing countries was just $106 billion—a shortfall of $119 billion from the 0.7 per cent promise and a betrayal of Goal 8 of the Millennium Development Goals which they had signed on to amid such fanfare.[79]

In practice, ODA is often unpredictable, poorly targeted and does not reach where it is needed. It is estimated that only around 24 per cent of bilateral aid actually finances investments on the ground. Even within the limited amount that was promised as assistance, it was never truly clear how much money could directly be linked to the environment. Based on a self-assessment made by OECD countries using the Rio markers for the period 2010–11, only 21 per cent of total ODA could be linked to the environment, to various degrees.[80] To address these shortcomings, developed countries pledged at the Copenhagen Summit to raise $100 billion a year to aid developing countries in mitigating and adapting to the effects of climate change. Yet the pledge itself is unsatisfactory; for one thing, developed countries have not truly promised to fund this amount, rather they have agreed to try to mobilize it. For another, the amount itself is more of a political pledge and not based on any reasonable scientific or economic assessment.

---

[79]Review of implementation of Agenda 21 and the Rio Principles, Stakeholder Forum for a Sustainable Future, January 2012.
[80]'Aid in Support of Environment', OECD, May 2013.

Ultimately, even this amount was subject to heated debate. The OECD had estimated that wealthy countries have already made 'significant progress' towards meeting their $100 billion a year promise. The report concluded that 'climate finance' reached $52 billion in 2013 and $62 billion in 2014. However, the Indian government roundly criticized this figure, arguing that the report was riddled with double-counting, mislabelling and misreporting. India said that the only credible figure was $2.2 billion in gross climate fund disbursements from seventeen special climate change funds, well shy of the often-touted $57 billion.[81]

Additionally, most of this finance is limited to mitigation activities. While most developing countries wanted a greater emphasis on adaptation finance, which includes finance that will enable states to institutionally adapt to climate change, the developed world was reluctant to provide it, assuming that accepting these demands would amount to an acknowledgement of responsibility based on historical emissions. Further, the benefits of mitigation projects are more tangible and far-reaching when compared to adaptation. According to the OECD, 77 per cent of total climate finance in 2013–14 was for climate change mitigation only, 16 per cent for adaptation only, and 7 per cent for activities designed to address both adaptation and mitigation. Over 90 per cent of private climate finance mobilized in this period targeted mitigation.[82] This gap in adaptation finance is particularly devastating for the poor and if future climate change finance comprises private investment and non-government grants, adaption efforts will continue to be seriously underfunded, perpetuating the existing injustice.

Despite their failure to live up to finance commitments for over three decades, the developed world attempted to change the narrative when negotiations were on for a new sustainable development agenda in 2010. They attempted to push for the principle of 'universality',

---

[81]'Analysis of a recent OECD Report: Some Credible Facts Needed', Climate Change Finance unit, Department of Economic Affairs, Ministry of Finance, Government of India, 2015.
[82]Climate Finance in 2013-14 and the USD 100 billion Goal, OECD.

implying that both developed and developing countries needed to implement change. Developing countries, however, interpreted this as an attempt by developed nations to diminish their role in providing aid—an interpretation which was only justified considering that almost all countries in the OECD had made significant cuts in aid following the financial crisis of 2008. When these countries met again at Addis Ababa in 2015, developed countries were again insistent that domestic mobilization and South-South transfers would have to pick up the burden. Ultimately, the Addis Ababa Action Agenda adopted at the conference failed to yield concrete new proposals for additional funding that could be swiftly implemented to meet the world's multiple challenges. Put simply, there was no new money brought to the table. Instead even the previous ambition of the rich countries to commit 0.7 per cent of gross national income as ODA remains only a statement of intent.

The Sustainable Development Goals (the successor to the Millennium Development Goals) also tell a similar story. While the goals themselves call upon developing countries to mobilize finance domestically, complex tax rules and thrifty multinational corporations might make this task impossible. It is estimated that developing countries will require between $3.3 and $4.5 trillion a year to implement the SDGs—which range from universal education, public health care and sustainable energy provision to universal access to clean drinking water and adequate sanitation—in a context where they already face a $2.5 trillion annual investment gap.[83] However, according some estimates, developing countries lost $5.9 trillion to illicit financial outflows, often in the form of tax avoidance or transfers to offshore banks, from 2002 to 2011,[84] and anywhere between $620-$970 billion in 2014 alone.[85] These are resources that

[83]Press Release, 'Developing countries face $2.5 trillion annual investment gap in key sustainable development sectors', UNCTAD, 24 June 2014.

[84]'Illicit Financial Flows from Developing World Nearly $6 Trillion in last decade', Global Financial Integrity, 19 December 2013.

[85]Christine Clough, 'New Study: Illicit Financial Flows in Developing Countries Large and Persistent', Global Financial Integrity, 1 May 2017.

could have been used to combat poverty through investment in basic public services. The developed world was also successful in undermining the concept of common but differentiated responsibility, which was bargained for in Rio. The SDGs place a disproportionate emphasis on raising finance domestically, ignoring the long history of injustice perpetrated on the Global South and ignoring the structural differences between the economic and technological capacity of the Global North and South.

Today, it is even more uncertain who finances whose development. In 2012, the developing countries received around $1.3 trillion in aid and investment. However, in that same year net outflows amounted to $3.3 trillion.[86] Almost all of this money is either interest payment on debts incurred during the 1980s, capital flight and tax evasion by TNCs from the North and royalty payments for intellectual property. In effect, this implies that development aid is flowing backwards and that the poorer countries are financing development in the rich ones.

Finally, it is also worth considering the extent to which climate change policies and international agreements are based on science, knowledge and literature developed in the Global North. The extent of this divide is evident from the fact that most scientific publications on climate change emerge from the Global North, with only a minuscule amount coming from developing and Least Developed Countries (LDC). 85 per cent of the research is produced by OECD countries compared to just 1 per cent by low-income countries.[87] This divide flows naturally from the greater wealth, access to education and funding for science.

A major constraint in bridging the North–South divide relates to the level of acceptance and credibility attached to scientific reports and consequent mitigation measures. The imbalance in research naturally favours the North, which, as we have pointed out over and over

---

[86]Jason Hickel, 'Aid in reverse: how poor countries develop rich countries', *The Guardian*, 14 January 2017.

[87]Malgorzata Blicharska et al., 'Steps to overcome the North-South divide in research relevant to climate change policy and practice', *Nature Climate Change*, 4 January 2017.

again, emits more carbon dioxide and is also less vulnerable to climate change. This status quo ultimately breeds distrust in developing and LDC, which are at a severe disadvantage while negotiating and seeking to come up with domestic plans to mitigate and adapt to climate change. Not only is research heavily focused in the North, the individuals responsible for much of the IPCC reports also tend to be heavily concentrated in the US or the UK.[88] The strong geographical patterns documented in the study we have been citing show that the global distribution and production of climate change knowledge is biased away from regions more vulnerable, but less contributory, to climate change. Such a knowledge divide between poor vulnerable regions and richer regions with high mitigation and adaptation capacity may imperil the integration of locally generated knowledge to provide contextually relevant advice.

However, the knowledge divide goes well beyond representation, but also implicates the manner in which issues are framed for consideration at international forums. For example, for the Global North, environmental damage is a result of normal human behaviour in industry or at home that needs to be tackled collectively. However, for the Global South, emissions are necessary for survival and not to lead a luxurious lifestyle. From a Southern perspective, this is problematic because it obfuscates the fact that per capita emissions in the industrialized North are exponentially higher than those in developing countries.

Ultimately, when the IPCC released its first assessment, the Northern perspective prevailed—there was no distinction between emissions generated by luxurious or survival modes of consumption. Instead all human emissions were lumped into the category of 'anthropogenic emissions'. Ultimately, all human lifestyles were held equally responsible for climate change, negating the Southern perspective on carbon inequality. This way of framing emissions had far-reaching consequences because it ultimately made its way into the

---

[88]Esteve Corbera et al., 'Patterns of authorship in the IPCC Working Group III report', *Nature Climate Change*, 6, 2016, pp. 94–99.

climate change regime and formed the basis of the Kyoto Protocol.

SUSTAINABLE DEVELOPMENT AND CLIMATE CHANGE TODAY
In today's world, the central challenge will be for governments to access the resources they need to meet the basic needs of their people without exacerbating climate change or transgressing environmental limits. This is a challenge that policymakers have grappled with ever since the agenda for sustainable development was set out in the Brundtland Report, published in 1987. Almost four decades later, governments are not any closer to implementing the policies and regulations that can meet the social, economic and environmental concerns of the world. Paradoxically, inequality has only widened, with, as we have seen, the richest 1 per cent owning just about as much of the world's resources and wealth as the rest of the population combined. At the same time humanity each year uses resources equivalent to nearly one-and-a-half Earths to meet its needs, and carbon dioxide emissions are currently set to increase by a catastrophic 3.2 °C by the end of the century. These figures lay bare the futility of today's sustainable development discourse and the failure of all actors involved to successfully meet these challenges.

Over the last two decades, emerging economies like China, India and Brazil have made great strides in narrowing the overall wealth gap between themselves and the Global North (though not per capita). Both China and India have successfully uplifted millions of their own citizens from poverty. However, while much progress has been made on this front, it is worth remembering that the gap between the industrialized North and the developing South continues to remain large and developing economies will have to sustain a high rate of growth to be able to successfully narrow it. However, they must do so in different circumstances, especially in the context of having to reduce energy consumption and emissions. Large swathes of Asia and Africa must lift the next billion individuals out of poverty without the same liberty to burn fossil fuels and emit toxic gases that their Western predecessors enjoyed. Reiterating what has been said many times in this chapter, the current state of development and growth has largely come about as a result of the carbon intensive economies of the West. On the other hand, developing countries have long argued that they are reluctant to change fundamental growth models unless action from the West is evident.

As the climate increasingly deteriorates, it is also worth noting that poverty and inequality will continue to be the mainstay of political discourse. Ever since the publication of the Brundtland Report, this is the complex intertwined challenge that policymakers have had to grapple with. Despite the countless speeches, scientific research and conferences that have dotted the history of this discourse, governments around the world are not much closer to guaranteeing the full spectrum of social, economic and political rights to all, nor addressing climate change. Consider for example that nearly 785 million people are unable to obtain clean drinking water, and 2 billion people lack access to sanitation, approximately 821 million people suffer from chronic undernourishment because they lack the resources to grow or purchase sufficient food to satisfy their dietary energy needs, and another 2.7 billion people lack modern energy for cooking, heating, lighting, transportation, or basic mechanical power. These figures also highlight the unbearable level of inequality which exists in society today.

It is in this context that the United Nations adopted the ambitious Sustainable Development Goalsm (SDGs), which we have referred to, whose aim is to 'free the human race from the tyranny of poverty and want and to heal and secure our planet'. However, just like the Millennium Development Goals, the SDGs continue to suffer from several methodical shortcomings. For one thing, the poverty benchmark is set at $1.9 a day. However, as the United Nations itself admits, this standard reflects the most extreme conditions of poverty falling well below 'a standard of living adequate for...health and well-being' as set out in the Universal Declaration of Human Rights (UDHR). The UN recommends that five and a half dollars a day is a more adequate benchmark and calculates that almost a third of all people in East Asia and the Pacific live in severe poverty, while in the Middle East and North Africa the figure is around 50 per cent. Most disturbingly, nearly half the world still lives on less than $5.50 a day. A five-dollar-a-day benchmark also calls into question the success of the MDGs. Under this benchmark the World Bank estimates that poverty consistently increased between 1981 and 2010, rising from approximately 3.3 billion to almost 4.2 billion over that period.[89] If the Millennium Campaign had used this more appropriate poverty threshold, the MDGs would clearly not have been met. Instead 14 per cent more people are living in five-dollar-a-day poverty now than in 1990. If we were to adopt an even more realistic benchmark of ten dollars a day, over five billion people around the world live in poverty—equivalent to over 70 per cent of the world's population.[90] (Of course, the purchasing power of the dollar is considerably greater in most developing countries than in the West, and five dollars, or 350 rupees, will buy a lot more in India than ten would in the US.)

On the other hand, the SDGs fail to address the systems which have so far reproduced inequality on a global scale. The income levels of the poorest half of humanity have been reduced to a tiny share thanks to supranational institutional arrangements which only the rich can influence. Wealthy individuals and associations have an unfair advantage in multinational agreements, which allow them to influence the formulation of policies for their own benefit. As a result, the poor continue to remain marginalized, unable to effectively fight corporate lobbying or influence government negotiations. The processes of globalization have only reinforced this divide. Supranational institutions, which are capable of shaping the evolution of global income and wealth distribution, continue to unfairly favour the West. Consider for example the WTO and TRIPS under which life-saving drugs have been placed outside the reach of those who need it the most due to strict patent laws.

The international politics behind climate change negotiations

---

[89]'Nearly Half the World Lives on Less than $5.50 a Day', World Bank, 17 October 2018.
[90]Rakesh Kochhar, 'Seven in Ten people globally live on $10 or less per day', Pew Research Center, 23 September 2015.

and the sustainable development discourse have also yet not managed to sufficiently address the inequity in today's climate governance. Today, as we have seen, the global rich are far more responsible for climate change, and are also the least likely to face its adverse consequences. A recent report from the World Bank found that most people live in countries where the poor are more exposed to disasters like droughts, floods and heat waves than the average of the population as a whole. In fact, while the LDC account for less than 1 per cent of the world's total GHG emissions, they are five times more likely to face intense weather events today than during the 1990s and represent close to 40 per cent of all casualties related to natural disasters.[91] While countries like China, India and Brazil have begun to close the gap in terms of total emission levels, such an analysis disguises the fact that the per capita emissions of those in the OECD countries continue to far outstrip those from the developing world. In fact, the lifestyle consumption of even the richest 10 per cent of Chinese citizens is considerably lower than their OECD counterparts. This difference is even more stark for India—where even the richest 10 per cent of Indian citizens have per capita emissions just one-quarter of the poorest 50 per cent of those from the US, while the poorest 50 per cent of Indians have a carbon footprint that is just one-twentieth of the poorest 50 per cent in the US.[92]

Despite the persistence of this divide, the conversation on climate change and sustainable development has made some headway over the last few years. In part this was because the scientific evidence on the matter is no longer subject to dispute—apart from a few vested interests in the US, represented in a handful of politically-motivated think tanks and politicians who continue to express scepticism about the science, a clear consensus has emerged on the adverse impact of climate change and inequality. Additionally, extreme weather events

---

[91]'Small Island Developing States in Numbers', Office of the High Representative for the Least Developed Countries, Landlocked Developing Countries and Small Island Developing States, 2015.

[92]'Extreme Carbon Inequality', Oxfam Media Briefing, 2 December 2015.

have continued to increase, helping to consolidate the opinion that climate change is no longer a far-fetched possibility but a tangible reality we must face today. Action to mitigate and adapt to these eventualities has also gained ground because of the rapidly falling prices of renewable energy—the cost of solar power is down by 80 per cent and wind power by 50 per cent since 2009. The argument that alternative energy was uneconomic is unlikely to hold for long. Developing countries were also emerging as market leaders in scaling up investment for green energy. In 2018, developing countries invested $177 billion in clean energy, $74 billion more than the developed world.[93]

It is likely that many of these converging developments helped lead to the success of the Paris Agreement under the UNFCC. After years of negotiations and scientific consensus, 2015 marked an epochal year in climate change politics. For one thing, 192 countries descended upon Paris to sign off on an agreement that will either go down in history as the event which prevented ecological catastrophe or the event where leaders from around the world failed to save our planet from catastrophic climate change (depending on whom you ask). The agreement seeks to 'strengthen the global response to the threat of climate change, in the context of sustainable development and efforts to eradicate poverty' including by 'holding the increase in global average well below 2 °C above pre-industrial levels and to pursue efforts to limit the temperature increase to 1.5 °C above pre-industrial levels'. In order to achieve these objectives each country was asked to communicate its own 'nationally determined contributions'. To be fair however, not everyone is happy with the 2 °C benchmark. A significant amount of research suggests that even if countries implement their national contributions perfectly, the cumulative reductions in harmful emissions would still fall short of preventing the Earth from warming over 2 °C. Some studies, for instance, calculated that if all countries accomplished their

---

[93]Vaibhavi Khanwalkar, 'Developing countries invest more in renewable energy than developing nations', *Moneycontrol*, 6 June 2018.

Intended Nationally Determined Contribution (INDC) pledges through 2030, the world would still be on track for a temperature rise of 2.9 to 3.4 °Celsius.[94]

Former US President Barack Obama's opening speech at the 21st Conference Of Parties (COP 21) included some ambitious claims. Early in the speech he proclaimed, 'The United States of America not only recognizes our role in creating this problem, we embrace our responsibility to do something about it.'[95] It isn't clear what responsibility he meant, because the United States consistently demanded that that differentiation and equity be left out of the Paris agreement, essentially shifting the cost of climate action from the rich countries to the poor.

The Paris Agreement ultimately represented a paradigm shift from the top-down model of the Kyoto Protocol, with adverse implications for several sustainable development principles laid down in Rio. The developed world no longer has to bear the burden of emission reductions, implying that they are no longer under the obligation to meet their 'fair share' of the mitigation efforts. While the United States appeared to be constructive in public, privately it was clear that the US remained adamant in its positions against binding mitigation and finance obligations. Some EU negotiators were said to have claimed that, 'If we insist on legally binding [commitments], the deal will not be global because we will lose the US.'[96] In fact, minutes before the final session, the United States demanded that a single word be changed: Developed countries 'should' rather than 'shall' undertake economy-wide quantified emission reductions.[97] Because the United States refused to budge in its position, the EU and the G77 reluctantly accepted this change in language, which would significantly reduce the impact of legally binding action.

---

[94]Vineeth Kumar, 'World will witness 2.9 to 3.4°C temperature rise even if Paris deal fully implemented', *Down to Earth*, 16 November 2016.

[95]Remarks by President Obama at the First Session of COP 21, Office of the Press Secretary, White House, 30 November 2015.

[96]Radoslav S. Dimitrov, 'The Paris Agreement on Climate Change: Behind Closed Doors', *Global Environmental Politics*, 16, No. 3, August 2016, pp. 1–11.

[97]Id.

Countries, due to their differential wealth and income levels, have differentiated capacity to take mitigation action, while the differentiated levels of continued per capita and historical emissions imposes differentiated moral responsibilities to do so. A civil society assessment of the INDCs made during the Paris Agreement stressed that 'the operationalization of equity and fair shares must focus on historical responsibility and capacity, which directly correspond with the core principle of the UN climate convention of "common but differentiated responsibility"—with respective capabilities.'[98] However, the assessment found that 'all major developed countries fall well short of their fair shares' while the 'majority of developing countries have made mitigation pledges that exceed or broadly meet their fair share'. The agreement itself also failed to drive home the necessity of structural transformation in economic development. Despite the fact that it is now necessary for 80 per cent of the fossil fuel reserves to remain underground, the chances of this realistically happening are significantly dampened in light of the $500 billion subsidies for the fossil fuel companies—a figure that is exponentially higher than any aid for developing countries or investment for renewable energy.

The Paris Agreement also reaffirmed the practice of carbon trading, which was so heavily criticized for creating perverse incentives for the developed world. The Paris Agreement fails to learn from the many flaws of market-based approaches and instead envisions an expansion of these highly problematic mechanisms. The Paris Agreement also failed to make any realistic headway in finance. Echoing the promises made at Copenhagen of mobilizing $100 billion per year, the agreement falls woefully short of any realistic estimates for the amounts actually required to mitigate and adapt to climate change. Meanwhile, the definition of 'mobilize' is purposefully broad, to include loans, private finance, grants with strings attached, and the reallocation of aid budgets. There has even been talk of calling the money sent home by migrants working in richer countries a form of climate finance, and counting it towards the total 'mobilized' by those rich countries. Unfortunately, this flew in the face of what campaigners and civil society have argued for ages—that finance is not a question of aid or charity, instead it is about the historical debt that the developed world owes. Sadly, but unsurprisingly, all talks on, and proposals for, climate reparations were thrown out of the window.

THE CENTRAL CONTRADICTIONS

Ultimately, the post-2015 development agenda which includes both the Paris Agreement and the SDGs are both apolitical and ahistorical. As we have said, and would like to reiterate, they ignore the reality of European colonialism, which led to the wide-scale plunder of Latin America, the African slave trade and the scramble for natural resources in Asia. Today's crises of poverty, inequality and environmental degradation were set in motion during this period of colonization and yet this narrative does not fit into the development paradigm acknowledged by the dominant powers.

These agendas also do not highlight or propose a restructuring of the global governance institutions which have perpetuated inequality for decades. The era of structural adjustment policies and wide-scale funding of private corporations who have had a disastrous impact on the developing world continues. Per capita income growth in the developing countries plunged to half the previous levels, and in Sub-Saharan Africa the GNP of the average country shrank by around 10 per cent during the 1980s and 1990s.[99] All told, developing countries lost roughly $480 billion per year in potential GDP, while multinational corporations raked in astonishing profits under the new economic regime.[100]

Perhaps it was only fitting then that President Trump ultimately chose to withdraw American support for the Paris Agreement. The idea of development, so enthusiastically put forward by Truman over

---

[99]Jason Hickel, 'The World Bank and the development delusion', LSE Blog, 16 November 2012.
[100]Id.

half a century ago, told a powerful story to the developed world—that their hard work and success had put them ahead in the great march to progress and that they had much to offer for the poorer countries who could not hope to cope. The advanced nations would instead stand as saviours to the developing world, helping them achieve what they could not themselves.

In one single stroke, Truman successfully erased the colonial draining of resources for over two centuries by the Europeans and America's own interventions in Latin America at the behest of banana and sugar companies, propping up authoritarian regimes in Nicaragua, Guatemala, Venezuela, and Mexico. Instead, the developed world would 'aid' the developing world. Today, the developed world gives close to $136 billion in aid every year, a figure proudly touted as evidence of their benevolence.[101] Hidden behind these figures are the massive outflow of illicit money as a result of laundering by TNCs, to the tune of $900 billion, or the $600 billion that developing countries pay in debt service, much of it on the compound interest of loans accumulated by illegitimate rulers long since deposed.[102] These figures reveal a pattern of extraction which has long been suppressed in the development narrative, fuelled by the benefits that rich countries reap from cheap labour, restrictive trade agreements and abysmal environmental standards.

Despite the force of history, the development narrative continues to parrot the old mantra of export-led growth which will eventually give everyone in the world a chance to enjoy a lifestyle similar to the developed world. However this hides the fact that if everyone on Earth lived like the average American, we would need five Earths to sustain us.[103] Even at existing levels of average global consumption, we are overshooting our planet's capacity by about 50 per cent each year, and this is almost entirely due to overconsumption in rich countries.

---

[101]Mark Anderson, 'Foreign aid close to record peak after donors spend $135bn in 2014', *The Guardian*, 8 April 2015.
[102]The Road to Development Justice, APWLD.
[103]Ecological Footprint, Global Footprint Network.

While the rich seek to preserve their way of life, they seek to prevent emissions from the South, which are caused due to their quest for basic necessities—food, water and energy—and not luxuries. Meanwhile, global inequality has been getting worse. The gap between the per capita incomes of advanced Western economies and those of developing regions like Latin America, Africa, and South Asia continues to widen and is now three times larger than it was in 1960.[104] It is perhaps telling that the only regions which have been able to buck this trend are China, India and some countries in East Asia—the only regions which largely escaped Western intervention in the post-colonial era.

[104]Jason Hikel, 'The Development Delusion: Foreign Aid and Inequality', *American Affairs*, Vol. 1, Issue 3, 2017.

CHAPTER 4

MAKING SPACE IN CYBERSPACE

In the previous chapter, we detailed how the global community failed in the governance of climate change and sustainable development. This chapter will argue the same of cyberspace. Cyberspace as a medium was born from the unipolarity of the late twentieth century—yet its nature has fundamentally changed as the balance of power shifted in the twenty-first century. For a medium with global reach and consequence, we ask if a truly diverse set of stakeholders actually managed it. Or is cyberspace, just like sustainable development, hostage to the interests and ambitions of a small community with outsized voice and influence?

A conversation on the management of cyberspace is useful for another key reason. It foreshadows the rise of a new superpower: China. Well before Beijing was making its weight felt on the high seas or through geoeconomic influence, China was carving out its own sovereign interest in cyberspace. This momentous shift in the power structure of governance only added a new twist to managing cyberspace. Whereas in the climate debates, some consensus was possible, given the unipolar power structure of the world, this has been exacerbated in regard to cyberspace, where the global community has largely failed to manage cyberspace through multilateralism or multi-stakeholder governance.

THE LIBERTARIAN INTERNET

The launch of Sputnik by the Soviet Union on 4 October 1957 was a wake-up call for the United States. As a part of the emerging geopolitical scenario post World War II, the space race was seen by many as a metaphor for state power. Intent on not falling behind on technological development, the US Defence Department issued Directive 5105, establishing the Advanced Research Projects Agency (ARPA) in 1958. ARPA's mission was: 'To assure that the U.S. maintains a lead in applying state-of the-art technology for military capabilities and to prevent technological surprise from her adversaries.' From this initiative came the Advanced Research Projects Agency Network (ARPANET), which sought to break up information into 'packets' that could be relayed from one computer system to another in order to communicate in a decentralized fashion.

The idea behind breaking information into packets was to create a network that would still work if a Soviet nuclear strike wiped out American communication systems. Because of this necessity, Lawrence Roberts—head of ARPANET—decided not to make a planned and centralized system.[1] In what was a strategic decision, influenced by military necessity, this very decentralization would become the hallmark of many of the values of the internet that we take for granted. *Because* ARPANET was flexible and decentralized, the functions of the internet that we are familiar with today, such as email, were born as unintended consequences. The decision by the internet's early innovators to design an open system meant that the medium could evolve as it did.

However, this development was only one part of the story that gave birth to the internet. For decades, communication infrastructure, generally postal or telecommunications, in most countries were state monopolies. The coordination of this network was premised almost completely on sovereignty. Internationally, they were governed by the International Telecommunications Union (ITU), an organization of the United Nations (that was originally founded as the International Telegraph Union in 1865), which resolves technical and financial

---

[1] *Funding a Revolution: Government Support for Computing Research*, Computer Science and Telecommunications Board, National Research Council, Washington DC: The National Academies Press, 1999, p. 169.

questions of international importance by arranging agreements between sovereign states. Even in the late 1980s, most experts from the world of telephony viewed it as an academic exercise, with no real commercial value. Unlike the public telephone networks, the internet initially attracted hardly any state interest in its control or oversight. Europe's relative indifference to the internet, and America's liberal policies on communication infrastructure, implied that the internet was pretty much in the hands of a few technical organizations and the engineers who developed it. The Internet Engineering Task Force (IETF), as it was known, was largely the only decision-making entity at the time.

The interesting characteristic of the IETF was that it was made up of mostly academic networks, and was fashioned very differently from most state and intergovernmental standards institutions. As a result, the internet's original management structure was almost entirely informal, and government indifference gave the IETF very liberal decision-making power. Because of this academic structure, those who worked on the internet in the early days did so with very little thought of security and regulations—an attitude which would underwrite much of the internet today. The real value of the internet back then was how free and open information was, and how much of it could be transferred on this medium. As Vinton Cerf, one of the internet's founders, described it, 'We were just rank amateurs, and we were expecting that some authority would finally come along and say, "Here's how we are going to do it." And nobody ever came along, so we were sort of tentatively feeling our way into how we could go about getting the software up and running.'[2]

In the early, heady days of the internet, cyber utopians were thrilled with the potential of the internet to erase physical differences and spaces. Such optimism no doubt stemmed from America's rise to unipolar prominence after the fall of the Berlin Wall and the

[2]'Excerpts from an Oral History Interview with Vinton Cerf, Vice President of data architecture, MCI Data and Information Services Division'. Interview by Judy O' Neill, Smithsonian Institution Oral and Video Histories, 24 April 1990, https:// americanhistory.si.edu/comphist/vc1.html.

collapse of the Soviet Union. The pioneers of Web 1.0 were certain that the internet would change the nature of human society, with its open, collaborative, and borderless structure. The individual would be digitized, free to choose the rules and laws that governed her virtual reality. In 1996, cyberguru John Perry Barlow issued the Declaration of the Independence of Cyberspace, the first of its kind: 'Governments of the Industrial World, you weary giants of flesh and steel, I come from Cyberspace, the new home of Mind. On behalf of the future, I ask you of the past to leave us alone. You are not welcome among us. You have no sovereignty where we gather.'[3]

These optimistic views were made possible by the American government's relatively lax regulatory policies. The US government adopted a light touch towards regulating the internet, which included financing research first through the Department of Defence (DoD), and later via the National Science Foundation (NSF).[4] This is because the 1980s also saw a shift in American thinking about the relationship between businesses and the state. The great depression of the 1930s and a failure to revive economic growth led to a questioning of Keynesian economics, which assumes higher government expenditure. Instead, with Ronald Reagan as president, 'deregulation' became the mantra. This same philosophy carried over into the regulatory and legal environment for internet developers as well. Only towards the late 1980s, when the registration of internet domain names began growing rapidly, did the US government decide to institutionalize the process. The end result of these deliberations was the creation of the Internet Assigned Numbers Authority (IANA), which functioned on the basis of a contract between the US Department of Commerce and the University of Southern California. The IANA, in effect, had become the sole monopoly over organizing critical internet resources. For a while, this arrangement worked well, but was thrown into disarray with the invention of the World Wide Web by Tim Berners-

---

[3]John P. Barlow, 'A Declaration of the Independence of Cyberspace', Hache Online, http://editions-hache.com/essais/pdf/barlow1.pdf.
[4]David Hart, 'NSF Shapes the Internet's Evolution', National Science Foundation, 25 July 2003, https://www.nsf.gov/discoveries/disc_summ.jsp?cntn_id=100662.

Lee at the Centre Europeén de la Recherche Nucléaire (CERN) in Geneva. Stimulated by this development, it soon became clear that the internet was moving beyond a mere technical innovation, and would have immense political and economic consequences.

At the time, the IANA was a one-man organization, run by Jon Postel, who was a professor at the University of Southern California. In 1995, Postel, realizing the need for a more stable and comprehensive Domain Name System (DNS) management system, wanted to move the IANA function under the umbrella of the Internet Society (ISOC), a policy-oriented network of internet technicians, established in 1992.[5] This move prompted the first politicization of internet governance. In March that year, Robert Aiken, president of the Federal Networking Council (FNC), shot off an angry email to the ISOC asking why they presumed that they had obtained jurisdiction over the root and if they did not make such a presumption, then who did it belong to?[6] The US government was furious with Postel's unilateral assumption of jurisdiction. They argued that mere technical experts could never understand the political and commercial implications of this new technology. In 1998, the Department of Commerce released a Green Paper on the administration of internet governance with the intention to move the administration of internet domain names into the hands of a private and non-profit organization.[7] In November that year, the Department of Commerce officially recognized the Internet Corporation for Assigned Names and Numbers (ICANN) as the organization that would inherit the responsibility for managing names and numbers. The US saw the ICANN—registered, improbably enough, under California state law—as international and private. What seems today an act of breathtaking unilateral effrontery was

---

[5]United Nations Dept. of Public Information and United Nations ICT Task Force, *Internet Governance: A Grand Collaboration: An Edited Collection Of Papers*, New York: United Nations Publications, 2004.

[6]Jack Goldsmith and Tim Wu, *Who Controls The Internet?: Illusions of a Borderless World*, Oxford: Oxford University Press, 2006, p. 35.

[7]United States Department of Commerce, 'Management of Internet Names And Addresses', ICANN, accessed 14 June 2019, https://www.icann.org/resources/unthemed-pages/white-paper-2012-02-25-en.

accepted at the time, in an era of unipolar US dominance.

The Clinton administration, which effected this transition, framed the narrative around internet control under the aegis of 'industry self-regulation'. One primary consideration of the US government was to keep the internet out of the hands of the ITU because of its one nation, one vote structure. Historically, the United States has shifted governance of new digital issue areas away from the ITU in order to secure its own preferences and interests free of inter-governmental mechanisms. Ira Magaziner, who was then a senior advisor to President Clinton, made the US opposition to an ITU role quite explicit when he stated, 'Technical management certainly should not be controlled by an intergovernmental organization or international telecommunications union.'[8] As has been noted, the Clinton administration framed the transition as a model of industry self-regulation, whereby the various private-sector stakeholders would come together, agree upon the proper membership and protocols for the new entity, and then assume responsibility for governing the internet, its root servers, and related protocols. This was another critical decision which would have unintended consequences in shaping global governance. The functioning of ICANN itself would give rise to new ideas of governance, which put businesses and civil society at an equal footing with states.

To many internet scholars, the self-governance narrative was primarily strategic. The EU, the transatlantic ally of the US, was skittish about American control over the internet, and was receptive to the idea that the ITU must take over. By framing internet governance in terms of it being private sector-led, the United States could legitimately claim that it had no oversight over its outcomes, thus pre-empting any attempt to multilateralize the internet. Of course, the idea of self-regulation itself implied that the internet was firmly in the hands of institutions which promoted US interests, such as the IANA, ICANN, ISOC, International Business Machines Corporation

---

[8]Henry Jenkins, David Thorburn (eds.), *Democracy And New Media*, Cambridge: MIT Press, 2004, p. 113.

(IBM) and MCI WorldCom (now Verizon Enterprise Solutions), thus ensuring that the US could have the best of both worlds. The US Department of Commerce White Paper, according to one prominent internet scholar, Milton Mueller, 'reflected a behind-the-scenes agreement that IANA–ISOC and their corporate allies would be the ones in control of the new organization and that a specific program acceptable to the trademark lobby, the U.S. Commerce Department and the Europeans would be executed.'[9]

Self-regulation also served to placate several technicians who were instrumental in developing the internet. That communication tools were a liberating force synonymous with freedom was a firmly held belief in such circles. In the early 1970s, Joseph Licklider and Robert Taylor, leading figures of ARPANET, believed that the internet would allow people to communicate more freely and productively. By keeping an arm's length distance between the US state and the technical resources of internet governance, the administration pacified concerns in the technical community about a 'government takeover' of the internet. For over two decades, this libertarian ethos of the internet, and its global spread, existed side-by-side without any contradictions. The internet's pioneers had successfully created a community of technical experts, primarily from the US and Europe, to manage the internet free from government control. Esoteric societies like ISOC and IETF at the time rendered decisions by 'consensus' with disagreement limited to technical, rather than political or economic, issues. As the internet integrated more and more with a globalized economy, however, such decision-making was increasingly impractical. The World Wide Web and the dot-com booms of the 1990s vastly increased the number of stakeholders with an interest in the internet, from commercial entities to end users. As a result, this libertarian ethos began disintegrating, spurred by new concerns of a digital divide between the Global North and the South, and by new rising powers who were keen to exert influence, if not control, over the medium.

---

[9]Shaun M. Powers and Michael Jablonski, *The Real Cyber War: The Political Economy of Internet Freedom*, Urbana: University of Illinois Press, 2015, p. 141.

WHO DOES THE INTERNET BELONG TO? THE RETURN OF THE STATE

The expansion of the internet truly took place in the late 1990s, after the US government removed legal restrictions on its commercial use. The move came as a part of the Clinton administration's 'Global Information Infrastructure Initiative', an ambitious project aimed at deregulating and liberalizing the telecom sector by removing trade protections and allowing private investment by Western companies in global communication infrastructure markets.[10] Then Vice President Al Gore announced the initiative at a 1995 World Telecommunication Development Conference in Buenos Aires, where he proudly declared that the internet would 'circle the globe with information superhighways on which all people can travel. These highways—or, more accurately, networks of distributed intelligence—will allow us to share information, to connect, and to communicate as a global community.'[11]

From the start, the US administration framed this new technology in democratic and market-centric terms, in line with America's vision of an international liberal order. According to Gore, the internet would spread the principles of participatory democracy and promote international cooperation along a new information superhighway. He also believed that 'the global economy also will be driven by the growth of the Information Age. Hundreds of billions of dollars can be added to world growth if we commit to the GII.'[12] Thus, by the late 1990s, the 'information society', as it would come to be known, was shaped largely by American imperatives and fashioned by the private sector. Government policy aided this endeavour by creating a political and regulatory framework that supported privatization and market liberalization.

---

[10]National Telecommunications and Information Administration, 'The Global Information Infrastructure: Agenda For Cooperation'. United States Department of Commerce, 1 June 1995, https://www.ntia.doc.gov/report/1995/global-information-infrastructure-agenda-cooperation.

[11]Cees J. Hamelink, 'The People's Communication Charter', Development in Practice, Vol. 8, No. 1, 1998, pp. 68–74, http://www.jstor.org/stable/4028865.

[12]Shaun M. Powers and Michael Jablonski, The Real Cyber War, p. 101.

Just like the traditional North–South divide in development, however, it soon became clear that inequities were setting into the digital domain as well. As a report by *Time* magazine highlighted, 'In the early 2000s the 15 percent of the world population that lives in the industrialized world enjoy five times better access to fixed-line and mobile phone services, nine times better access to internet services, and own 13 times more personal computers than the 85 percent living in poor and middle-ranking countries.'[13] And just like the development debates, the Global North was almost evangelical in its belief that free markets would hold the answer. It was here that the ITU stepped in with the idea of a World Summit on Information Society (WSIS) which took place in Geneva in 2003, with a follow-up summit in Tunis in 2005. Having been sidelined by the forces of liberalization and the ascendance to free market trade, the ITU was keen to reinvigorate its historical role in shaping the politics and economics around communication networks.

In the broader context of global governance, the WSIS was also one of the last in a series of summits convened since the 1990s, of which the highlight had been the Rio Earth Summit on the environment that we have already discussed. Following the end of the Cold War, and America's rise as the world's sole superpower, a space opened up for new and innovative approaches in solving global problems like climate change and creating the 'information society'. For the first time, it was possible to navigate past the treaty-based, inter-governmental and bureaucratic nature of global governance. In this context, it is noteworthy that a new wave of public advocacy groups, or civil society, mobilized around the summit. Spurred on by globalization, these non-state actors attempted to broaden the scope of the discussion beyond control over internet infrastructure and towards topics such as human rights, cultural imperialism and inequality. For a long time, meaningful civil society participation in the UN was somewhat the exception rather than the norm. This began to change with the Rio Earth Summit in 1992, when

---

[13]Simon Robinson, 'Tackling the world's technology gap', *Time*, 18 November 2005.

NGO participation exploded onto the scene, forcing the UN to formalize a 'consultative relationship' between accredited NGOs and the UN. Because of this, the historically technocratic ITU had to respond to criticism about the lack of effective stakeholder participation. Ultimately, pressure from such groups culminated in the ITU commissioning a 'civil society division' meant to facilitate the full participation of civil society organizations in the WSIS process. In hindsight, as we shall see, this development was both a result of globalization and a significant contributor to shaping the future of internet governance.

Not all countries were pleased with the introduction of civil society into internet governance. Autocratic states, such as Pakistan, Iran, Russia, and perhaps most vocally, China, attempted to exclude any reference to media and human rights in the official text. Civil society was not the only source of consternation. Just as in the climate debates, Brazil and India proactively sought to ensure that intellectual property rights would not be used against the interests of developing countries. Developing countries, spearheaded by Senegalese President Abdoulaye Wade, were also insistent that the developed world promote the idea of a 'Digital Solidarity Fund'.[14] Except for the nations who would have to pay, the idea caught the imagination of other participants by storm. While the idea itself never took hold, it reflects the line of thinking NGOs had developed in the Rio Earth Summit.

Whatever disagreements states had about NGO participation, the fact that they would now be 'partners', rather than outside observers in global governance, was a truly extraordinary development. It was at WSIS that the expression 'multi-stakeholder' became the buzzword; it was an approach that would accommodate the voices of civil society and businesses in decision-making. This new discourse was visible throughout the WSIS process, and even made its way into

---

[14]United Nations General Assembly, 'General Debate Of The 63rd Session (23–27 September & 29 September 2008)', UN, accessed 14 June 2019, https://www.un.org/ga/63/generaldebate/senegal.shtml.

academic literature. That the multi-stakeholder process would be a true innovation became the commonly held belief amongst the summit participants.

However, as we shall discuss later in this chapter, looking at the muti-stakeholder model in hindsight, it became clear that it was the Global North and its businesses and civil society networks that were effectively represented. This early strain in the practical understanding of this model was visible at one of the most contested debates at the WSIS, which was over open source software. Developing countries believed that open source software was a cheaper and more reliable alternative to proprietary software sold by American corporations, led at the time by Microsoft. Unfortunately for the developing world, the cost of Microsoft software was prohibitive, and governments would have saved billions of dollars if they switched to free and open source software. In responding to the mounting pressure from open source software advocates, Microsoft worked with lobby groups in the US. Bill Gates even warned against the use of such software at a conference in Seattle.[15] It was perhaps due to such lobbying that the draft of the WSIS declaration of principles went from outright 'support' of open source software for the developing world to promoting awareness about 'different software models, and the means of their creation, including proprietary, open-source and free software'.[16]

For these very reasons, perhaps, the most important development at WSIS was that more and more countries increasingly began voicing disapproval with US control over the core infrastructure of the internet, specifically the ICANN. The debates over self-regulation, globalization and privatization of the internet were divided broadly into two groups. First, those who preferred that the ITU deal with these issues, such as China, Brazil, South Africa and India, and those who sought reforms in the ICANN structure without dismantling it, such as the EU and the US. The debate around

---

[15]Mathew Broersma, 'MS leads lobby against open software', *ZDNet*, 13 August 2002.
[16]'Plan of Action', *World Summit on the Information Society*, Geneva 2003–Tunis 2005, 12 December 2003, https://www.itu.int/net/wsis/docs/geneva/official/poa.html.

multilateral administration was quite procedural. Because the ITU is an intergovernmental organization that operates under the aegis of the UN, governments argued that they could exercise greater influence over the economic and political impact of the internet on their countries. During the WSIS, the ITU was keen on putting itself forward as the most appropriate institution for managing the internet. Interestingly enough, this position found support even from the EU, which by now was quite uncomfortable with the ICANN and US role on the internet. This was unacceptable to the US, because for many internet libertarians, a defining feature of internet governance was America's "soft touch" approach, meaning that there would be no interference in the internet's operations.

This view was in for a rude shock in 2005, when the Bush Administration actively intervened with the ICANN to prevent the registration of a '.xxx' top level domain name to distinguish porn websites.[17] Innocuous as the decision was, and heavily fuelled by domestic conservative politics, to the international community, the move was significant. It was a reaffirmation of their belief that American unilateralism over the internet would pose a strategic threat to their political and economic sovereignty. The US did itself no favours when it unilaterally declared in June 2005 that it would 'maintain its historic role in authorizing changes or modifications to the authoritative root zone file'.[18] Expressing a strong desire to maintain a 'market-based approach and private sector leadership', the US government made it clear that ICANN would operate under its oversight. To many delegates at the WSIS, America's position was just another example of the digital divide they had sought to address at WSIS. The Brazilian delegation, for example, noted that the digital divide is not simply about financial inequalities and access

---

[17]Declan Mccullagh, 'Bush Administration Objects To .xxx Domains', *CNET*, 15 August 2005.
[18]National Telecommunications and Information Administration, 'U.S. Principles on the Internet's Domain Name and Addressing System', NTIA, accessed 14 June 2019, https://www.ntia.doc.gov/other-publication/2005/us-principles-internets-domain-name-and-addressing-system.

to computers and phone lines. The divide is also tied to 'political inequalities, arising from the inability of developing countries to influence Internet decision-making.'[19]

Ultimately, the WSIS concluded with little or no change in the way the internet was governed. The US was successful in keeping the UN and the ITU out of such debates, and the final text recognized that the ICANN would follow the multi-stakeholder model and approved of the 'private sector taking the lead'. The only real concession was the creating of an Internet Governance Forum (IGF) which would operate under the auspices of the UN. However, it was only a forum for countries to 'discuss' internet-related issues without the power to enforce any changes. Media outlets in the West saw this as an unmitigated victory for the US and its allies. The *BBC*, for example, announced that the '...US has won its fight to stay in charge of the Internet.'[20] The extent to which America wanted to keep the UN out of internet governance was made clear when Ambassador David Gross, the former coordinator for International Communications and Information Policy at the State Department during the Bush administration, reminisced that, 'My number-one accomplishment [while in government] was keeping the Internet stable and secure in the face of suggestions for the creation of, or establishment of, a multilateral institution taking over control.'[21] In all fairness, it must be acknowledged that this position found considerable support amongst advocates of free media and free expression, who were anxious that greater governmental involvement by countries without a free-speech tradition would compromise free media, especially within developing countries.

CATALYSTS: THE ARAB SPRING, L'AFFAIRE SNOWDEN AND THE RISE OF INFORMATION SOVEREIGNTY

While debates around internet governance continued at the IGF

---

[19]Gustavo Capdevila, 'Internet: Groups Meet To Hash Out Who's In Charge', *Inter Press Service English News Wire*, 10 January 2005.
[20]'US Retains Hold Of The Internet', *BBC*, 16 November 2005.
[21]Ryan David Kiggins, 'Wired World: United States Policy and the Open Door Internet', Ph.D, Diss., Gainesville: University of Florida, 2011, p. 42.

for half a decade or so, the internet and communication platforms themselves were undergoing a massive change. Over three decades ago, Robert Noyce and Gordon Moore—whose famous articulation of the speed of technological development, 'Moore's Law', continues to hold today—developed the world's first microprocessor. A decade later, Steve Jobs introduced the Apple personal computer. These developments in hardware were complemented by Berners-Lee's invention of the World Wide Web, which connected many of these computers to a common network.

While these technologies were revolutionary at the time, they were limited to a few industrialized countries who could afford these platforms. Today, the internet is truly ubiquitous. Nothing exemplifies this more than the rise (and continued exponential rise) of social media. Facebook launched in 2004 as the brainchild of an ambitious Harvard student, Mark Zuckerberg. It was an immediate hit. In the first month of coming online, almost half the campus had signed up for it. By the end of the year, it had stormed several American universities. As the *Stanford Daily* exclaimed at the time:

> Classes are being skipped. Work is being ignored. Students are spending hours in front of their computers in utter fascination. Thefacebook.com craze has swept through campus... Modeled after social networking Web sites like Friendster.com, this site provides Stanford students with a network of their peers... A student with just over 100 friends can have a network of over 1,500 people. 'I signed up on Tuesday morning and I was immediately addicted,' [a student] said. 'Nothing validates your social existence like the knowledge that someone else has approved you or is asking for your permission to list them as a friend. It's bonding and flattering at the same time.'[22]

The rise to power of Web 2.0 platforms revolutionized how individuals communicated and shared information. Zuckerberg said as much in a 2009 interview: 'Think about what people are

---

[22]Shirin Sharif, 'All the Cool Kids are Doing It", *Stanford Daily*, 30 April 2004.

doing on Facebook today. They're keeping up with their friends and family, but they're also building an image and identity for themselves, which in a sense is their brand. They're connecting with the audience that they want to connect to. It's almost a disadvantage if you're not on it now.'[23] No longer was the internet a mere commercial or communicative tool. The internet was slowly turning into an extension of human personality. This was the beginning of the age of the smartphone—affordable, accessible and always online. It is also the age of Facebook, Twitter, Instagram and a whole raft of social media.

In the 2014 and, even more so, the 2019 Indian elections, political parties resorted extensively to social media. Aside from issuing messages through social media memes, digital posters and WhatsApp forwards, the indirect impact of social media (as a source for 'mainstream' media stories) made it an indispensable communications tool for politicians. And that's where the trouble started.

WhatsApp is the favoured medium, first, because 82 per cent of India's internet users have downloaded the app,[24] and, second, because it's targeted to specific people; a party can create groups defined by their interests, their caste or religious identity, or a specific issue or cause, and bombard them with messages to reinforce their biases and convince them the party is with them.

The problem, however, is that the use of social media is not always benign. 'Fake news' has been derided enough in the contemporary world, but it exists because it has been manufactured to serve the political interests of its disseminators. The danger, therefore, is that a lot of votes will be cast on the basis of false information.

Having been made aware of the political misuse of its messaging services, WhatsApp took steps to limit the damage, limiting forwards in some countries, for instance, to just five recipients in order to make it more difficult for lies to go viral. It also decided to block numbers

[23]Fred Vogelstein, 'The Wired Interview: Facebook's Mark Zuckerberg', *Wired*, 29 June 2009.
[24]Sahir, 'WhatsApp Usage, Revenue, Market Share and other Statistics (2019)', *Digital Information World*, 11 February 2019.

identified by the Election Commission of India as guilty of spreading 'fake news'.[25] But this has done little to stop the dissemination of disinformation; at best it might slow it down, as the guilty parties scramble to find alternative numbers and create yet more groups.

The fears of democrats are not unfounded: people have been killed on the basis of fake WhatsApp rumours. It is striking that when the Easter church bombings took place in Sri Lanka in April 2019, one of the first reactions of the government was to shut down social media in that country. But the stakes are different when it comes to political messaging: in India, where all political parties have a vested interest in seeing themselves re-elected, they tend to turn a blind eye to the excesses of their own partisans.

Social media offers a marvellously useful set of communication tools that democratizes the expression of public opinion. But in the hands of unscrupulous politicians, who see it as a means of manipulation, social media can undermine democracy itself. Once you have voted for the wrong people on the basis of false information, there is nothing you can do about it till the next election. In that chilling fact lies the WhatsApp danger to Indian democracy.

Which is why who controls the internet is only one question amongst many that are agitating cyberspace. For many governments, it is necessary that democratic norms and values translate from the offline world to the online one. Freedom of speech and expression and the right to privacy are just some of the human rights that most liberal democracies attempt to safeguard, even on the internet. The trigger for many of these debates has been the exponential growth of the internet, along with a change in its characteristics. Yet, it is evident that there really is no global consensus on these norms. Despite the libertarian origins of the internet, the values which underwrote its spread have not truly spread as desired. Two events over the past few years highlight that it is not easy to guarantee these rights—even for the citizens of the more liberal countries.

---

[25]'WhatsApp Blocks Numbers Spreading Fake News During Lok Sabha Election', *Business Today*, 13 April 2019.

The first was undoubtedly the turmoil which engulfed the Arab world in 2011. The protests itself began with the creation of a Facebook page that mourned the killing of a young Egyptian by the state police.[26] Soon, thousands of people organized at Tahrir Square in downtown Cairo in what was to become an uprising that would overwhelm the Middle East. These angry movements spread, and eventually four of the world's most autocratic dictators— Zine al-Abidine Ben Ali of Tunisia, Muammar Gaddafi of Libya, Ali Abdullah Saleh of Yemen, and Hosni Mubarak of Egypt—were cast out of power. Popular democratic movements, which began in Tunisia, ultimately led to what is now known as the 'Arab Spring'. While some debate continues to exist on the issues, it is undeniable that social media and the internet (in addition to older technologies like satellite television broadcasts) had a transformative role to play in these protests. While the proximate cause of the protests itself was an inflammable combination of ruthless policing, youth unemployment, absence of political freedom and lack of social mobility, the undeniable fact that platforms like Twitter and Facebook amplified this frustration was a momentous event in history.

For many in the West, it was an affirmation of the democratic potential of the internet. Western media glorified the role that their technology companies had to play in bringing democracy to the Middle East. 'How an Egyptian Revolution Began on Facebook', read one headline in the New York Times.[27] For the first time, disgruntled citizens were able to connect in a virtual space and aggregate in a physical one. These movements lent weight to the utopian idea of a borderless post-sovereign world fantasized by many technocrats. To many, it lent credence to the words of Nicholas Negroponte, director of MIT Media Lab, that the internet was beyond the reach of national laws, not because these 'laws aren't relevant', but because

---

[26]Jennifer Preston, 'Movement Began With Outrage and a Facebook Page That Gave It an Outlet', New York Times, 5 February 2011.

[27]Jose Antonio Vargas, 'Spring Awakening: How an Egyptian Revolution Began on Facebook', New York Times, 17 February 2012.

'the nation-state is not relevant'.[28]

Western governments (whose own relevance was seemingly unquestioned though surely just as vulnerable) were paradoxically thrilled with these developments. In November 2011, an American senator, the late John McCain, proudly proclaimed that, 'A year ago, Ben-Ali and Gaddafi were not in power. Assad won't be in power this time next year. This Arab Spring is a virus that will attack Moscow and Beijing.'[29] The United Nations Secretariat was equally quick to jump on the bandwagon, with Special Rapporteur Frank La Rue declaring in 2011 that the internet should be considered in human rights terms and that achieving universal access to the internet should be a priority for all states. That the Arab Spring was influential in arriving at this report is evident from La Rue's remarks:

> The Special Rapporteur believes that the Internet is one of the most powerful instruments of the 21st century for increasing transparency in the conduct of the powerful, access to information, and for facilitating active citizen participation building democratic societies. Indeed, the recent wave of demonstrations in countries across the Middle East and North African region has shown the key role that the Internet can play in mobilizing the population to call for justice, equality, accountability and better respect for human rights.[30]

The Arab Spring, however, was not the first ever instance of the network effect. In 1999, the WTO was rocked by what were later called the Seattle Protests. Angered by the power and authority exercised by transnational corporations and elites, millions of Americans used email to coordinate and disrupt the WTO meetings. To some internet historians, the Seattle Protests were one

---

[28]Quoted in *Who Controls The Internet?: Illusions of a Borderless World*, p. 3.

[29]Steve Clemons, 'The Arab Spring: "A Virus That Will Attack Moscow And Beijing"', *The Atlantic*, 19 November 2011.

[30]Human Rights Council, 'Report of the Special Rapporteur on the promotion and protection of the right to freedom of opinion and expression, Frank La Rue', UNGA, 16 May 2011, accessed 14 June 2019, https://www2.ohchr.org/english/bodies/hrcouncil/docs/17session/A.HRC.17.27_en.pdf.

of the earliest manifestations of 'networked movements' which are capable of assimilating digital technologies into the fabric of their mobilization.

Speaking at a G8 meeting later in 2011, former French President Nicolas Sarkozy was prescient in his critique of the Arab Spring. He warned the executives of Google, Facebook, Amazon and eBay who were present at the meeting: 'The universe you represent is not a parallel universe. Nobody should forget that governments are the only legitimate representatives of the will of the people in our democracies. To forget this is to risk democratic chaos and anarchy.'[31]

The Arab world was quick to prove him right, and to demonstrate that protecting human rights online requires democratic state foundations. This is the fundamental difference between the networked protests of 1999, and the Arab Spring. Mass demonstrations by themselves can run out of steam quickly unless state institutions and structures can support and enable democratic conversations. Fast forward a few years, and it becomes clear that those who saw the Arab Spring as 'democracy's fourth movement' overestimated the potential of the internet to transcend boundaries and sovereigns. Five years after the advent of the Arab Spring, winter set in on the Arab world. After a period of 'techno-utopia', the Middle East saw the resurgence of authoritarian governments and failed states. While the 'Twitter revolutions' of 2011 were successful in some states, especially in Tunisia, countries like Bahrain successfully squashed all protest, while Syria and Libya descended into civil war. Any gains made in Egypt were ultimately undone by a military coup in 2013, leading to a brutal crackdown on civil liberties. Bashar al-Assad, despite confident predictions to the contrary backed up by Western military support to Syrian rebels, continued to hold on to power, and Russia and China used the Arab Spring as a pretext to crack down further on their populations.

To say that Russia and China followed the events in the Arab

---

[31]Eric Pfanner, 'G-8 Leaders To Call For Tighter Internet Regulation', *New York Times*, 24 May 2011.

world closely is an understatement. For authoritarian regimes, the threat of 'networks' is an ever-present risk. By most accounts, these authoritarian regimes viewed the Arab Spring as democratic movements that were ostensibly furthered by Western interests. And why shouldn't they have seen them that way? In 2012, internet users in Iran were bombarded with online advertisements which read 'Accessing a free internet is your inalienable right!'. Underneath the advertisements was a prompt which linked to various tools which circumvented the internet. Such tailored ads on Facebook, Google and other social media platforms were delivered to several countries in the Middle East. The campaign resulted in over 1.5 million people clicking on the ads, and almost half a million downloads of the tools. The ads, it appears, were a part of the US Department of State's attempt to promote freedom of speech in authoritarian regimes hostile to American interests.[32]

It is unsurprising then that almost immediately after the spread of discontent in 2011, China, Russia and a few Central Asian states such as Tajikistan and Uzbekistan, asked the then UN Secretary-General Ban Ki-moon to circulate their proposed International Code of Conduct for Information Security (the Code) as a formal UN document at the 66th session of the General Assembly.[33] The document was clear in its demands—that the free flow of information must not have an adverse effect on domestic stability. The document referred to the use of communication technologies that 'are inconsistent with the objectives of maintaining international stability and security', as well as the responsibility to 'prevent other states from...undermin[ing] the right of the countries, which accepted this Code of Conduct, to independent control of ICTs.' For the first time, there was a concerted attempt to emphasize the

---

[32]Fergus Hanson, 'Internet Freedom: The Role Of The U.S. State Department', Brookings, 25 October 2012, accessed 14 June 2019, https://www.brookings.edu/research/internet-freedom-the-role-of-the-u-s-state-department/.
[33]'The UN and Cyberspace Governance', Observer Research Foundation, 1 February 2014, accessed 14 June 2019, https://www.orfonline.org/article/the-un-and-cyberspace-governance/.

multilateral nature of internet governance, i.e., to promote state control. The Code 'underlin[es] the need for enhanced coordination and cooperation among States' and 'stress[es] the role that can be played by the United Nations and other international and regional organizations.' This was in clear contrast to America's preferred multi-stakeholder approach which involved civil society and the private sector through less traditional groups such as the Internet Governance Forum.

This code of conduct was really the first step in what was to become China's assault on the idea of internet freedom. In fact, Hillary Clinton's senior advisor Alec Ross somewhat prophetically told the *Washington Post* that, 'If the great struggles of the 20th century were between left and right...the conflict of the 21st century will be between open and closed.'[34] Such moral grandstanding, of course, preceded the year 2013, and revelations by a certain whistle-blower.

If offline rights are difficult to replicate online in the most autocratic parts of the world, the expectation was that liberal democracies would fare better. In 2013, however, this expectation was put to rest. That summer, led by journalists from *The Guardian* and other newspapers around the world, details of the mass electronic surveillance by the National Security Agency (NSA) began to emerge. An NSA contractor, Edward Snowden, revealed that the US government was collecting massive amounts of metadata from American citizens and individuals from around the world. Under the aegis of a programme known as PRISM, and empowered by the Foreign Intelligence Surveillance Act, America was able to collect data from Facebook posts, Google emails, Twitter chats, and even call data from companies like AT&T and Verizon.

Following these revelations in the US, he was hailed, at times, as an American patriot who protected the values of freedom, and at others as a traitor who compromised national security. Whichever side of the debate you fell on back then, almost all of Snowden's

---

[34]Will Englund, 'Russia hears an Argument for Web Freedom', *Washington Post*, 28 October 2011.

detractors and supporters could agree that it marked a new turning point in international relations—a new convergence of foreign policy choices and global internet governance.

If the Arab Spring exemplified the democratic potential of the internet, the Snowden revelations did exactly the opposite. The vast troves of data individuals generate every day were now capable of being intercepted, catalogued, and analysed. The very same instruments— social media companies and other tech giants—which empowered marginalized and oppressed citizens, also served to collect information on a massive scale, which could be misused by both governments and companies. The advent of new technologies for 'big data' analysis only made these efforts easier. That America—a self-proclaimed exemplar, and a self-professed defender, of democracy—was instrumental in this blatantly intrusive and arguably illegal action only served to embolden the detractors of a free internet.

What was most troubling was that the US had set a terrible benchmark for protecting the right to privacy online. The US, which was the primary champion of internet freedom, had now provided governments a roadmap for mass surveillance, with the connivance of global tech companies. What came as a rude shock to many of the United States' friends was that it was conducting surveillance on its closest political ally—the EU—by intercepting private communications on a massive scale, even going so far as to wiretap high-ranking officials in the EU. That America used data from the most prevalent internet platforms, like Google, Yahoo, Amazon, and others, to acquire information about individuals around the world offended sensibilities in many states.

To some extent, the events of 2013 can be traced back to the terror attacks of 9/11. The benign hegemony that the US exercised over the internet truly ended after that year. In prosecuting its war on terror, the US began employing its digital power as an instrument of state policy. As one issue of *Foreign Affairs* explains: 'In the aftermath of the 9/11 attacks, the United States began to exploit interdependence, deliberately using its economic power as an instrument of national security... Despite publicly promoting an open and secure Internet, it has privately undermined the encryption of online communications and surreptitiously created vast international surveillance systems in cooperation with close allies.'[35]

Of course, the Snowden revelations ultimately shed light on this hypocrisy, and irreparably damaged the ideal of 'internet freedom' as espoused by the US and its allies. The narrative around the internet was a carefully crafted strategy which focused on human rights and internet access, intended to back authoritarian countries like China and Iran into a corner. Suddenly, however, the US now emerged as the principal antagonist against internet freedom, and could no longer claim to be the arbiter of its moral values.

To the US allies, especially Germany, the revelations were a complete breach of trust, and were popularly referred to as 'Handygate'. Handy, in German, translates to cell phone, and Merkel was known as 'Handy-Kanzlerin' or Cell Phone Chancellor, because of her savvy adoption of new technology.[36] Soon after the leaks, a furious Angela Merkel called then US President Barack Obama and told him that, 'This is just like the Stasi,' the East German security and surveillance service.[37] At the time, the White House assured Berlin that the United States was not monitoring the conversations of Angela Merkel. Such assurances did little to placate Merkel, who ultimately chose to internationalize the issue. She found a willing partner in former Brazilian President Dilma Rousseff, who was another victim of NSA surveillance. Soon after Snowden's revelations that the NSA had spied on President Rouseff and Brazil's national oil company, Petrobas, she cancelled a planned state visit to Washington, and introduced laws which would have forced American companies to store their user data in Brazil. Addressing the UN later that year, she accused the US of violating international law, arguing that, 'In

[35]Henry Farrell, Abraham Newman, 'The Transatlantic Data War', *Foreign Affairs*, January–February Issue, 2016.

[36]Ian Traynor in Brussels, Philip Oltermann in Berlin, and Paul Lewis in Washington, 'Angela Merkel's call to Obama: are you bugging my mobile phone?' *The Guardian*, 24 October 2013.

[37]Adam Segal, *The Hacked World Order: How Nations Fight, Trade, Maneuver, and Manipulate in the Digital Age*, New York: Hachette, 2016, p. 210.

the absence of the right to privacy, there can be no true freedom of expression and opinion and therefore no effective democracy. In the absence of the respect for sovereignty, there is no basis for the relationship among nations.'[38]

If the US allies were stunned by Snowden's revelations, its rivals were less so. To them, the NSA leaks were merely a reaffirmation of their long-held belief that the US was using the internet to advance its own geopolitical interests. Days after the revelations, the *China Economic Weekly*, owned by the *People's Daily*, ran a headline entitled, 'He's watching you' with the image of a World War II-era American military helmet with an NSA logo inscribed on it.[39] The article called American companies like IBM, Microsoft, Google, Cisco, Oracle, Qualcomm, Intel and Apple, the 'eight guardian warriors' who had 'seamlessly infiltrated China'.

The end result of these revelations was that most governments, democratic or otherwise, became more assertive in demanding that the internet be placed under state control, whether it was to protect privacy, national security or to fight terrorism. Russian President Vladimir Putin went so far as to call the entirety of the internet a 'CIA' project and adopted a set of legislations that would place severe restrictions on the internet; blocking websites, criminalizing illegal blogging and even going so far as to regulate them. It was China, however, which truly led the charge against the US and its conception of the internet with its demand for 'cyber sovereignty'.

A NEW CYBER POWER

Two decades ago, no one could have predicted the kind of power China could exercise over the internet. In a speech at Johns Hopkins University in 2000, former US President Bill Clinton joked about China's efforts to regulate the internet: 'Good luck! That's sort of like trying to nail Jell-O to the wall.'[40] He was convinced that the United

---

[38]Julian Borger, 'Brazilian president: US surveillance a "breach of international law"', *The Guardian*, 24 September 2013.
[39]Adam Segal, *The Hacked World Order*, p.151.
[40]'Clinton's Words On China: Trade Is the Smart Thing', *New York Times*, 9 March

States would benefit economically from greater access to Chinese markets and that the internet would spread liberty in China. Two decades later, it appears that China has proved him wrong.

If China was suddenly leading the rally against perceived American domination over the internet, it is because over the years its own cyber power has grown exponentially. An important aspect of this rise has been the rejection of Western media companies in Chinese social affairs. To keep them away from the market, China has employed a multifaceted approach of censorship, government monitoring, unfair trade regulations and enormous spending on Chinese national industries. In China, access to the internet is a privilege granted by the state, and not a freedom to be enjoyed.

These imperatives have also led China to advocate for a model of the internet that is completely at odds with a libertarian vision. Just months after Hillary Clinton argued for global recognition of a universal right to the internet, China released its first ever English-language State Council White Paper outlining its vision for 'internet sovereignty'. 'Within Chinese territory the internet is under the jurisdiction of Chinese sovereignty', 'The internet sovereignty of China should be respected and protected', was the line parroted by state officials.[41] In China, restrictions on internet freedom were justified by the need to preserve state interests and social harmony.

Already China is well ahead of the game in creating a system of de facto control over the internet. The government uses variations of IP blocking, DNS filtering and redirection, URL filtering, packet filtering, connection reset, and network enumeration to control Web access throughout China. Usually, it censors topics that are considered sensitive, such as the 1989 Tiananmen Square crackdown or positive references to the Dalai Lama. Microblogging sites that are popular amongst Chinese are most heavily controlled; just like in Russia, new users must authenticate their identity and undergo police verifications.

2000.

[41]China Foreign Ministry, 'Protecting Internet Security', Beijing: Govt. White Papers, accessed 14 June 2019, http://www.china.org.cn/government/whitepaper/2010-06/08/content_20207978.htm.

Offences in China are notorious for how vaguely they are defined, and for the farcical criminal proceedings that enforce them. A user might 'disturb' social stability by 'spreading rumours, calling for protests, promoting cults or superstitions and impugning China's honour.'[42]

Information censorship, however, was only one objective of the Chinese state. Eliminating the use of foreign technology companies is another. Google's spat with the Chinese government in 2010 is a perfect example. Officially, Google entered the Chinese market in 2006, and was public in its intention not to share any information about dissidents or blocked content with the government. However, the tech giant courted some controversy by adhering to the government's legal requirement to censor some of its search results. The company justified breaching its own core principles 'in the belief that the benefits of increased access to information for people in China and a more open internet outweighed our discomfort in agreeing to censor some results'.[43] The Chinese government was never content with Google's stated objectives, viewing them with suspicion and mistrust as a nefarious extension of American power on China's soil.

In 2010, this struggle reached a boiling point when Google issued a statement revealing that Chinese hackers had infiltrated Google's servers to steal proprietary information, and information on Chinese dissidents. Google then announced plans to negotiate an unfiltered search engine with China. When negotiations failed in March 2010, Google automatically redirected all google.cn search traffic to google. hk, which is based in Hong Kong and thereby not under effective Chinese jurisdiction. Criticizing this move, the overseas edition of the *People's Daily*, the main newspaper of the Chinese Communist Party, reported: 'For Chinese people, Google is not god, and even if it puts on a full-on show about politics and values, it is still not god,' said a front-page commentary piece. 'In fact, Google is not a virgin when it comes to values. Its cooperation and collusion with

---

[42]Shaun M. Powers and Michael Jablonski, *The Real Cyber War*.
[43]'TEXT-Google's statement on China operations', Reuters, 13 January 2010.

the U.S. intelligence and security agencies is well-known.'[44]

The dispute between Google and China was really an early clash of values between two incompatible visions of the internet and, indeed, broader political cultures. A democratic and open internet inherently contradicts China's style of functioning, which mixes free markets with authoritarianism. To the Chinese, Google represented everything they resented: American technological dominance, its large market share in China, its political values and the ever-present threat of American surveillance. It is no coincidence that the clash took place around the same time China was marking its rise as a global superpower.

China was never satisfied with the kind of de-nationalized liberalism commonly associated with the internet. Its own political economy rests heavily on the fundamental primacy of the state and its role in ensuring social harmony. Neither was it satisfied with the role America had to play in the internet governance regime. To China, both of these features were a part of the same problem—the US 'internet freedom' agenda was merely a tool to propagate America's hegemony and to subvert other states with its own values.

China's move to push out foreign tech firms also plays well with its intention to ramp up its own technology companies. At the first meeting of the internet security and informatization group in China, President Xi Jinping called developing domestic technologies and ensuring cybersecurity 'two wings of a bird'—equally important elements in China's ambition to become a global superpower.[45] The Snowden revelations only crystallized the long-standing unease that the Chinese government had over its reliance on Western technology firms. Through 2008–13, China targeted US technology companies in what appeared to be a concentrated effort to stunt their growth in Beijing's market. Microsoft software, for example, was banned from government computers on the pretext that it constituted a national

---

[44]'Google is not God', *China Daily*, 25 March 2010.
[45]Shannon Tiezzi, 'Xi Jinping Leads China's New Internet Security Group', *The Diplomat*, 28 February 2014.

security risk. In 2009, the popular video sharing site YouTube was blocked by China's censors. According to *Xinhua*, China's state news agency, the primary reason was the uploading of a video that showed Tibetan protestors being beaten by Chinese police officers. Similarly, Facebook was permanently blocked on the pretext that activists from the Uighur region were using it to communicate and network.

At the same time, indigenous Chinese variants of these very websites saw their market share soar. Baidu, for example, has emerged as China's largest search engine. YouTube clones like Youku and Tudou quickly occupied the space that the video platform had earlier occupied. Weibo and other such companies have emerged as social media companies that compete with Facebook and Twitter. To the Chinese, replacing foreign tech with home-grown internet companies represents a perfect intersection of interests between national security imperatives and its broader economic goals. The Snowden revelations only provided the cover for China to act against American companies under the guise of information security.

To China, which by 2013 was emerging as a revisionist power in global governance, the Snowden revelations were a rude shock. If anything, its position on national sovereignty over cyberspace has further toughened. Cyber sovereignty emerged as China's official slogan in international fora. The shift in Chinese policy is evident from President Xi's proclamations. In the first World Internet Conference in China in 2014, he called for a 'multifaceted, democratic, and transparent governance system for the international Internet'.[46] By the time 2015 rolled in, President Xi was more categorical when he said, 'No country should pursue cyber hegemony, interfere in other countries' internal affairs, or engage in, connive at or support cyber activities that undermine other countries' national security.'[47]

Ever since the US government began to take a more hands-off approach to the internet, other governments, led by China and Russia

---

[46]Kamlesh Bajaj, 'As Trump Dampens US's Internet Freedom Agenda, the Race to Cyber Supremacy Reaches New Levels', *The Wire*, 21 August 2017.
[47]PTI Beijing, 'No nation should have hegemony over Internet: Xi', *Hindu BusinessLine*, 16 December 2015, Updated 22 January 2018.

have wanted to increase control over it. For the longest time, an epistemic community of civil society, technical experts and academia resisted calls for government 'capture' of the internet. Ultimately, China has shown that even if technical functions of the internet remain international, the internet itself is capable of being controlled and stymied. It is keen, now, to change to norms and narratives that have shaped how the internet has evolved. 'Information sovereignty' is a crude term; it marks the return of Westphalian sovereignty over the one medium which was born to stay free from it.

Ironically, the development of technology looks likely to serve this retrogressive approach. China has clearly understood that in the contest for global power and influence, success will, in significant measure, depend upon a country's ability to develop and control technology and to make the right investments in what will be the essential technologies of the future. In keeping with its totalitarian instincts, China has also decided that these would have to be proprietary national technologies. For too long, in Beijing's view, the race has been surrendered by default to the US. By proscribing and restricting the operations of major US players—notably Google, Facebook, Amazon and WhatsApp—in its own internet market, China not only curbed the extent of US influence but encouraged the development of home-grown alternatives in Baidu, Alibaba, Weibo, Wechat and Tencent, which have also become household names.

While China's methods were disruptive, its ambition to dominate emerging technologies is born from its understanding of US hegemony over technology. If the Snowden revelations made clear that the US would happily undermine digital protections for foreign citizens, the Cambridge Analytica scandal, which allowed a private firm to mine data of millions of Americans for electoral targeting, in 2018 served to highlight just how powerful and unaccountable Silicon Valley is. As we now pass through an age where most powers understand the strategic value of dominating emerging technologies, the race to control them will only grow fiercer.

The convergence of three structural factors will drive this trend: the politics of nationalism, the weakening of the post-war order, and the rapid rise of the digital economy. Indeed, India has taken stock of this emerging 'techno-nationalism' and is responding in its own way. The Modi government's decision to introduce new, more restrictive e-commerce rules to favour domestic companies suggests that New Delhi, too, sees merit in facilitating the rise of domestic technology enterprises as an alternative to permitting multinational giants unhindered access to the Indian market. And for good reason. New Delhi's ambitions of growing to a $5 trillion economy is contingent on its willingness to protect its long-term interests: the growth and resilience of its domestic technology sector; the projection of Indian technological solutions in different jurisdictions; guarding against supply chain risks; protecting the rights of its citizens and the security of its critical infrastructure. The emotive call has gone up to 'resist data colonialism'. Given the increasingly zero-sum nature of global competition over emerging technologies, it is unlikely that India will be able to achieve these through partnerships or multilateral efforts.[48]

Whether or not India desires a global competition over emerging technologies, history will conspire against it. The emergence of breakthrough technologies during periods of bi- or multi-polarity has always resulted in a geopolitical tug of war for control over such technologies. In the twentieth century it was the US and Russia for Information and Communications Technology (ICT) and space technologies. A century before that, Britain and the US competed for ownership and the intellectual property of the first and second industrial revolutions. We are in the midst of another such period—both China and the US have adopted policies that respond to their national interest. And as the history of American unipolarity teaches us: the winner takes all. Unless New Delhi can emerge as a technology power in its own right, it will forever be dependent on, and vulnerable to, American or Chinese propositions. The unilateral decision by the US to divest Huawei, a company that generated $107

---

[48]This section is based on Samir Saran and Kanchan Gupta, 'In rising e-commerce storm, India must protect its own ship', ORF, 20 May 2019.

billion in revenue in 2018, of essential digital technologies under its control should worry all ambitious digital societies. It only serves to highlight how self-serving the US 'globalist' approach to technology has always been. Meanwhile, the cosy relationship between China's tech sector and the Communist Party makes brand ChinaTech an omnipresent security risk. India cannot relegate itself to choosing between two bad options—it must develop its own indigenous systems that are responsive to its jurisdiction.

India and other developing countries will realize that the promise of technology will not always be utopian. Indeed, we are at a point in history where the assumption that technology inevitably aids liberalization is increasingly being questioned. The onset of artificial intelligence (AI), in particular, allows governments to conduct even more effective surveillance of their citizens. AI offers tools to monitor, understand, and control internet users with a greater degree of precision and specificity than ever before. AI will offer authoritarian governments a way to circumvent the historical pattern by which economic development had almost always led to increased democratization. By giving powerful governments a tool for social control, AI will allow authoritarian states to both keep tight control of dissidence and encourage economic growth and prosperity.

This has become apparent in China's systematic construction of what amounts to a digital authoritarian state by using surveillance and machine learning tools to stifle any restiveness among its people. One tool it has created is the 'social credit system' under which every citizen is awarded points for conformist behaviour, and loses points for conduct disapproved of by the authorities: too many demerit points can result in prohibitions like denial of permission to purchase air tickets, travel abroad, etc. The Chinese government has established— and demonstrated to other potential emulators abroad—a capacity to selectively censor subjects it considers taboo, to sanction behaviour of which it disapproves, and to curb internet dissidence, while at the same time, allowing information it deems useful (to promote economically productive activities) to flow freely.

This development is not about China alone. Other states are

paying attention. And Beijing has decided to take its effort abroad by making common cause with like-minded authoritarian states in a new digital alliance to complement its foreign policy efforts. In 2017, President Xi announced that China would develop a digital counterpart of its physical infrastructure-building Belt and Road Initiative. President Xi declared that China would work to promote digital connectivity and the integration of big data to build 'the digital silk road of the 21st century'. Digital connectivity infrastructure is to be built in parallel with the physical connectivity planned under the BRI.

The now seemingly out-of-date idea of sovereign borders melting away in the face of rampant techno-globalism rested upon the assumption that all states shared the same values in the international system. As China leads a serious challenge to the old consensus on the nature and structure of the international order, and as other countries emulate it in preferring authoritarian nationalism to internationalist liberalism, techno-globalism is giving way to a new phenomenon of technological nationalism.

This has inevitably aroused concerns in the US and other countries that, with its progress in AI, its emerging lead in 5G network technology, and its deep surplus of investible funds, China will emerge as a viable global competitor for US technological dominance. Several like-minded countries have begun to buy or emulate Chinese systems. China's 5G technology and equipment are likely to become the gold standard in the Eurasian region and beyond. The US, in turn, is fighting back, pressuring its allies not to use Chinese technology and threatening to sanction Germany for contracting with Chinese firm Huawei in developing its 5G network. A new US–China technological cold war is looming. Huawei's offer to license its 5G technological platform to a US company to manufacture there has not so far found any willing takers.

China's techno-nationalist success, as political scientist and columnist Pratap Bhanu Mehta argues, is 'not seamless integration into a global system; rather it is the artful use of the rhetoric of integration into the world economy to advance national technological goals.'[49] President Xi's rhetoric about digital connectivity and its link to the existing Chinese project of the BRI evidently aim at prompting a more accommodative response from potential partner countries to the spread of Chinese technology.

COLONIALISM.COM

The normative and technical battles between America and China show that states have clearly understood the geopolitical implications of the internet for some time now. Their struggle to exert control over the medium only goes to show how important the internet now is to global economic and political relations. However, states are far from being the only actors in cyberspace. Today, a select handful of technology giants are racing to control the internet. In 1981, Tom McPhail coined the term 'electronic colonialism'—a vision of the internet colonized by mass media companies whose intent was to capture the minds and attention spans of large parts of the world.[50]

While the internet was still in a relatively nascent state then, the term itself assumes added significance in light of the changing nature of the information economy. As early as 1995, a prescient Irving Goldstein, former president of Intelsat, predicted that information 'will be for the twenty-first century what oil and gas were for the beginning of the twentieth century. It will fuel economic and political power.'[51] Yet it was clear that the information revolution, unlike the French Revolution, is one with much liberté, some fraternité and no égalité. It is yet to deliver the goods, or even the tools to obtain them, to many of those most in need.[52]

Today, among the major dividing lines between rich and poor, between North and South, are fibre-optic and high-speed digital lines. If 'digital divide' is an overused phrase, it represents a reality

---

[49]Pratap Bhanu Mehta, 'We might enter an "RSS meets Jio" ideological world', *Indian Express*, 1 May 2019.

[50]Thomas L. McPhail, *Electronic Colonialism: The Future of International Broadcasting and Communication*, Newbury Park: SAGE Publications, Inc., 1987.

[51]Shaun M. Powers and Michael Jablonski, *The Real Cyber War*, pp. 75–76.

[52]Shashi Tharoor, 'The great digital divide', *The Hindu*, 20 November 2005.

that cannot be denied. Fifteen per cent of the world's population control about 90 per cent of access points to the internet for the 85 per cent of the world's population living in low and lower-middle income countries.[53]

The world is yet to find ways to ensure that the enormously powerful tools that we now possess, in the form of new information technologies, are used to guarantee, in the words of the UN Charter, 'better standards of life in larger freedom'. Greater access to information and communication technologies can improve the lives of farmers and assist micro-entrepreneurs. It can prevent AIDS and other communicable diseases, promote women's equality and foster environmental protection. Indeed, all over the developing world, e-commerce, distance education, telemedicine and e-governance are already improving the quality of life for countless people.[54]

But much more can be done if the information revolution is to fully deliver on its promise to the developing world—and we must give serious thought to what and how. At the first phase of the WSIS in Geneva in 2003, the world promised to achieve a host of targets by 2015—linking, via technology, villages and communities, universities and primary and secondary schools, scientific and research centres, public libraries, cultural centres, museums, post offices and archives, health centres and hospitals, and local and central government departments. This has not yet happened four years after the target date. Other targets included improving the availability of information in all languages on the internet, and ensuring that everyone in the world has access to television and radio; here progress is undeniable.

But access to the internet is of little value if the information that it contains is—almost exclusively—in a language you don't understand, or if it fails to deal with the life-and-death questions that affect your society. The governments meeting in Geneva agreed 'to encourage

---

the development of content and to put in place technical conditions in order to facilitate the presence and use of all world languages on the internet.' Such concerns seem almost quaint a decade and a half later, when the battleground has shifted. Fast forward to 2017, when *The Economist* issued a special report, noting that 'Data is the new oil'.[55] This prediction has more than a hint of truth to it. In 2017, Alphabet (Google's parent), Amazon, Microsoft and Facebook were valued at an amount greater than the GDP of Norway, a country flush with oil. China's BAT—Baidu, Alibaba and Tencent—have all displayed similar trajectories. The immense valuation of these firms reflects their ownership over consumer data—a digital deposit of social, economic and cultural interactions that overlap with our lives. Popular internet critics like Evgeny Morozov dub their economic models as 'data extractivism'.[56]

'Data is the new oil' has already become the defining cliché of the twenty-first century. And not unlike the colonial conquests of the past, a new rat race seeks to monopolize it. Only, this time, things are different. If states were the primary antagonists in the nineteenth and twentieth century, today Apple, Google, Facebook, Amazon and a long list of electronic giants already have the ability to shape how we think, act and consume. The parallels between the inequitable natural resource extraction of the industrialized North for much of the twentieth century, and today's data oligarchs is more than simple reductionism. The value that personal data generates for these firms is immense: for one thing, more data yields more advertisement revenue. The ad revenue model of business is only one part of the story. Today big data analytics and machine learning have made it possible for these very companies to develop new technologies and products.

It is these new technologies and products that have led to the fragmentation of the Web, and the concentration of market power

---

[55]'The world's most valuable resource is no longer oil, but data', *The Economist*, 6 May 2017.

[56]Evgeny Morozov, 'There is a leftwing way to challenge big tech for our data. Here it is', *The Guardian*, 19 August 2018.

in the hands of a few technology companies. In August 2010, *Wired* magazine announced the 'Death of the Web',[57] based on the premise that platforms are becoming the primary mode of access to the internet. Since the first use of the World Wide Web, the internet has been an open and interoperable collection of websites. Today, power platforms are suddenly replacing this understanding. Berners-Lee has raised similar concerns about the 'platform economy'. In 2010, he wrote: 'Each site is a silo, walled off from the others. Yes, your site's pages are on the web, but your data are not.' Websites like Facebook and YouTube are like walled gardens in an infinite forest that is the internet. The more users they bring onto their platforms, the more data they generate, and the less their competitors are able to develop successful business models which depend on the economies of scale.[58]

There are accordingly two races which are currently ongoing. The first is to monopolize the user base. For technology companies, it was always evident that the largest consumers would not come from the developed world. Asia and Africa, which together host over two-thirds of the world's population, would naturally be their target.

The dynamics of this narrative were best displayed in India's fight against 'Free Basics', Facebook's ambitious plan to connect the world to the internet. At first blush, Facebook's offer was tempting: access to the internet at reduced costs for over a billion potential users. Zuckerberg's offering, however, came with a catch—access to the internet equals access to Facebook, which would act as a gatekeeper of sorts. The weakness then was that such a platform harvested huge amounts of personal data, while choosing which third-party platforms could sign on to it. Ultimately, Facebook could give preferential treatment to those products and services that either paid them better, or restrict services that might emerge as competitors. More importantly, perhaps, because Zuckerberg was reaching markets that were new to the internet, it would have given the platform

---

[57]Chris Anderson and Michael Wolfe, 'The Web Is Dead. Long Live the Internet', *Wired*, 17 August 2010.
[58]Luther Lowe, 'It's Time to Bust the Online Trusts', *Wall Street Journal*, 31 October 2017.

unlimited power to shape the cultural and economic experiences of those who accessed the internet through Facebook.

In an op-ed Mark Zuckerberg wrote for the *Times of India*, he asked: 'Who could possibly be against this?' As it turns out, millions of Indians were. 'We've been stupid with the East India Company,' said a user on the popular social platform 'Reddit', referring to the British Raj. 'Never again!', she went on to add.[59] If the parallels to colonialism seemed somewhat unnecessary, sample the sarcastic words of then Facebook board member, Marc Andreessen: 'Anti-colonialism has been economically catastrophic for the Indian people for decades,' Andreessen wrote. 'Why stop now?'[60]

India, however, was not the only battleground. While the tide of techno-evangelists from Silicon Valley might have been somewhat curbed here at home, it continued to flow unabated in other parts of the world. Africa, for example, continues to present a far more lucrative goldmine for technology companies, with much less resistance. Technologies offered by almost every other Western tech company frames a narrative around digital exclusion. However, their global reach and approach demonstrate that their entry into new markets is not really an attempt to propose specific solutions to local communities. Instead, it is a catchall remedy that is steeped in Western world views, benefiting a limited set of actors.

Ultimately, getting people online, or more accurately, online on certain platforms, was only one part of the race. What comes next is far more important—control over behaviour. If data is the new oil, then attention is the currency. The ability of Big Tech, a catchall phrase for the largest technology companies, to guide our thoughts, preferences and behaviour is significantly aided by new developments such as the internet of things, big data and algorithmic analysis. As *Wired* magazine explains, 'The paramount value of the devices, in a sense, lies not in the hardware itself but the interconnectedness

---

[59]Adrienne Lafrance, 'Facebook and the New Colonialism', *The Atlantic*, 11 February 2016.
[60]Saritha Rai, 'Marc Andreessen Unwittingly Likens Facebook Free Basics To Colonialism, Kicks Up India Twitter Storm', *Forbes*, 10 February 2016.

of that hardware. As the devices talk to each other, by building an aggregate picture of human behavior, they anticipate what we want before even we know.'[61]

And the attention they garner is enormous. Around the beginning of 2019, there were 4.4 billion active internet users. It was estimated that as of April 2019, 56.1 per cent of the world's population had internet access, and 81 per cent of the developed world's.[62]

In October 2012, Facebook passed the one billion users mark; a year later this had crossed two billion, with over 2.418 billion monthly active users as of 31 March 2019.[63] But that's just Facebook; its related services, such as WhatsApp, Facebook Messenger and Instagram all account for another half a billion users, give or take. Google tells a similar story, with more than a billion people using its search engine to make over one trillion searches every year. YouTube, the popular video streaming platform, crossed the one billion mark in 2013, with users uploading hundreds of millions worth of hours every year. Apple's CEO Tim Cook was quite frank about what was happening. 'Some of the most prominent and successful companies have built their businesses by lulling their customers into complacency about their personal information,' said Cook at a 2015 dinner at the Electronic Privacy Information Center (EPIC), 'They're gobbling up everything they can learn about you and trying to monetize it.'[64]

What Apple thought was right, however, is irrelevant. Today, companies are looking to modulate user behaviour to generate profit, a model some refer to as surveillance capitalism. Like oil, data is only useful once it has been refined and analysed. Which is why Facebook undertook an experiment in 2014 to determine if different posts

---

[61]Marcus Wohlsen, 'What Google Really Gets Out Of Buying Nest For $3.2 Billion', *Wired*, 14 January 2014.

[62]'World Internet Usage And Population Statistics May, 2019 – Updated', Internet World Stats, accessed 14 June 2019, https://www.internetworldstats.com/stats.htm.

[63]'Number of monthly active Facebook users worldwide as of 1st quarter 2019 (In Millions)', Statista, accessed 14 June 2019, https://www.statista.com/statistics/264810/number-of-monthly-active-facebook-users-worldwide/.

[64]Geoffrey Smith, 'Apple's Tim Cook Accuses Facebook and Google of Violating User Privacy', *Time*, 3 June 2015.

on a user's timeline would change their emotions. Uber similarly experiments with its drivers, using insights from addictive gaming to ensure that their workers continue to drive longer hours. All of these new technologies have traded consumer privacy for greater commercialization. Despite the grandstanding in the tech industry, there seems to be very little support for privacy on the inside. As early as 1999, Scott McNealy, then CEO of Sun Microsystems, famously declared, 'You have zero privacy now anyway. Get over it.'[65] Overtly or not, this is a sentiment most technology companies share.

This is because personal data is today's raw material; it flows largely from developing countries who are dependent on new platforms and is harvested on the cloud and manufactured into intelligent services and products, with the value being captured by tech companies in the West and in China. If American and Chinese companies continue to maintain their monopoly on the data market, it is because they have been proactive in shaping the global political economy of the internet. Actors in the platform ecosystem develop business models for a globalized networked infrastructure and services. They perform best where privacy statutes and data protection regimes are the least developed, while data flows are most open. Countries which are on the verge of digitizing their economies have still not grappled with the inequality that traditional social institutions foist, and the rise of the platform economy threatens to aggravate these differences.

Because most platforms are US corporations, the US government has been aggressive in placing cross-border data flows front and centre in its economic relations. As the digital economy will soon permeate and restructure all sectors, from banking to finance and trade, data, and control over it, has become a hot button issue in international trade relations. Already data flows generate close to $3 trillion in GDP every year. For the economically developed G20 countries, control over data is critical to their growth. For developing countries, however, innovation is gridlocked due to lack of access to this very data.

---

[65]Polly Sprenger, 'Sun on Privacy: "Get Over It"', *Wired*, 26 January 1999.

As platforms and data become the new drivers of globalization, trade agreements are increasingly adopting new, non-traditional agendas. The now defunct Trans-Pacific Partnership, for example, was the first such agreement to introduce new digital issues—cross-border data flows, online privacy, cybersecurity, and safe harbour protection for internet intermediaries. Social movements have articulated concerns about the opaque negotiations surrounding the digital agenda of such agreements. While civil society members have had a tough time being a part of these negotiations, platform owners have almost certainly been involved in these negotiations. Jack Ma of Alibaba, for example, has consistently advocated for new policy-making frameworks which emphasize the role of multinational corporations in international rule-making. Ma is only the spearhead of a larger Chinese effort to reshape the rules of the internet. As part of its ambitious BRI infrastructure initiative, China has also outlined a vision to develop 'an information silk road'. State-owned Chinese telecommunication companies are increasingly investing in Asian countries to develop digital infrastructure; even private players like ZTE are investing in fibre-optic cables in countries like Afghanistan.

China's domestic market only gives it the added heft to shape such infrastructure. Already, according to McKinsey, China is the world's largest e-commerce market, accounting for more than 40 per cent of the value of e-commerce transactions worldwide. Mobile payments in China amount to approximately eleven times that of the US, fuelled by the widespread adoption of e-wallets across its cities.[66] One in three of the world's 262 unicorns are Chinese, making up 43 per cent of the global value of these companies.[67] In 2015, the Chinese government signed off on its 'Made in China 2025' and 'Internet Plus' initiatives that aim to digitize China's economy by integrating artificial intelligence, robotics, and digital services into

---

[66]Jonathan Woetzel, Jeongmin Seong, Kevin Wei Wang, James Manyika, Michael Chui, and Wendy Wong, 'China's digital economy: A leading global force', McKinsey Global Institute, accessed 14 June 2019, https://www.mckinsey.com/featured-insights/china/chinas-digital-economy-a-leading-global-force.
[67]Ibid.

manufacturing processes.

Developing countries, then, are caught in a catch-22 situation. They cannot step back from digitization, because of the enormous economic and social value they bring. At the same time, they do not benefit at all from the vast troves of natural resources they possess in the form of individual data. Uber's integration with local transport infrastructure highlights this dichotomy the best. The data it generates of traffic patterns is of enormous value to governments. Who owns this value, however? Can states compel Uber to release its data?

The digital order of today then is eerily parallel to the colonial conquests of the past. A handful of countries, mostly from the developed world, with the exception of China, now control almost all the data flow networks. The structural dependency of developing countries is today higher than it ever was, leading some to dub today's order as 'digital colonization'.

WHICH STAKEHOLDERS?

Clearly, the questions that haunt cyberspace are many. Who controls its core functions? Can a political map be drawn over the internet's boundaries? Whose vision of the internet do we adopt? How do we regulate the platform giants? And who's the 'we' in these questions? The conventional wisdom in internet governance circles is that many of these decisions need to be made with multiple stakeholders. Ever since WSIS, the US has repeatedly announced its intention to sever the links between the Department of Commerce (DoC) and the ICANN, and shift the management of the DNS to a private international 'multi-stakeholder' body. Ultimately, it was the Snowden revelations that changed this equation. Soon after her speech at the UN, former Brazilian President Dilma Rousseff called for a new global meeting to revitalize the debates on internet governance. The NETmundial Initiative, organized in 2014, was the result of this call. Fadi Chehadé, then CEO of ICANN, met with Rousseff and supported her call for this meeting. Most organizations connected to internet governance, including ICANN, IETF, Interactive Advertising Bureau (IAB), World Wide Web Consortium (W3C), and the

ISOC, met in Uruguay on 7 October 2013, and issued a statement distancing themselves from the US government and its actions, calling for an 'environment in which all stakeholders, including all governments, participate on an equal footing'.[68]

While the US administration might deny that the Snowden revelations and the new NETmundial Initiative changed its policy on internet governance, most observers agree that this was the case. In the face of hostile international pressure, the Obama administration unilaterally decided to allow ICANN's contract with the DoC to lapse. News reports at the time suggested that officials in the administration warned President Obama that any delay in effecting a transition would result in the UN's oversight of the internet. Ultimately the US agreed to transfer oversight of the internet's core functions to an international 'multi-stakeholder' body.

Seen in this light, one must wonder why the US, and its corporate allies, were so insistent on a 'multi-stakeholder' body. What does it mean in practice, and what does it seek to achieve? Unlike multilateral decision-making, which involves greater state representation, the multi-stakeholder model puts states on an equal footing with businesses and civil society representatives. As discussed in earlier parts of this chapter, such a model was part of a wider trend in reimagining global governance for the twenty-first century. However, the idea was never fully developed nor critically evaluated at the time, because of America's overwhelming influence in the early 2000s. Today, the only stakeholders with a real voice in internet governance debates are the incumbent corporations and civil society members from the Global North. To understand just how pervasive and entrenched such voices are, it is useful to take the example of the NETmundial Initiative.

From the beginning, civil society representatives viewed the initiative with scepticism, primarily because it was launched by the

---

[68]ICANN (Internet Cooperation for Assigned Names and Numbers), 'Montevideo Statement on the Future of Internet Cooperation', 7 October 2013, accessed 14 June 2019, https://www.icann.org/news/announcement-2013-10-07-en.

ICANN and the WEF, well known for organizing an exclusive annual meeting for the world's political and economic elite in Davos. This is one of the reasons why several civil society groups, such as the ISOC and the Just Net Coalition (JNC), decided to abstain from participating in this new initiative. If that weren't enough, at the conference, the International Chamber of Commerce's Business Allied to Support the Information Society (ICC BASIS) proposed five business representatives to the coordinating committee—Facebook, Google, Microsoft, 21st Century Fox and ICANN. Clearly, these were all American companies. The implicit suggestion in this recommendation was that American businesses and technicians somehow commanded greater legitimacy, either due to historical reasons or market-based dominance, in deciding the contours of a new internet governance model. This line of thinking however provoked some further thought. If technical expertise and market share were genuine indicators of legitimacy, why was it that so few representatives from Chinese firms like Alibaba, Baidu or Tencent were being proposed for inclusion?

Until recently, most debates on internet governance turned on the dichotomy between multilateralism—negotiations between states—and multistake-holderism, a hypothetical middle ground between a classical government approach and the free markets. Unfortunately, very little thought has gone into actually studying what the multi-stakeholder body means in practice. While this model has indeed succeeded in wresting some power away from the state, in the sense that more businesses and civil society groups now have some say, it has not necessarily led to a wider range of views or global representation of interests and concerns. If anything, this body only concentrates representation from actors in the developed West, while ignoring large swathes of the developing world which lack civil society networks and powerful business lobbies.

That most business and civil society members at NETmundial were American raised serious questions about the legitimacy of such multi-stakeolder deliberations. Primarily, this is because most stakeholders in America are aligned by what some refer to as 'disciplinary neoliberalism'. Private sector expansion in the technology and communications sector was always a part of America's foreign policy and national interest. For the private sector, this was a beneficial relationship, as the government would advance their interests in global governance forums through regulations on intellectual property and data protection laws. Ultimately, such disproportionate representation by actors who are well established in internet governance has done more to undermine the vision of an open and globalized internet. Despite the fact that the NETmundial Initiative was conceived to reimagine how a plurality of voices could have a say in internet governance, it completely failed to do so. Multi-stakeholderism, as it currently operates, runs the risk of bringing together assemblies largely of the already-converted, and consequently missing out on the value of diverse perspectives.

From the very beginning, there were two objectives that NETmundial sought to achieve. First, were the issues that stung President Rousseff, regarding surveillance, and second came the issue of America's unilateral oversight of the internet. Before the conference began, Brazil was a proponent of multilateralism; in 2011, along with India and South Africa, Brazil had called for the establishment of a new body that would be located within the UN to establish principles relating to internet governance. At the time, it was suggested that this organization would absorb existing bodies like the ITU, IETF and the ICANN. However, this was not meant to be. Whether or not it was geopolitical pressure, the final statement at NETmundial shied away from criticizing the US surveillance programme, and, ultimately, even endorsed the principle of multi-stakeholderism.

It is interesting that such debates over communication infrastructure find parallels in history as well. In the 1970s, there was a raging debate in the United Nations about the balance of power asymmetry, led primarily by the 'Non-Aligned Movement'. As has been discussed, what was sought, at the time, was a New International Economic Order, in which the developing world would have greater political and economic sovereignty, along with the equitable distribution of the world's resources. As a part of this debate that raged from the mid-1970s to the 1980s, developing countries demanded a New World Information and Communication Order (NWICO).

At the time, global communication systems were beset by structural inequalities, media and information flowed mostly from the Western world to the rest, and most media companies were foreign-owned. In the beginning, this fight manifested itself around the question of satellite control. There was a fear that the United States would use its dominance over satellite communications and transmit unwanted information and media into developing countries. Because of this, the debates at the NWICO centred around Western domination of news content, and the importance of Western-controlled technology over information media, against which developing countries sought to assert their own national sovereignties.

These debates were most heated at UNESCO, which dealt with cultural and communication issues. The developing world introduced 'The Declaration on Mass Media', which proposed certain amendments to the free flow of information doctrine, centred mostly on national sovereignty.[69] However, by this time Western governments had begun rallying their press against such amendments. Freedom of information and its free dissemenation globally, they argued, was a fundamental human right. Despite intense diplomatic pressure, the final version of the free flow of information doctrine was amended to read 'free flow and a wider and better-balanced dissemination of information'.

In order to address the competing visions of communications and media, the UNESCO commissioned a report by Seán MacBride, an Irish Nobel laureate and chairman, Commission on International Communication, for UNESCO, which built on earlier debates by making wide-ranging recommendations to cover a range of different media, including television, radio and satellite. The MacBride Report,

---

[69]'Declaration on Fundamental Principles concerning the Contribution of the Mass Media to Strengthening Peace and International Understanding, to the Promotion of Human Rights and to Countering Racialism, apartheid and incitement to war', UNESCO, 28 November 1978, accessed 14 June 2019, http://portal.unesco.org/en/ev.php-URL_ID=13176&URL_DO=DO_TOPIC&URL_SECTION=201.html.

for the first time, gave the NWICO a general framework and a detailed set of recommendations. The release of this report, however, provided the impetus for the newly-elected governments of Ronald Reagan and Margaret Thatcher, both of whom were introducing neoliberal market reforms, to charge UNESCO with attempting to water down basic human freedoms. The World Press Freedom Committee, which had strong links to the Western media industry, lobbied aggressively against UNESCO, to the extent that by mid-1980, the feverish campaign culminated in the US and the UK pulling out of UNESCO.[70]

The US and the UK, of course, were the largest sponsors of UNESCO. After they pulled out, the NWICO gradually receded into obscurity. The parallels between the NWICO and the 'internet freedom' agenda are stark. The same rhetoric that was employed to ensure control over new media infrastructure in the late 1980s was used to dominate the narratives around the information society. This time, however, 'multi-stakeholderism' became the preferred vehicle to protect this interest. In October 2016, the United States finally relinquished its unilateral oversight over technical functions of the internet to a new international 'multi-stakeholder body'. At home, the announcement was denounced as 'America's Internet Surrender', as the *Wall Street Journal* put it, arguing that, 'Russia, China, and other authoritarian governments have already been working to redesign the Internet more to their liking, and now they will no doubt leap to fill the power vacuum caused by America's unilateral retreat.'[71]

For decades, American control over the internet was regarded as illegitimate; after all, how could one state control the twenty-first century's most important resource? Still, one must wonder whether this multi-stakeholder system will be different. Even today, decisions are taken by a select few interest groups and voices from the non-English speaking Global South are limited. By transitioning internet

---

[70]Associated Press, 'Britain Following Lead of U.S., Will Withdraw From UNESCO', *Los Angeles Times*, 5 December 1985.

[71]L. Gordon Crovitz, 'America's Internet Surrender', *Wall Street Journal*, 18 March 2014.

governance to a new international body, the United States defined the limits of reform and change. That governments are lumped in the same bag as businesses and civil society only allows America to retain de facto influence over the internet.

A NEW MEDIUM

Since its inception as an American military project in the early 1960s, the internet has come a long way. Today, it makes up a significant part of most economies and life would be unimaginable for most individuals without it. The pervasiveness of this medium, however, has also seen it become a medium that is capable of being used for destructive purposes. Sometime in 2007, local authorities in Tallinn, a city in Estonia, decided to remove a Soviet memorial from the city's downtown. Formerly a part of the Soviet Union, the country was keen to forget its cold-war heritage. As soon as the decision was announced, however, the Russian government warned that removing the statue would be considered an insult to Russia. At the time, such warnings were largely ignored. The next day, Estonians woke up to realize that their access to the internet was almost completely blocked. They could not access online newspapers, social media websites, government sites or even financial services. Only a few days later did the Estonian government realize that it was a massive distributed denial-of-service (DDoS) attack that had crippled the small state's internet infrastructure. Speaking to *Foreign Policy*, Toomas Hendrik Ilves, then President of Estonia, said that, 'Looking back on it, it was the first, but hardly the last, case in which a kind of cyber-attack...was done in an overtly political manner.'[72]

The Estonian attacks marked a turning point in the history of the internet. For the first time, Russia showed to the world that the internet was now fair game in broader geopolitical struggles. Far from its libertarian origins, the internet is now a space for conflict and aggression. Since the cyber attacks on Estonia, almost every

---

[72]Emily Tamkin, '10 Years After the Landmark Attack on Estonia, Is The World Better Prepared for Cyber Threats?', *Foreign Policy*, 27 April 2017.

state has used cyberspace as a domain to further military interests, the US included. In 2012, US officials made public the details of a cyber attack on the computers which ran Iran's nuclear programme. Code named 'Olympic Games', the virus would infiltrate Iranian systems and physically manipulate the state of Iran's centrifuges that were used to enrich uranium.[73] Stuxnet—as the virus was called— eventually found itself in thousands of computer systems around the world. Thankfully, the joint American and Israeli team which created it programmed it such that it would activate only when it saw a configuration of a specific company that ran the Iranian centrifuges.

While the US was busy developing weapons for cyberspace, China was engaged in a massive espionage campaign which targeted high-tech corporations in the United States, Japan, and Europe.[74] By the time China's activities came to light, it had hacked into the database of defence contractors and even the Pentagon, stealing secrets from sensitive weapons programmes such as the F-35 fighter jet and missile systems. China's actions didn't stop there, however, it also raided financial institutions, think tanks and media outlets. *Foreign Policy,* for example, carried a story in 2014 about China's cyber espionage against solar power companies in order to steal market strategies and pricing information, which was later used to undercut them in competitive markets.[75] The sheer scale and intensity of China's activities led General Keith B. Alexander, then head of NSA, to call these and other economic espionage cyberattacks on American companies the 'greatest transfer of wealth in history' and estimated that American companies had lost $250 billion in stolen information.[76]

Sophisticated cyberspace strategies are not limited simply to

---

[73]Ellen Nakashima and Joby Warrick, 'Stuxnet was work of U.S. and Israeli experts, officials say', *Washington Post,* 2 June 2012.

[74]Ellen Nakashima and Paul Sonne, 'China hacked a Navy contractor and secured a trove of highly sensitive data on submarine warfare', *Washington Post,* 8 June 2018.

[75]Shane Harris, 'Exclusive: Inside the FBI'S Fight Against Chinese Cyber-Espionage', *Foreign Policy,* 27 May 2014.

[76]Josh Rogin, 'NSA Chief: Cybercrime constitutes the "greatest transfer of wealth in history"', *Foreign Policy,* 9 July 2019.

state actors. As has been noted, ISIS has been at the forefront of using the power of social media to serve its own nefarious ends. ISIS maximized its audience by exploiting the reach of social media platforms like Facebook and Twitter, and even resorted to using encrypted messenger systems like Telegram. Abu Musab al-Zarqawi, the ideological progenitor of ISIS, realized the value of these tactics early on, when he uploaded low-quality videos of killings and other violence on the internet. ISIS information propaganda was so well developed that *Vice* magazine called the group 'total social media pros'. By some accounts, ISIS was releasing over 40,000 tweets a day.[77] The group developed several Android and iOS apps, which gave access to user's media accounts, allowing ISIS to coordinate hundreds of thousands of accounts simultaneously. As early as 2002, even the late Osama bin Laden understood the value of new media. In a 2002 letter to Mullah Omar, former head of the Taliban, Osama bin Laden wrote, 'It is obvious that the media war in this century is one of the strongest methods; in fact, its ratio may reach 90 percent of the total preparation for the battles.'[78] Terrorist operatives have leveraged every feature of the internet—from its ability to facilitate massive information flows to the ability to encrypt communications—to promote propaganda, recruit and radicalize individuals and finance their operations. It is important to understand that, like war, terrorism is simply politics by other means. Terrorism is ultimately an expression of alternative political values and norms for organizing societies—albeit fuelled by violence. And like mainstream politics, terrorist organizations have co-opted technology as a force multiplier in achieving their objectives.[79]

2016 perhaps marked the year in which cyber operations truly matured. Russian trolls, government agencies and allied companies gamed the internet to disrupt a system that many would have

[77]Faisal Irshaid, 'How Isis is spreading its message online', *BBC*, 19 June 2014.
[78]Dylan D. Schmorrow and Denise M. Nicholson (eds.), *Advances In Design For Cross-Cultural Activities Part I*, Boca Raton: CRC Press, 2012, p. 100.
[79]Samir Saran and Kabir Taneja, 'Technology and Terror: A new era of threat in a borderless online world', ORF, 21 May 2019.

considered impossible just a few years ago—the American national elections. The inspiration for this technique comes from Russian General Valery Gerasimov, who, after forty years of experience with the Soviet Union and the Russian military, outlined a vision for twenty-first-century warfare that erased the boundary between peace and war. 'In the 21st century...wars are no longer declared and, having begun, proceed according to an unfamiliar template,' he wrote for *Russian Military Journal* in February 2013, outlining an asymmetric, multifaceted approach to warfare which involves 'a permanently operating front through the entire territory of the enemy state'.[80]

Russia's sophisticated use of social media influence operations reached over 126 million users, by the conservative estimates of social media companies who testified to the US senate. Fake accounts, bots, hashtags, and paid targeted advertisements were the preferred weapons of choice for the Russians. While many speculate that Moscow's ultimate objective was to propel Trump to power, the design of these operations reveal that the real intention was to subvert democratic processes, in order to cast doubts on their feasibility. According to Facebook, Russian operatives spent close to $100,000 on purchasing ads with socially divisive messages, such as LGBT rights, race relations, gun rights, police brutality, and so on.

Even setting aside Russian influence operations, social media was at the forefront of the 2016 American presidential elections. Early on in the race, it was evident that buzz generated on Facebook or Twitter would be an important aspect of success. Social media had now become a public space, where individuals engaged in political discourse. Unfortunately, unlike the old town halls and public squares of the twentieth century, social media is not a neutral platform. Its algorithms and code generate information that create echo chambers, targeting and tailoring news and information to conform with the biases inherent in most individuals. The polarization that social media is capable of causing will perhaps have long-lasting, unintended and

---

[80]'Valery Gerasimov, 'The general with a doctrine for Russia', *Financial Times*, 15 September 2017.

difficult-to-trace consequences for years to come in most countries.

It is, however, China which has truly envisioned the most dystopian future for the internet. By 2020, as we have mentioned, the CCP plans to implement a 'social credit system', which would give each of the 1.3 billion people under its control a unique score based on the aggregation of all their activities. This citizen score comes from monitoring an individual's social behaviour, based on shopping habits, utility bill payments, social media interactions, and it becomes the basis of that person's trustworthiness, which would also be publicly ranked. Citizens with a lower ranking, for example, would suffer from low credit scores, be denied access to public spaces, such as housing rentals, and utilities like high-speed internet; their chances of employment go down and they would be, in fact, prohibited from working in certain government jobs. As the government document states, the social credit system will 'allow the trustworthy to roam everywhere under heaven while making it hard for the discredited to take a single step.'[81]

From the earliest representations of dystopian futures, such as George Orwell's famous book, *1984*, the risk of an ever present 'big brother' has haunted societies. The idea of an imperious and opaque state, capable of peering into the innermost lives of its powerless citizens, has been a cautionary theme for decades now. China, it seems, sees this vision as the future. Beijing's leadership over cyberspace only makes this idea far more worrying, considering that its model of the internet now competes head to head with the status quo. The cyber utopians of the early 1990s never predicted how easy it would be to transform the internet into a tool for surveillance, or how easy it would be to spread fake news and propaganda. Instead, they focused on the potential of technology to empower these very same people who were oppressed by authoritarian tools. In a cruel paradox, while the internet has transformed politics, it is still not clear if it has done so in a manner that is conducive to democratization.

[81]Pete Hunt, 'China's Great Social Credit Leap Forward', *The Diplomat*, 4 December 2018.

Going forward, it is possible that the internet of yesterday is increasingly resembling a 'splinternet'. President Donald Trump already has called to 'close the internet' in areas where its rivals operate. Xi Jinping has reasserted the idea that each state must have sovereign control over the internet. The EU has passed a new data protection regulation that will hamper its transatlantic alliance and set restrictive regulations on content, digital markets and privacy. For a mix of political, commercial and security reasons, states are now intent on redrawing the map of the internet to suit their own geographical boundaries.

To many who have been a part of the internet's growth over the past decades, the nature of the internet has truly morphed. The internet governance landscape is marred by conflicting normative visions, competing commercial realities, and cyber geopolitics. Today, the internet is fragmenting along well understood international divisions. For almost half a century, the US attempted to create an ostensibly rules-based order. It advocated for the expansion of participatory democracies, a free press, the protection of human rights and market freedom. However, the emergence of regional powers like India and global powers like China have already threatened the coherence of this foreign policy. Globalization has simultaneously spurred the rapid diffusion of information and communication technologies and a diffusion of cultural values. These trends, however, have not necessarily bridged the political differences between communities. Instead, it has sharpened those fault lines, and the internet, once envisioned as a bridge, is now a contested medium. Rapid technological change, the blurring of boundaries between war and peace, and the primacy of the private sector have only compounded the challenges to global governance, especially that of the internet.

The inexorable march of freedom which began with the collapse of the Soviet Union seems to have halted, and year after year, civil society groups report that countries are moving away from democracy and human rights. The internet which was the spearhead of this march is now turning on the very societies that built it, and is now a weapon in the hands of those who do not bother with democratic norms and institutions. Slowly but surely, the libertarian internet is morphing into something entirely different. The emerging implications for global governance are deeply dismaying. Just as the contest among liberal democratic, fascist, and communist social systems defined much of the twentieth century, so the struggle between liberal democracy and digital authoritarianism, but also that between transnational technocratic colonialism and assertive techno-nationalism is set to define the twenty-first.

CHAPTER 5

THE NORMATIVE FOUNDATIONS OF
A NEW WORLD ORDER

AN IDEA

In November 2016, the election of Donald Trump to the presidency of the United States sent shockwaves around the world. Indeed, people from across the globe watched with awe how the unlikeliest of candidates ran what many would consider the most un-American campaign possible, and won. Trump's victory, some believed, heralded the end of the liberal rule-based international order. The morning after his victory, a *New York Times* editorial argued that Trump 'will plunge the United States into an era of unknowns that has little parallel in the nation's 240-year history'.[1]

To be fair, American hegemony in global governance was eroding well before Trump took office. In fact, a few weeks before Trump assumed the presidency the American intelligence community released a report which forecast a tectonic shift in international affairs: 'For better and worse, the emerging global landscape is drawing to a close an era of American dominance following the Cold War,' the report argues. 'So, too, perhaps is the rules-based international order that emerged after World War II.'[2]

Some trace the beginning of this period of 'liberal internationalism' to Britain's advocacy for free trade and freedom of navigation on the seas. Yet, this openness coexisted uneasily with its imperial ambitions

---

[1]David E. Sanger, '"Strange New Land": America in a Time of Trump', *New York Times*, 9 November 2016.
[2]Jamie Seidel, 'Prepare for "a dark and difficult future", warns US National Intelligence Council', News Corp Australia Network, 10 January 2017.

and devastating colonialism. Its true normative vision, as many scholars would agree, was articulated by President Woodrow Wilson in the months preceding World War I. As tensions in Europe continued to boil over in the early twentieth century, America could no longer ignore the looming presence of Germany near their shores. When the United States finally entered World War I, it did so under the guise of a new moral universality. Articulating America's historic sense of free values, President Wilson made it clear that American intervention did not seek to restore the balance of power in Europe, but to 'make the world safe for democracy'—in other words, to build a world order that was compatible with American domestic institutions and values.

Even after World War I, Wilson was keen on expanding his liberal internationalism across the world, and to create a multilateral and cooperative international order through which sovereign states would interact to keep peace and trade. In his now famous 'fourteen points' laid out in a speech to Congress delivered in January 1918, Wilson not only articulated American war objectives, but also what was arguably a blueprint to organize global politics. Two notable features of this organization stand out: 'A steadfast concert of peace', Wilson believed, 'can never be maintained except by a partnership of democratic nations.'[3] And, he added, by 'the removal, so far as possible, of all economic barriers and the establishment of an equality of trade conditions among all the nations.' A belief in democratic peace, the self-determination of those who were colonized and free markets underpinned America's ambition of creating a 'new world'. 'What we seek,' Wilson declared at Mount Vernon on 4 July 1918, 'is the reign of law, based on the consent of the governed and sustained by the organized opinion of mankind.'[4]

Wilson envisaged a new global institution to secure this world view—a 'League of Nations' that would guarantee sovereignty

---

[3] G. John Ikenberry, Thomas J. Knock, Anne-Marie Slaughter, and Tony Smith, *The Crisis of American Foreign Policy: Wilsonianism in the Twenty-first Century,* Princeton: Princeton University Press, 2009, p. 53.

[4] Id at pp. 11–12

'pursuant to the principle of self-determination.' At a time when Europe was still largely a colonial power, the idea itself seemed revolutionary. For Americans, however, these norms were the basis of their own domestic institutions: 'These are American principles, American policies,'Wilson declared,'We could stand for no other.And they are also the principles and policies of forward-looking men and women everywhere, of every modern nation, of every enlightened community. They are the principles of mankind and must prevail.'

Despite this grand ambition, Wilson's plan for an international order could not fructify. The isolationist US Senate would not allow the United States to join the League at all, and without American involvement, Wilsonian principles could not effectively manage great power competition within the League of Nations. As Kissinger writes:

> The League of Nations was impotent in the face of the dismemberment of Czechoslovakia, the Italian attack on Abyssinia, the German derogation of the Locarno Treaty, and the Japanese invasion of China. Its definition of aggression was so vague, the reluctance to undertake common action so deep, that it proved inoperative even against flagrant threats to peace. Collective security has repeatedly revealed itself to be unworkable in situations that most seriously threaten international peace and security.[5]

In the end, this experiment in building a liberal word order failed to prevent a new interwar period between rival European powers.

To some, it might have seemed like the onset of World War II was a testament to the failure of the Wilsonian imperative. However, even after the end of this great war, the principles, values and norms espoused by Wilson continued to influence American policy; and this time, the United States was unquestionably the most powerful actor in the international system by virtue of its military and economic dominance. At the end of World War II, the United States of America had uncontested air and naval power projection abilities; it accounted

---

[5]Henry Kissinger, *World Order*, NewYork: Penguin Books, 2014.

for almost 50 per cent of the world's GDP; held almost half the world's gold reserves; and accounted for almost three-fifths of the world's oil reserves.[6] President Truman was not exaggerating when he declared that: 'We are the giant of the economic world. Whether we like it or not, the future pattern of economic relations depends on us. The world is watching to see what we do.'[7] Leveraging this extraordinary power, the United States went on to create the institutions of the post-war international order which still define it today: the United Nations, the North Atlantic Treaty Organization (NATO), the World Bank, the International Monetary Fund and the World Trade Organization (which was, prior to 1995, the General Agreement on Tariffs and Trade). Simultaneously, Washington implemented the Marshall Plan, an economic scheme that would revive and reintegrate a Europe that was ravaged by war, and would also go on to create a new framework of alliances in Asia, especially with Pakistan in South Asia and with Japan, the Philippines and South Korea in East Asia.

At the same time, this fledgling international order was also buttressed by America's domestic norms and values, giving it a new, ostensibly universal, ideological, ideational and cultural appeal. Human rights and democracy became deeply embedded in the international system, first with the Universal Declaration of Human Rights adopted by the UNGA in 1948. Articulating the notion of universal individual rights, the document outlined a vision where such rights deserved recognition around the world—independent of a sovereign government's political preferences. This was followed by a stream of conventions and treaties which continued to expand a vision for human rights, often articulating norms which gave the international community the right to intervene in the affairs of sovereign states, such as the 'responsibility to protect'.

Thus, a Western liberal world order emerged; anchored by the United States (with Europe and Japan emerging as key partners), it

---

[6] Wilson Centre, 'A short history of America's economy since World War II', *Medium*, 23 January 2014.
[7] Speech by Harry S. Truman, 'Address On Foreign Economic Policy', Baylor University, 6 March 1947.

was, at first, a loose assortment of multilateral institutions and security partnerships which stabilized the world economy and prevented the outbreak of war. Once the Soviet Union collapsed in 1989–91, the liberal order began to spread outwards, towards Asia, Eastern Europe and Latin America. Piece by piece, the institutions which came to define it expanded as well, with enormous implications for the rest of the world. The 1990s became the heyday of globalization—a process that many believed was rendering the old Westphalian notions of sovereignty and great power rivalries obsolete. As multilateral institutions continued to expand their role, a new era was born in which international rules and norms not only defined behaviour between states, but also affected domestic societies. This increase in the scope, density and intrusiveness of the international order led to a new social contract between the citizen, the state and the global community.

President George H. W. Bush called for a 'new world order' based on democratic states at the UNGA in 1990, a sentiment reciprocated by the G7, who made the promotion of democracy a key feature of its blueprint for a twenty-first century peace. This hubris was understandable—in 1900, there were no democracies; by the middle of the century, there were almost thirty such countries; and in 2005, a democratic surge had swept across the globe, with 91 of the world's 193 countries recognized as democracies.[8] In advancing his thesis of the 'end of history' Francis Fukuyama wrote that:

> As mankind approaches the end of the millennium, the twin crises of authoritarianism and socialist central planning have left only one competitor standing in the ring as an ideology of potential universal validity: liberal democracy... Two hundred years after they first animated the French and American revolutions, the principles of liberty and equality have proven not just durable but resurgent.[9]

---

[8]Max Roser, 'Democracy', Our World in Data, https://ourworldindata.org/democracy.
[9]Peter F. Nardulli, *Popular Efficacy in the Democratic Era: A Reexamination of Electoral Accountability in the United States, 1828-2000,* Princeton: Princeton University Press,

A MULTI-CONCEPTUAL WORLD ORDER[10]

Looking at the world at the end of the twentieth century, it was easy to see why Fukuyama was enamoured of the idea of the world inexorably marching in one direction. Charles Krauthammer celebrated the triumph of the US vision of the world by proudly proclaiming a 'unipolar moment'—the onset of a period of single-power dominance to replace the binary superpower stand-off the world had witnessed during four decades of the Cold War. But as we move towards the third decade of the twenty-first century, the era of the American imperium appears to be in crisis. For the first time, hostility towards this system appears to come from within. Economic anxiety, stimulated by the adversity of hyper-globalization and cultural withdrawal brought on by the millions of refugees making their way into Europe, have produced a West that is increasingly hostile to globalization and multiculturalism.

Trump's first agenda in office was to challenge every sacred assumption of the earlier era: he sought to 'build a wall' to keep out foreigners, trash NATO, renege on the Trans-Pacific Trade Agreement and the Paris Agreement. Across the Atlantic, Britain voted to exit the European Union, amidst a populist authoritarian surge in Europe that has claimed many countries such as Hungary and Poland. Just twenty-six years after the publication of Fukuyama's essay, a 2015 Freedom House report stated that the 'acceptance of democracy as the world's dominant form of government—and of an international system built on democratic ideals—is under greater threat than at any point in the last 25 years.'[11]

Even as the transatlantic consensus is in crisis, broader economic and political shifts are underway: as has been noted throughout the book, power is increasingly moving East and South, away from

---

2007, p.1.

[10]This section is based on Samir Saran, 'India in vanguard of new order: Raisina 2019', ORF, 14 February 2019.

[11]Arch Puddington, 'Discarding Democracy: A Return to the Iron Fist', Freedom House, accessed 15 June 2019, https://freedomhouse.org/report/freedom-world-2015/discarding-democracy-return-iron-fist.

the Atlantic system. The *Economist Intelligence Unit* was blunt in its predictions: 'The share of world real GDP (at PPP) accounted for by North America and Western Europe will be halved from 40% in 2010 to about 20% in 2050, while developing Asia's share is predicted to almost double from 27% in 2010 to almost half in 2050.'[12] While China has undoubtedly been the main cause—as well as beneficiary—of this transformation, other emerging powers such as India, Turkey and Brazil have also seen their share of production and output grow. As a result, these powers have been clamouring for a greater voice in global governance institutions; and, in some cases, have created new ones such as the BRICS New Development Bank and Contingent Reserve Arrangement (a financial mechanism), the Asian Infrastructure Investment Bank (AIIB), and China's Belt and Road Initiative. To make matters more complex, power is also diffusing vertically: the rising power of private wealth, through corporations and philanthropic organizations, an increasingly vocal civil society, new regional alliances, and the velocity of information flows across the internet have diluted the power of nation states.

At the same time, due to globalization, the world is far more interdependent than ever before, with supply chains, power grids, sea cables and infrastructure criss-crossing the planet. Challenges like climate change, disease, poverty, food supply and internet governance are also becoming intertwined with the international system. In this complex and networked world, old state hierarchies could well give way to new networks of cities, transnational corporate interests, and grassroots social movements which are capable of influencing economic and political outcomes.

The traditional order of state hierarchy is becoming less and less relevant with these developments, and so is separation between domestic and foreign policy. As a result of this complexity, world politics will not be defined solely by governments. Formal and informal networks ranging from non-governmental organizations

---

[12]Laza Kekic, 'Globalization to Remain Concentrated in Asia', *CNBC*, 18 March 2012.

to terrorists will challenge established state-led mechanisms. While governments will continue to be the most influential voices, the global table of decision-making is growing more and more crowded by the day, limiting their scope of action.

Richard Haass writes that, 'These days the balance between order and disorder has shifted toward the latter.' The future of the international order, he writes, is 'one in which the current international system gives way to a disorderly one with a larger number of power centers acting with increasing autonomy, paying less heed to U.S. interests and preferences.'[13] These complex shifts tell us something important: that the international order today is multi-conceptual—different powers, institutions, actors and ideologies are competing to stake a claim in shaping an emerging order. Unlike the Cold War era, there are no binary ideological competitions; instead, parochial nationalism and religion appear to be shaping state identities. Apart from a diverse array of states ranging from authoritarian to democratic, new non-state actors are either lending heft to state authority or undermining it. The new alphabet soup of institutions that emerging powers have created are often uncertain about a new global consensus, but agree on what they do not want— the universalization of the Western-led liberal order. Clearly, while the demand for global governance will remain strong, supplying it through institutional mechanisms, normative principles and a diverse array of actors will increasingly become difficult.

The United States intelligence community agrees with this assessment, finding that by the mid-2020s, the 'powers at the center of [regional] spheres [are attempting] to assert their right to privileged economic, political, and security influence within their regions.'[14] Reflecting on these trends, former US Secretary of State Henry Kissinger argues that, 'The contemporary quest for world order will

---

[13]Richard N. Haass, 'The Unraveling: How to Respond to a Disordered World', *Foreign Affairs*, November–December 2014.

[14]National Intelligence Council and Office of the Director of National Intelligence, *Global Trends: Paradox of Progress*, Washington DC: Government Printing Office, 2017, p. 54.

require a coherent strategy to establish a concept of order *within* the various regions and to relate these regional orders to one another.'[15] Yet developing such inclusive, open regional orders is easier said than done. In fact, the liberal international order is today clearly fractured; parts of it continue to defend its traditional values such as democracy and free markets; in other regions, there is contest over the norms and rules of governance, and in some areas, order has collapsed completely.

Reacting to Trump's victory, Chancellor Merkel stated that, 'Germany and America are connected by values of democracy, freedom, and respect for the law and the dignity of man, independent of origin, skin colour, religion, gender, sexual orientation, or political views... I offer the next President of the United States close cooperation on the basis of these values.'[16] For many in the West, this was a clear signal from Merkel that Germany would resist illiberal forces—after all, the EU has been the poster child for multilateralism for human rights and liberal democracy, and for free trade. In Brussels, there was probably a collective sigh of relief when France voted for Emmanuel Macron in France, who has so far defended the cause of liberal values—multilateral governance, open trade, human rights, and diversity. At the World Economic Forum in 2018, headlines were awash with the hope that France and Germany would collectively push back against Trump's 'America First' Agenda.

However, the Atlantic system is not as coherent as one might wish. In Eastern Europe, for example, Russia under Vladimir Putin is intent on reviving its traditional sphere of influence. In a 2014 address following Russia's annexation of Crimea—an act in itself that shook the very foundations of the international order, since it rearranged sovereign territorial borders—Putin was furious about the Western-backed protests which thrust former Ukranian President Viktor Yanukovych out of power: 'If you compress the spring all the

---

[15] Henry Kissinger, *World Order*.
[16] AFP, 'Does Donald Trump's victory spell the end of the West?', *The Hindu*, 2 December 2016.

way to its limit, it will snap back hard,' he said.[17] For Putin, NATO's unbridled expansion, ostensibly illegal interventions in Afghanistan and Iraq, and American support for the Arab Spring all added up—to put it in his words—to 'compress the spring'. Putin's challenge to the West, however, is more than territorial. Russia's unconcealed influence operations in America and Europe—manifest in support for far-right parties' hints at a more insidious agenda; one which culminates in Europe and America abandoning their normative foundations, resulting in a West that is undecided, unsure, and incapable of shaping an universal international agenda.

Hungarian Prime Minister Viktor Orbán is perhaps Exhibit A in Putin's coup de grace. Under his rule, Hungary has undergone a massive transformation from a liberal state to Putin's puppet in the EU; he has fiercely criticized EU sanctions on Russia and has embarked on major energy projects with the country. Orbán also supports Russia's narratives of 'ethnic homogeneity', pitting Christianity against Islam—an explicit rejection of European multiculturalism. Russia has successfully supported, without any military intervention, the rise of a raft of illiberal democrats ranging from Orbán himself to Marine Le Pen in France.

At the same time, together with other revisionist powers such as China, Moscow has invested in new regional institutions which are capable of acting as normative buffers against the West: the Shanghai Cooperation Organisation (SCO), for example, brings together China, Russia, four of the Central Asian states, and, most recently, India and Pakistan. The SCO regularly issues public criticisms of 'American imperialism', and the imposition of its norms on other countries. The SCO enshrines 'respect for civilizational diversity' or the 'Shanghai spirit', routinely rejecting the imposition of democratic and free-market-based conditionalities on global governance. Just like the BRICS, the SCO enshrines respect for state sovereignty and non-interference, and promotes the 'democratization of international relations'.

---

[17]Joshua Yaffa, 'Can Putin Get His Way on Syria?', *New Yorker*, 28 September 2015.

Farther East, the Islamic world is occupied in a tumultuous catastrophe which does not seem to end. The entire region is facing governance crises: large swathes of the map have been dominated by terrorism and perverse manifestations of nationalism. State authority has collapsed almost entirely in many countries, and across the Muslim world, from Libya, Yemen, Gaza, Lebanon, Syria, Iraq, Afghanistan, Nigeria, Mali, and Somalia, there is a real possibility that many of these states will fall out of the international system altogether, other than in name. Religion has metastasized into a weapon and political, sectarian, ideological and geopolitical disputes and rivalries have merged into an unending spiral of civilizational wars. Syria and Iraq—ground zero for these disruptions—have become symbols of disintegrating statehood, embroiled in conflict and manipulated by a boggling array of external powers.

No doubt, a major source of this crisis was the United States itself, whose disastrous interventions across the region after the events of the 9/11 attack sparked an ideological fervour against the West in a manner that seemingly validates Samuel Huntington's 'clash of civilizations' thesis. Part of the backlash is cultural. As Coral Bell puts it, 'The US has become "the Great Satan" because it has become "the Great Tempter", tempting the young people of Islamic communities away from their traditional ways to the more relaxed and permissive ways of the contemporary West.'[18] In many ways, the Middle East is testament to the follies of empire and the hubris of hegemony. From Kosovo to Somalia to Libya, the United States intervened and overcommitted itself in areas that had little to do with its direct national security interests under the guise of globalism and democracy. In the Middle East, this unsustainable endeavour has ultimately mired America in some of the longest running conflicts it would ever fight. The rise of ISIS and its ideological defiance to the norms and rules of a Westphalian world in itself are worrisome;

---

[18]Coral Bell, 'The end of the Vasco da Gama era: The Next Landscape of World Politics', Lowy Institute Paper 21, 15 November 2007, https://www.lowyinstitute. org/sites/default/files/pubfiles/LIP21_BellWEB_1.pdf.

and even after its demise, its call for a pan-Islamic caliphate, amplified inevitably by the internet, will undoubtedly resonate with young, disillusioned Muslims across the world.

In Asia, the regional balance of power is stuck in an uneasy contest between China and the United States, with other regional powers hedging one way or another. For many this was nothing unexpected; Singapore's Lee Kuan Yew was prescient when he said that 'the size of China's displacement of the world balance is such that the world must find a new balance... It is not possible to pretend that this is just another big player. This is the biggest player in the history of the world.'[19] For decades, many Asian states integrated with China economically, while relying on the United States for military security. Today, this 'dual hierarchy' is under strain: At a time when American foreign policy itself is uncertain, Beijing now seeks complete pre-eminence in Asia and considerable influence in the rest of the world—a twenty-first-century refinement of its historic role as the 'middle kingdom'. While most states in Asia have attempted to hedge between the two competing systems, they find themselves increasingly a fractured group, with some seeing no alternative to acquiescing in China's rule, and others refusing to abandon a rules-based order altogether.

NORMATIVE SHIFT

'The dominance of a single great power,' wrote American scholar Robert Keohane in his widely acclaimed book, *After Hegemony*, 'may contribute to order in world politics, in particular circumstances, but it is not a sufficient condition and there is little reason to believe that it is necessary.'[20] Indeed, at many historical junctures, states and communities have grappled with the quest for creating a stable international order. More often than not, the catalyst for these

---

[19]Graham Allison, Robert D. Blackwill, and Ali Wyne, *Lee Kuan Yew: The Grand Master's Insights On China, the United States, and the World*, Cambridge: The MIT Press, 2013, p. 42.
[20]Robert O. Keohane, *After Hegemony: Cooperation and Discord in the World Political Economy*, Princeton: Princeton University Press, 1984, p. 46.

junctures is conflict that destroys established orders. Both the world wars and the end of the Cold War in 1991 were such important junctures. For America, the task in the late twentieth century was building an international order in an era where it initially gauged that it had no conceivable challengers.

Writing for the *Financial Times*, commentator and journalist Gideon Rachman argued that the 'western age of optimism' stretching from the end of the Cold War to the 2008 financial crisis was underpinned by five key principles: 'The first was a faith in the onward march of democracy... The second, linked belief was a faith in the triumph of markets over the state... [the] third key belief was in the transforming power of technology, as a force driving forward prosperity, democracy, and globalization. The fourth idea, which knitted all these notions together, was the theory of the "democratic peace": the belief that in a world in which democracy and capitalism were on the rise, the risk of conflict between nations inevitably diminished. The fifth and final idea—a sort of insurance policy—was the faith [that] in the last resort the US military could defeat any power on earth.'[21]

These were the normative elements of America's unipolar moment, and today, all five appear to be under considerable stress. The consequences of the change in power equations, however, are not simply material but normative as well, since hegemony, spheres of influence, and regional orders are often shaped by principles and norms. As author Robert Gilpin writes in *War & Change in World Politics*, states 'enter social relations and create social structures in order to advance particular sets of political, economic, or other types of interests.'[22] Indeed, powerful states, as a matter of course, will seek to influence the hierarchies and networks within their spheres of influence. Such international social structures underwrite a given hegemonic order through ideas, values, norms and institutions. This is

---

[21]Gideon Rachman, 'Zero-Sum World', *Financial Times*, 23 October 2010.
[22]Robert Gilpin, *War & Change in World Politics*, Cambridge: Cambridge University Press, 1981, p. 9.

why hegemonic transitions often disrupt the status quo in more ways than just a military balance of power; in other words, the shifts are not merely material, but also normative. As a great power rises, it seeks to normalize its own cultural, economic and political orientation into the international system. World War II and the Cold War are a testament to these trends; the wars themselves were not merely about great power competition, but also pitted fascism and communism against liberal, free-market democracies. For this same reason, a redistribution of power today will not simply change actors on the global high table, but will also challenge the normative foundations of a Pax Americana that is now more than seven decades old.

Countries have specific ideas, ideologies and religious beliefs which shape their political, cultural and economic milieus. Larger powers tend to have a unique normative understanding about global institutions as well, which is why in different historical eras, the international system would reflect the world view of a dominant hegemon. For centuries, East Asia was ordered in a hierarchical system which had China at the centre of its cultural and economic relations. Pax Britannica, on the other hand, was founded through commercial ventures, underpinned by a global network of trading nodes and, from the second half of the nineteenth century onwards, a strong missionary sense of bringing civilization to the world. Pax Americana, which upheld Britain's trading impulses, also brought with it the ideas of a more egalitarian and democratic social order built in its own image.

Today, globalization and the consequent interdependence it fostered will make normative shifts all the more complex when such transitions take place. Pax Americana is not simply giving way to a new powerful nation-state, but is beset instead by multiple power centres that include non-state actors. For the first time since the end of World War II, as we have noted, the world will be more connected and interdependent than ever, but will not be anchored by Western economic power, nor by its norms and values. A new world order will be characterized by multiple competing and interacting orders; it will be a world that is at once multipolar and interdependent. The consequences of normative shift then are enormous. Some in Washington believe that emerging powers will embrace the international order, underwritten by the globalization of its universal norms and values. According to political theorist John Ikenberry, 'The United States' global position may be weakening, but the international system the United States leads can remain the dominant order of the twenty-first century.'[23] To ensure that new powers are accommodated within this order, 'The West should sink the roots of this order as deeply as possible.' This is arguably feasible because, unlike Germany and Japan in the first half of the twentieth century, the new emerging powers are not explicitly seeking to overturn the existing international order. 'China and other emerging great powers,' Ikenberry writes, 'do not want to contest the basic rules and principles of the liberal international order; they wish to gain more authority and leadership within it.'

That Ikenberry should highlight China as the primus inter pares of the rising powers is not a coincidence; the country is increasingly viewed as a global competitor, one that is capable of displacing the United States in the existing international system. China, which is arguably the most prominent normative challenger, also embodies a set of universal values that it seeks to spread. In fact, a common refrain in Beijing about the current international order is its absence during its formation. China's own rise is a reflection of its ability to project its own economic accomplishments and unique political system. There is longing in China for the revival of its status as the Middle Kingdom, where it was the centre of global political, economic, and security affairs. China is not simply a rising power with material wealth—it embodies, articulates, and projects its own ideas and norms in ways that make it a global leader.

A CENTURY OF HUMILIATION

In the late eighteenth century, Imperial Britain was running a massive trade deficit with the Chinese empire, mostly over tea,

---

[23]G. John Ikenberry (ed.), *Power, Order, and Change in World Politics*, Cambridge: Cambridge University Press, 2014, p. 54.

porcelain, and silk. To remedy this situation, they sent Britain's first envoy to China, Lord George Macartney, in 1793 to establish trade relations with the last imperial dynasty, the Qing Dynasty, bearing gifts that bore testament to Britain's industrialization. Unsurprisingly, the Chinese emperor had little interest in this man, where he came from, or in the idea of 'diplomatic relations'; at the time China had never established a relationship of parity with any other country—ever. From the first meeting, the cultural differences were apparent: refusing to 'kowtow'—or prostrate—before the Chinese emperor, as was the custom in the East Asian tributary system, Macartney proposed instead that he would bow on one knee as he would in England; and that a Chinese official must do the same before the portrait of King George III which he carried.

Shooed away rather ambivalently, it would take Macartney two years to travel back to Britain and deliver the message that the Qianlong emperor had written to King George III: 'Our Celestial Empire possesses all things in prolific abundance and lacks no product within its borders. There is, therefore, no need to import the manufactures of outside barbarians in exchange for our own produce.'[24] As an emerging empire, Britain would not be easily dissuaded from its attempt to penetrate the Chinese market. Searching for goods to trade with the Qing Dynasty, the English ultimately found their answer in a produce that was available in abundance in the fertile lands of East India: opium. As Pankaj Mishra writes: 'The export of opium exponentially increased revenues and quickly reduced Britain's trade deficit with China; mass Chinese intoxication became central to British foreign policy. But the easy availability of the drug quickly created a problem of addiction in the country. In 1800, the Chinese forbade the import and production of opium; in 1813, they banned smoking altogether. Still, the British kept at it: by 1820, there was enough opium coming into China to keep a million people addicted, and the flow of silver had been reversed.'[25]

[24]Peter Worsley, *The Third World*, Chicago: University of Chicago Press, 1970, p. 2.
[25]Pankaj Mishra, *From the Ruins of Empire: The Revolt Against the West and the Remaking*

Taking exception to this development, which was miring the dynasty in chronic drug abuse, the Chinese entrusted a faithful commissioner of the Canton region, Lin Zexu, to end this fiendish trade. Clamping down on the smuggling of opium, Lin would harass British merchants, seize their goods, impound their vessels and arrest hundreds in China. 'We mean to cut off this harmful drug forever,' Lin wrote to Queen Victoria in 1839. Meanwhile, Lord Macartney was about to pen down a prescient observation: 'The Empire of China', he wrote, 'is an old, crazy, first-rate man of war, which a fortunate succession of vigilant officers have contrived to keep afloat for these hundred and fifty years.' It has managed to overawe its neighbours 'merely by her bulk and appearance... But whenever an insufficient man happens to have the command on deck,' Macartney cleverly observed, '...she may drift some time as a wreck, and will then be dashed to pieces on the shore.'[26] And dashed to pieces she was. Failing to negotiate terms of trade amenable to themselves, the British chose to do what any other imperial power would: they dispatched a large naval flotilla, equipped with iron hulls and powerful cannons. Faced with such an overpowering and technologically advanced foe, the Chinese relented, and signed the Treaty of Nanking, which amongst other things gave the British docking rights in China, low tariff rates, millions of pieces of silver in wartime repatriations, and complete sovereignty over Hong Kong.

In some ways, the Opium Wars—as *The Times* of London would first label it—marked the culmination of a slow reversal of fortune for both the great Asian empires at the time: China in East Asia and India in South Asia. In the 1400s, both these countries, along with the Islamic world, were comparable in economic power to Europe. With the voyages of Christopher Columbus, who sailed across the Atlantic, and Vasco da Gama who reached Indian shores in the late

---

of Asia, London: Penguin, 2012, p. 103.

[26]Helen H. Robbins, *Our First Ambassador to China: An Account of the Life of George, Earl of Macartney, With Extracts from His Letters, and the Narrative of His Experiences in China, As Told By Himself, 1737-1806*, New York: Cambridge University Press, 2011, p. 386 [see https://archive.org/details/ourfirstambassad00robbuoft/page/n10].

fifteenth century, the relationship between European empires and the rest of the world was transformed. Over the next few hundred years, through conquest and trade, they built colonies across Asia and Africa, in the process fuelling their own military, naval, and industrial prowess. Still, as late as 1600, according to the British economic historian Angus Maddison, India accounted for 22 per cent, and China 29 per cent of the world economy.[27] By the twentieth century, the tables had turned; the West had ascended to the top through the Industrial Revolution, and economic strength was mirrored in imperial power as well: Britain and her colonies alone accounted for over a quarter of the world's land area. According to British archaeologist and historian Ian Morris, 'By 1914, Europeans and their colonists ruled 84 percent of the land and 100 percent of the sea.'[28]

The global order and the fledging international system during the first half of the twentieth century was shaped almost entirely to preserve the balance of power in Europe and the stabilization of their colonies abroad. As the foundations of the twenty-first century were being cemented, China and India were cut down to size, a historical aberration that would obscure the extent of their power and influence across the centuries. For China, which endured for so long on the unshakable belief of its own primacy, centrality, and the universality of its norms, values and ethics, this new period was the dawn of what the Chinese see as a 'century of humiliation'. The new world order was no longer based on the hierarchical order of the Middle Kingdom, but was instead a system premised on juridical equality and state sovereignty. It was also based on Anglo-Saxon and Judeo-Christian religious norms and institutions. Democracy, not empire and free trade, and certainly not tributaries, would define this era. The West would underwrite these values, first through colonization, and then through American power.

---

[27]Manas Chakravarty, 'World history by per capita GDP', *Livemint*, 25 August 2010.
[28]Ian Morris, *War: What is it Good For?: The Role of Conflict in Civilisation, From Primates to Robots*, London: Profile Books, 2014.

TRANSITION

Following the decolonization movements and the end of World War II through the second half of the twentieth century, Asia slowly began to see a reversal in its fortunes. This commenced, first, with the East Asian 'tiger economies' of Japan, South Korea and Taiwan in the 1970s. Japan's economic growth was so staggering that some in America were concerned that the United States might be overshadowed by its former adversary; as late as 1989 pundits were foreseeing the primacy of 'Japan As Number One'. But with a population of just over 100 million, Japan would never be able to shift the balance of economic power alone. This task would fall upon China and India, each home to over a billion citizens each. Beginning in the 1980s, China would grow at an extraordinary pace, followed by India from the 1990s onwards. Then, in 2014, something extraordinary happened: the IMF announced that China was the world's largest economy, when measured by purchasing power, overtaking the United States, which had maintained this status since at least 1872.

China's rise, if anything, was simply the culmination of a larger trend. Today, we are witnessing a gradual shift in global economic power—from West to East, and from the Atlantic to the Pacific and Indian Oceans. The magnitude of this shift cannot be understated; the United States National Intelligence Council (NIC) noted in its 2012 forecast that 'in a tectonic shift, by 2030, Asia will have surpassed North America and Europe combined, in terms of global power, based upon GDP, population size, military spending, and technological investment.'[29]

This transition, however, raises complex questions of world order and its normative foundations. In Europe, centuries of war and conflict finally gave way to an equilibrium beginning with the Treaty of Westphalia and culminating with European integration after World War II. In Asia, no such congruence exists, with identity, norms,

---

[29]PTI, 'US sees India as rising economic powerhouse by 2030', *Economic Times*, 10 December 2012.

cultural traditions, and regimes competing for primacy. The old divides between East Asia, South Asia, West Asia (the 'Middle East' in the West's geocentric language), and Central Asia are blurring, but cultural, philosophical, and religious influences have always transcended these divides, and are now competing in a common space at the same time as momentous shifts in global economic power are taking place. If multipolarity is the new normal, it is most visible in Asia, where there is no unifying political and economic architecture. The liberal international order, grounded in transatlantic values, has no parallel in Asia.

Former Australian Prime Minister Kevin Rudd once remarked, 'Very soon we will find ourselves at a point in history when, for the first time since George III, a non-Western, non-democratic state will be the largest economy in the world. If this is the case, how will China exercise its power in the future international order? Will it accept the culture, norms and structure of the post-war order? Or will China seek to change it? I believe this is the single core question for the first half of the twenty-first century, not just for Asia, but for the world.'[30] For China, the answer undoubtedly is shaped by its understanding of history. 'Our nation is a great nation,' President Xi Jinping declared in a 2012 speech. 'During the civilization and development process of more than 5,000 years, the Chinese nation has made an indelible contribution to the civilization and advancement of mankind.' From the norms, rules, and institutions of economic relations and collective security, China is offering a new vision for the world order.

THE RISE OF NON-MARKET ECONOMICS

In the 1990s, the collapse of the Soviet Union and the liberalization and democratization of Eastern Europe seemingly ended the notion that a country could generate economic growth through state interventionism and management. Even China, whose

---

[30]Kevin Rudd, 'Kevin Rudd: The west isn't ready for the rise of China', *New Statesman*, 11 July 2012.

revolutionary birth in 1949 was driven by communism, began to generate economic prosperity only after its leaders embraced some style of market-based capitalism in the 1970s. Across the Atlantic, America and Europe were driving a new era of private-industry-led prosperity, with Margaret Thatcher privatizing key state enterprises in the power, transport, and communication sectors. During the heyday of globalization, Bill Clinton declared that, 'The era of big government is over', during his State of the Union address in 1996.[31] Preaching the virtues of free-market capitalism around the world, global financial institutions would cajole and cudgel much of the world to embrace the US-endorsed 'Washington consensus'.

In May 2000, the Clinton administration successfully clinched a deal that many in Washington believed would universalize this consensus: getting China into the World Trade Organization. By improving trade relations with the world's most populous country, Clinton believed that he would cement his legacy by underscoring the role of free markets in advancing American foreign policy. 'By joining the WTO, China is not simply agreeing to import more of our products; it is agreeing to import one of democracy's most cherished values: economic freedom,' Clinton declared in 2000. Clinton's belief that China's entry into the WTO would result in a more liberalized economy and democracy was common at the time; even George W. Bush declared in November 1999 that, 'Economic freedom creates habits of liberty. And habits of liberty create expectations of democracy... Trade freely with China, and time is on our side.'[32] Prominent free-market advocates like Thomas Friedman believed that 'China's going to have a free press', and that 'globalization will drive it'.[33] In retrospect, it is clear that this was never true: the Chinese Communist leaders watched with alarm the collapse of

[31]Robert Higgs, 'The Era of Big Government Is Not Over', *The Good Society: A PEGS Journal*, Vol.9, No. 2, 1999, p. 97, https://www.jstor.org/stable/20710961?seq=1#page_scan_tab_contents.

[32]Wash Everett, 'Excerpts of George W. Bush's Speech in Washington State', *New York Times*, 18 May 2000.

[33]Gideon Rachman, 'Why America and China will clash', *Financial Times*, 19 January 2010.

the once-impregnable superpower, the Soviet Union, and drew the conclusion that it was not perestroika (economic restructuring) that was to blame, but glasnost (democratization and opening up space for pluralist dissent) that had laid the Soviet Union low. With market reforms succeeding, Beijing needed perestroika but firmly refused to indulge in any form of glasnost. Even in more recent years, China has continued to hold back on any political reform process, creating a unique blend of state-led and communist party-controlled industries with some elements of a market economy under an authoritarian, indeed even totalitarian, state. A managed exchange rate, a vast array of state-owned enterprises, and control over land, labour, housing, and credit would allow the state to maintain its hold over the economy while retaining absolute control over the polity.

Rather than temporary aberrations which delayed the path towards a fully transparent Western-style free-market approach, the retention of this economic model has proven to be an enduring feature of the Chinese economy, allowing it to enjoy high economic growth while insulating it from the vagaries of globalization.

In the intervening years, China's economic growth has been staggering. Deng Xiaoping's programme of 'reform and opening up' (economically, of course) in 1978 undoubtedly played the key role in this transformation, and China's entry into the WTO paved the way for it to lift hundreds of millions out of poverty, enhancing its international influence and eventual emergence as a power capable of shaping international rules and norms to its own advantage.

Deng Xiaoping, often referred to as the chief architect of China's economic reforms, famously described his approach as 'crossing a river by feeling the stones'. He was not simply alluding to the pace of economic reforms, but also the political consequences they would have. Through the 1970s and 80s, the party would maintain a balance between these two spheres, with the political protests and subsequent massacre at Tiananmen Square marking a turning point in the country's history.

The decision to crush the student protests at Tiananmen Square—overtly Western-inspired as they were, with mock-ups of the Statute of Liberty being brandished by the protestors as totems of their idealism—was taken by the government of an impoverished country whose leadership adamantly refused to enter another cycle of revolutionary upheaval. Since then, Deng Xiaoping and his successors have pursued a model where political suppression has gone hand in hand with the relentless pursuit of prosperity. They reasoned that the Chinese would live without political freedom if it guaranteed them a chance for material well-being, and so the government's single-minded drive was for economic growth, aimed at enriching millions of Chinese. While most of the world embraced the Washington Consensus, Beijing chose to champion state-owned firms, leveraging control over the financial system to channel low interest capital to domestic industries, while using the legal system against foreign companies seeking to enter the Chinese market. China's leaders do not place the free market above the state; instead, control over the market is key to maintaining social stability, economic growth, and the legitimacy of the party. At the same time, they rejected Western norms; in 2013, an internal Communist Party memo entitled, 'Document No. 9' explicitly warned against 'Western constitutional democracy' and other 'universal values' (which, of course, had been the very values cited by the Tiananmen Square protestors).[34]

In 2000, Gordon Chang, prominent China sceptic and author of *The Coming Collapse of China*, predicted that China's state-owned enterprises (SOE) would not 'see the second decade of the new millennium', and that they could not remain state-linked while at the same time reforming and becoming competitive with foreign businesses and in foreign countries.[35] Clearly, he underestimated the will of the CCP. In 2007, Premier Wen Jiabao called the Chinese economy 'unstable, unbalanced, uncoordinated, and unsustainable'.[36] Rather than pursue reforms, however, the Party consolidated SOEs, killing off or merging the inefficient companies, and pursuing policies

[34]Chris Buckley, 'China Takes Aim at Western Ideas', *New York Times*, 19 August 2013.
[35]Gordon G. Chang, *The Coming Collapse of China*, New York: Random House, 2001.
[36]Tom Holland, 'Wen and and now: China's economy is still "unsustainable"', *South China Morning Post*, 10 April 2017.

that would promote industries in key emerging sectors. By 2015, ninety-eight of China's state-owned enterprises had made it onto the list of the Fortune 500 companies, second only to America's 128. SOEs are at the heart of China's political economy, where economic performance underpins the legitimacy of the party.[37] A 2011 investigative report by a Hong Kong based consultancy firm highlighted how senior executives in many of China's state-owned firms were CCP members, concluding that the roles of SOE Chairman and CEOs are 'synonymous with the Party'.[38]

If predictions about the collapse of China's state-dominated economy were plentiful, few anticipated the global financial breakdown of 2008. In a crisis which destroyed one of America's largest investment banking firms, Lehman Brothers, European and American markets plunged into chaos, virtually sinking the weakest of them, such as Greece and Iceland, into uncontrollable debt. Half a decade after the crisis, Spain, for example, which was the thirteenth largest economy in the world, registered an unemployment rate of 57 per cent for those under twenty-five years of age. The financial crisis of 2008 was not simply an economic tsunami; it marked a turning point in the future of the international order. It is unsurprising then that President Xi—widely acknowledged to be the most powerful Chinese leader since Deng—was emphatic at the 19th Party Congress in 2017 that China's system is 'blazing a new trail for other developing countries to achieve modernization' and offers 'a new option for other countries and nations who want to speed up their development'.[39]

Indeed, the election of Donald Trump as president in the United States and Britain's vote to exit the European Union only strengthens his claim. During the World Economic Forum, 2017, in Davos, Switzerland, President Xi made an impressive case for continuing with globalization, even as the West seemed to have had enough of

---

[37]Scott Cendrowski, 'China's Global 500 companies are bigger than ever—and mostly state-owned, *Fortune*, 22 July 2015.

[38]John Lee, 'China's Corporate Leninism', *American Interest*, 10 April 2012.

[39]Simon Denyer, 'Move over, America. China now presents itself as the model "blazing a new trail" for the world', *Washington Post*, 19 October 2017.

it. Exhorting the audience to 'rise to the challenge', he said that, 'history is made by the brave'.[40] The 'Beijing consensus', as some refer to it, which combines authoritarianism with a development-focused economic approach, has increasingly been gaining traction. To be fair, Xi is entitled to such rhetorical confidence; in 2011, *The Economist* noted that, 'the global financial crisis exposed critical weaknesses in Western economies. China, by contrast, suffered only a brief slowdown in its fast-paced growth before surging back into double digit expansion.' Thus, while China's share of world trade was less than 1 per cent in 1970, today it is not only the world's leading exporter, but also the centre of dense and intertwined trading networks that span continents.

Xi's embrace of globalization undoubtedly marks a turning point in history. For the first time since the end of the Cold War, the global economy was dependent not on a liberal free market, but on a hybrid combination of political repression and state-directed capitalism.[41] China's economic achievements and ambitions are not merely of academic value, they represent a challenge to the orthodox belief that free markets can exist side by side with democracy. In his book, *The End of the Free Market: Who Wins the War Between States and Corporations?* Ian Bremmer writes that for almost two decades, 'Private wealth, private investment, and private enterprise appeared to have carried the day. But as the sun sets on the first decade of the twenty-first century, that story has already become ancient history. The power of the state is back'—and back in a way that would 'threaten free markets and the future of the global economy'.[42] Taking a cue, seemingly, from Bremmer's analysis, in 2015, the *Wall Street Journal* published a front-page story about the rise of 'state capitalism' which was creating a new global economic paradigm:

[40]Ceri Parker, 'China's Xi Jinping defends globalization from the Davos stage', World Economic Forum, 17 January 2017.
[41]Samir Saran, 'World in flux: India's choices may help manage disruptions', ORF, 25 January 2018.
[42]Ian Bremmer, *The End of the Free Market: Who Wins the War Between States and Corporations?*, New York: Penguin, 2010.

'Since the end of the Cold War, the world's powers have generally agreed on the wisdom of letting market competition—more than government planning—shape economic outcomes,' *WSJ* reported. 'China's national economic strategy is disrupting that consensus.'[43]

At Davos in 2018, President Trump claimed that, 'When the United States grows, so does the world.' Replace America with China, and that statement would still hold true; indeed, China's trading empire now extends from Southeast Asia, across the Eurasian landmass, through Africa and even encompasses the Latin American markets, reducing the world's economic dependency on America and Europe. China's economic success has undermined the belief that the Washington Consensus is the only pathway to prosperity for the world, and inspired a new wave of autocratic rulers to emulate its success. The next wave of globalization will be based on non-market economics—and China's instrument of choice is the Belt and Road Initiative.

BELT AND ROAD TO HEGEMONY

In April 2016, China Ocean Shipping Company (COSCO), a Chinese state-owned infrastructure behemoth, pledged over 300 million dollars to buy and upgrade the once-sleepy Greek port of Piraeus.[44] Farther to the east, along the sprawling jungles of Laos, hundreds of Chinese engineers are digging away at mountains to build new tunnels and bridges to construct a 260-mile railway line—a $6 billion project that will eventually connect eight Asian countries.[45] In Pakistan, a 3,000-kilometre-long development corridor slices through mountains, plains and deserts, stretching from Kashgar in China to the ancient fishing port of Gwadar, which cradles the

---

[43]Jason Dean, Andrew Browne, and Shai Oster, 'China's "State Capitalism" Sparks a Global Backlash', *Wall Street Journal*, 16 November 2010.

[44]George Georgiopoulos, 'China's Cosco acquires 51 pct stake in Greece's Piraeus Port', Reuters, 10 August 2016.

[45]Ashley Westerman, 'In Laos, A Chinese-Funded Railway Sparks Hope For Growth—And Fears Of Debt', *NPR*, 26 April 2019.

Arabian Sea.[46] Once a dusty town in a desert region that housed around 50,000 Pakistani fishermen, Gwadar is now the place that China and Pakistan aspire to turn into a new Dubai, making it a city that will ultimately house two million people. In 2017, China took over the Sri Lankan port of Hambantota, and built its first overseas base in the African country of Djibouti, right next to American and French naval bases.[47]

Writing at the turn of the twentieth century, English geographer Halford John Mackinder believed that the country which integrated Europe, Asia, and Africa into one single 'World-Island' would ultimately rule the world: 'Who rules East Europe commands the Heartland; who rules the Heartland commands the World-Island; who rules the World-Island commands the World,' he wrote in 1919.[48] Almost a century later, President Xi announced two new development and trade initiatives: 'The Silk Road Economic Belt' and the 'Twenty First Century Maritime Silk Road', collectively known as the One Belt One Road (OBOR) and now rebaptized the Belt and Road Initiative (BRI). Through a vast network of transportation, telecommunication and energy infrastructure projects, Beijing seeks to physically redraw the global map by diluting the cartographic divides between Asia, Europe and Africa. The BRI, Xi believes, will tie China to the rest of the world in a prosperous 'community of common destiny'.

The appellation of 'Silk Road' is no coincidence; it conjures up images of an era when ancient trading routes connected imperial China to the Roman empire through Central Asia. Along this route, merchants would exchange ideas, science, inventions, art and religion along with profitable trade in goods and services. Indeed, it was through the Silk Road that China would embrace Buddhism, even as trade between China, Central Asia, India, and Persia extended

---

[46]Zofeen T. Ebrahim, 'Gwadar fisherfolk worry about One Belt One Road', *Business Standard*, 30 May 2017.

[47]Lee Jeong-ho, 'How the tiny African nation of Djibouti became the linchpin in China's belt and road plan', *South China Morning Post*, 28 April 2019.

[48]Phil Tinline, 'The father of geopolitics', *New Statesman*, 30 January 2019.

both east and west, culminating in the Mediterranean Sea. To many, the phrase 'Silk Road' brings forth visions of caravans travelling across vast Asian deserts, benefiting multiple empires. For China, it evokes memories of a time when the western world had still not emerged, and the Zhongguo, or Middle Kingdom, was at the centre of world affairs.

The German geographer Ferdinand von Richthofen coined the term 'Seidenstrassen' or 'Silk Roads' in 1877 for the ancient overland trade route through Central Asia.[49] The plural is appropriate: there were, in fact, many Silk Roads, which can be clustered broadly into two: overland Silk Road and maritime Silk Road. The overland Silk Roads stretched from West China to the Mediterranean; the maritime Silk Roads started from Southeast China and traversed the South China Sea, through the Strait of Malacca, to Sri Lanka and India, then crossing the Arabian Sea to reach the Gulf countries and East Africa.

The two sets of Silk Roads were much travelled. It is through them that Chinese silk and tea, the Chinese inventions of paper-making, gunpowder, the movable-type printing press, and the compass, Buddhist scriptures, and Indian music and dance, all crossed from South and East Asia to Europe. It was through the Silk Roads, in return, that Indian astronomy and the idea of the calendar, the faiths of Buddhism and Islam, and Indian plants and herbal medicines were introduced to China. Thanks to the intrepid Chinese Admiral Zheng He, who steered his naval armada across the Indian Ocean seven times in the early fifteenth century, the Chinese wok became the favourite cooking vessel of the housewife of Kerala in Southwest India, and Chinese fishing nets still dot the waters off Kochi.

In 1410, near the Sri Lankan coastal town of Galle, Admiral Zheng erected a stone tablet with a message to the world. His inscription was in three languages—Chinese, Persian, and Tamil—and his message

---

[49]Daniel C. Waugh, 'Richthofen's "Silk Roads": Toward the Archaeology of a Concept', Seattle: University of Washington, 2010, http://faculty.washington.edu/dwaugh/publications/waughrichthofen2010.pdf.

was even more remarkable: it called for the blessings of the Hindu gods for his efforts to build a peaceful world of trade and maritime commerce.[50] So 600 years ago, a Chinese sailor-statesman called upon Indian gods as he set out to develop commercial links with the Middle East and East Africa through the Indian subcontinent.

Six hundred years later, the appeal was echoed. In September 2013, in an address at Kazakhstan's Nazarbayev University, President Xi launched a new foreign policy initiative he called the 'Silk Road Economic Belt', calling for international cooperation and joint development of the Eurasian region. He presented five specific goals: the strengthening of economic collaboration, improvement of road connectivity, promotion of trade and investment, facilitation of currency conversion, and bolstering of people-to-people exchanges.

Soon enough—the very next month—the other shoe dropped. President Xi addressed the Indonesian parliament and called for the re-establishment of the old sea networks—a twenty-first-century 'Maritime Silk Road' to jointly foster maritime cooperation, international connectivity, scientific and environmental research, and fishery activities. China's Premier Li Keqiang repeated this call at the Asia-Pacific Economic Cooperation (APEC) and East Asian Summits.

Since then, President Xi's ideas to promote the modern twin Silk Roads have become official Chinese policy, moving from speeches to formal adoption by both the Communist Party's Central Committee and the country's rubber-stamp parliament as objectives to be pursued by the state. Xi has made it clear in subsequent declarations that the revival of the Silk Road economic initiative known as the Silk Road Economic Belt is intended to revive ancient ties of friendship in the contemporary globalized world.

There is undoubtedly a domestic motive as well for Xi's international initiative. The gap between eastern and western China has increased in the course of the country's breathless if uneven economic growth. The concentration of development in the cities and special economic zones (SEZs) in the east has generated

---

[50]Shashi Tharoor, *Pax Indica*.

energy and environmental constraints and bottlenecks. Through this new Silk Road initiative, Beijing clearly hopes to make western and southwestern China new engines for China's next phase of development.

But there is, obviously, in both grounding and appeal, a major international dimension to the initiative. Chinese diplomats have pointed to a constellation of mechanisms and platforms built or strengthened in recent years that could serve the initiative: the SCO; the Bangladesh-China-India-Myanmar Corridor; the China-Pakistan Corridor; the Chinese-built railway from Chongqing in western China to ports in Germany, Holland, Poland; and the new and incipient energy corridors between China and Central Asia, as well as Myanmar. In addition, given China's enormous investible surplus, its great enthusiasm for establishing the BRICS NDB and AIIB is not surprising. With China having a prominent role in each of them, it would not be difficult for Beijing to use these new financial institutions to provide financing for Silk Road-related programmes.

The maritime Silk Road is more problematic. At a time when Chinese assertiveness in its eastern waters has already created anxiety among its near-neighbours—Japan, Vietnam, the Philippines, and Singapore have all expressed varying degrees of concern—the new Silk Road initiative has evoked geopolitical apprehensions in the target countries that are historically well-founded.

Back to history: Admiral Zheng's seven expeditions between 1405 and 1433 included the use of military force in what are present-day Indonesia, Malaysia, Sri Lanka, and India to install friendly rulers and control strategic chokepoints across the Indian Ocean. He intervened in the dynastic politics of Sri Lanka and Indonesia, abducted local rulers and brought back prisoners to Nanjing, the Ming capital (and later executed them). Zheng also seized the famous Tooth Relic of the Buddha at Kandy, long a symbol of Sri Lankan political sovereignty.[51] In Sumatra, in 1407, he conducted 'regime change' by abducting

---

[51]Kapila Bandara, 'Chinese sailor Zheng He's Lanka voyages far from friendly', *Sunday Times*, 5 October 2014.

and later executing the local king and replacing him with a more pliable one. The littoral countries on Zheng's route therefore recall his adventures not merely as trade promotion but as direct military intervention in their affairs, under the pretext of ushering in a harmonious world order under the emperor of China.[52] Reminding them of this painful past may not entirely be in Beijing's interest.

There is no doubt that the Silk Roads initiative of the Chinese government, with the substantial influx of money and the significant investments it will bring to the partner countries, could boost the economies of several countries in Asia and Europe that are willing to claim and seek to revive ancient links to the Middle Kingdom. For China, the success of the initiative will open new avenues for investing its vast monetary reserves.

But it will also mark a major step towards recreating the Chinese world order of ancient times known as tianxia, which referred to all regions of the known world that acknowledged the suzerainty of the Chinese Son of Heaven, the sacred imperial title of the Chinese emperor. This is why the seemingly benign talk of a new Silk Road could have significant geopolitical implications. Many in Asia still remember Japanese efforts before and during World War II to create a 'Greater East Asia Co-Prosperity Sphere' by force of conquest. Might China be seeking the same objective without needing to resort to World War III to achieve it?

The Belt and Road Initiative combines Chinese money, infrastructure planning capacity and maritime power into one grand strategy. According to the Asian Development Bank, developing countries in Asia will require $26 trillion in infrastructure investment in the coming years. Leveraging this economic need, the BRI provides China with the opportunity to use its growing economy for political gains. To support this massive infrastructure surge, Beijing has injected millions of dollars into public financial institutions such as the Chinese Development Bank (CDB) and the Export-

---

[52]Shashi Tharoor, 'China's Silk Road revival raises concerns', *Korea Herald*, 19 October 2014.

Import Bank of China (EXIM). Borrowing heavily and at low interest rates from the People's Bank of China, these banks can generously give loans to Chinese companies working on massive projects across the world. This easy money enables Chinese SOEs to bid for projects at extremely competitive rates that most foreign companies cannot offer. It is no coincidence then, that the BRI has almost no international participation. According to a study by the think tank Center for Strategic & International Studies (CSIS), as of 2018, of all the contractors involved in the BRI, '89 percent are Chinese companies, 7.6 percent are local companies and 3.4 percent are foreign companies (non-Chinese companies from a country other than the one where the project was taking place). In comparison, out of the contractors participating in projects funded by the multilateral development banks, 29 percent are Chinese, 40.8 percent are local, and 30.2 percent are foreign.'[53]

By China's estimate, the BRI would cover roughly '4.4 billion people, 65 countries, and a combined economic output of $23 trillion, or 29 percent of global GDP.'[54] It is unsurprising then, that Xi Jinping could claim that, today, 'China has the capability and the will to provide more public goods to the Asia–Pacific and [to] the whole world.' While official government channels are careful to avoid speaking about undermining and eventually overturning the existing international order, Chinese scholars are less reticent. 'One Belt One Road is an attempt and a pathway for China to change from being a regional power with worldwide influence to a world power with comprehensive power,' wrote Xue Li, the director of the International Strategy Office of a leading official think tank, Institute of World Economics and Politics (IWEP) of the Chinese Academy of Social Sciences (CASS).[55] With this prowess, China is rapidly

---

[53]Jonathan E. Hillman, 'China's Belt And Road Initiative: Five Years Later', Center for Strategic & International Studies, 25 January 2018, accessed 15 June 2019, https://www.csis.org/analysis/chinas-belt-and-road-initiative-five-years-later-0.
[54]'How will the Belt and Road Initiative advance China's interests?', *ChinaPower*, accessed 17 June 2019, https://chinapower.csis.org/china-belt-and-road-initiative/.
[55]Howard W. French, *Everything Under the Heavens: How the Past Helps Shape China's Push for Global Power*, New York: Knopf Doubleday Publishing Group, 2017, p. 258.

becoming the world's most extensive, and eventually indispensable commercial empire. Xue called the project 'China's Marshall Plan'.

As Xi Jinping's first public act as the Chief of the Communist Party of China in 2012, he accompanied members of the new Politburo to the national museum in Beijing which hosts tribulations to the 'Chinese Century of Humiliation'. Here he unveiled a new display—'The Road to Rejuvenation', vowing 'to realize the great rejuvenation of the Chinese nation and accomplishing the "Chinese Dream".' The Belt and Road Initiative is now a prominent part of this dream, which includes, among other things, becoming a 'moderately prosperous society' by 2021; a global technology leader by 2035; and developing China into a great, modern, socialist country that is 'prosperous, strong, democratic, culturally advanced, harmonious, and beautiful' by 2049, the centenary of the founding of the People's Republic of China.

The new Silk Road is now essential to China's renewed nationalism and muscle flexing. By building interwoven transport infrastructure, energy and power grids, and new supply routes, Beijing aims to cast a wide net of economic dependency that will draw smaller nations into China's economic embrace. At its heart, as we have seen, the BRI is a roadmap for a Sino-centric world order; underwritten by new institutions such as the AIIB, and new trade regimes such as the Regional Economic Comprehensive Partnership (RCEP). Beijing's grand strategy is to weave the world into a Sinicized economic, cultural, and security network that will allow it to first reconstitute the Asian order, and eventually the global order, with new ideas, norms, and rules.

Today's state capitalists are entering markets directly, at times 'shaping these markets not just for profit',[56] Hillary Clinton explained, 'but to build and exercise power on behalf of the state.' In Europe, America, India, Japan, and Australia, strategists and foreign policy pundits have begun to use the term 'geo-economics' to describe

---

[56]Robert D. Blackwill and Jennifer M. Harris, *War by Other Means*, Cambridge: Harvard University Press, 2016, p. 37.

China's mercantilist state-run economy and foreign economic relations. As early as 2008, a report by the US National Intelligence Council predicted a multipolar world predicated on rivalry around finance, trade, investment, and technology. China, the report assessed, was poised to have 'more impact on the world over the next 20 years than any other country'.[57] The report also highlighted something significant: that developing countries, including China and Russia, were using state capitalism to influence market power and encourage industry. 'Whether mercantilism stages a comeback and global markets recede' resulting in states 'descending into a world of resource nationalism'—a process that would increase 'the risk of great power confrontations' was an open question in the report. China seems implicitly to have responded in the affirmative.

In developing countries, China's loose purse strings and political influence have translated into a toxic client-state relationship. India need to look no further than their closest southern neighbour, Sri Lanka, to observe Beijing's imperial ambitions play out. As the nearly twenty-six-year-old civil war was coming to an end in the island state, Western nations unleashed a barrage of accusations against Mahinda Rajapaksa, the country's former president, for egregious human rights abuse. China, on the other hand, was silent, choosing instead to extend billions of dollars in soft loans to the country. Eventually, China Merchants Port Holdings Company, a state-owned enterprise, signed a deal that would give them a 70 per cent stake in the strategically located Hambantota Port, located on the southern coast of the country. Unable to pay Beijing's loans, Sri Lanka eventually had to give away the port to China on a ninety-nine-year-long lease, a debt-for-equity swap that many now refer to as 'debt trap diplomacy'.

Such projects are a part of the Chinese government's plans to support modernization through a model which 'offers a new option for other countries and nations who want to speed up their

---

[57]National Intelligence Council and Office of the Director of National Intelligence, *Global Trends: Paradox Of Progress*, Washington DC: Government Printing Office, 2017, p. vi, https://www.dni.gov/files/documents/nic/GT-Full-Report.pdf.

development while preserving their independence; and it offers Chinese wisdom and a Chinese approach to solving the problems facing mankind'.[58] Chinese wisdom, however, often translates into serving Chinese interests; unlike the IMF and World Bank, China often secures its loans by collateralizing strategically important natural assets, such as the Hambantota Port, which links trade routes from Europe, Africa, the Middle East, and Asia. Development aside, China also buys up political influence using such strategies; in 2017, when China extended $24 billion in loans to the Philippines, President Rodrigo Duterte announced that 'it is time to say goodbye' to the United States—a country that it has long enjoyed close economic and security partnerships with.[59] Similarly, then Malaysian Prime Minister Najib Razak, who was facing a stormy crisis over a banking scandal which involved his family (and is being pursued in the matter by the new government of Malaysia), declared that he was a 'true friend' of China after securing deals worth over $30 billion.[60]

The same pattern of economic and political expansion is visible in Africa. When President Xi visited African leaders in 2015, he came promising almost $60 billion in new loans and other finance mechanisms, promising African leaders something they long believe has been denied to them by the West: 'China supports the settlement of African issues by Africans in the African way.'[61] There is also a rather less positive view of what China is trying to do in Africa. Over the years, dubious financial investments, rent-seeking resource exploitation and a complete disregard for human rights have proved the hallmark of China's investments in Africa. With cheap access to credit from Beijing, Chinese state-owned enterprises have systematically extracted

---

[58]'Socialism with Chinese characteristics enters new era: Xi', *Xinhua*, 18 October 2017.

[59]Lindsay Murdoch, '"It's time to say goodbye": Rodrigo Duterte dismisses US to embrace China', *Sydney Morning Herald*, 20 October 2016.

[60]Tom Miller, 'China's Clout has few limits. Shouldn't we be worried about its new Silk Road', *Gulf News*, 5 September 2017.

[61]Eswar Prasad, 'Path to Influence', International Monetary Fund, *Finance & Development*, September 2017, Vol. 54, No. 3, accessed 17 June 2019, https://www.imf.org/external/pubs/ft/fandd/2017/09/prasad.htm.

raw material from Africa to fuel China's own economic expansion, with little or no growth in local capacity visible in these states. In 2013, Lamido Sanusi, the then governor of the Central Bank of Nigeria, made headlines when he wrote that, 'China takes our primary goods and sells us manufactured ones. This was also the essence of colonialism.'[62]

The money China pours into Africa also comes with political strings attached, with the amount of aid correlating with support for Chinese foreign policy objectives. The Economist, in fact, calculates that China increases aid by a substantial margin every time an African state votes along with China on certain issues in the United Nations—a strategy that has served Beijing very well. Increasingly, African countries are forced to show deference to Beijing's interests in other areas as well: in 2014, South Africa refused to host the Dalai Lama, and in 2016, São Tomé and Principe cut off ties with Taiwan. Beijing's actions in China have earned it the unenviable moniker of a 'new colonial power', a title that it has been embarrassedly trying to play down. In May 2017, Chinese Premier Li Keqiang visited four nations in Africa, and remarked that, 'I wish to assure our African friends, in all seriousness, that China will never pursue a colonialist path like some countries did or allow colonialism, which belonged to the past, to reappear in Africa.'[63]

China's investment patterns in Asia and Africa are quite similar: in exchange for finance, China demands access to natural resources, strategically located ports and supply routes and political favouritism. As the Hambantota experience shows, China often shackles countries in debt by offering opaque loans and other financial incentives. In fact, China often invests heavily in countries that have a terrible governance record, allowing them to bypass irritating concerns like human rights and environmental consequences. Explaining very succinctly why these loans help, Ugandan President Yoweri Museveni—who restored

---

[62]Lamido Sanusi, 'Africa must get real about Chinese ties', Financial Times, 12 March 2013.
[63]'China in Africa: Investment or Exploitation?' Al Jazeera, 4 May 2014.

peace and order to his country without being unduly troubled by concerns of democratic governance—bluntly stated that the Chinese 'don't ask too many questions' and 'come with big money, not small money.'[64] This is not very surprising. China has long been suspicious of what it sees as Western-led attempts to democratize everyone: in the 1980s, Deng Xiaoping once complained to a visiting business delegation about Western talk of 'human rights, freedom, and democracy' that were designed, he believed, 'only to safeguard the interests of the strong, rich countries, which take advantage of their strength to bully weak countries, and which pursue hegemony and practice power politics.'[65]

Legitimacy, for the Chinese state and party, comes from competence, and not necessarily democracy, said Eric X. Li, a Shanghai-based venture capitalist, during a TED Talk in 2013. 'When the Chinese Community Party took power', he said, 'China was mired in civil war, dismembered by foreign aggression, [and] average life expectancy at that time [was] 41 years. Today China is the second-largest economy in the world, an industrial powerhouse, and its people live in increasing prosperity.'[66] Whether or not this competent delivery of development necessarily translates into sound and productive development projects abroad is an open question. China's failure to adhere to sound investment norms has produced dozens of 'white elephant projects' across the world, according to a report by the Oxford Saïd Business School. The report claims that almost half of the projects that Beijing invests in are not economically viable at the outset, and 17 per cent have generated returns that are lower than forecast. On human rights and environmental concerns, the United Nations says it has been vocal about what it sees as 'significant gaps from a human rights perspective'[67] in the funding

---

[64]Anja Manuel, 'China Is Quietly Reshaping The World', *The Atlantic*, 17 October 2017.
[65]Xintian Yu, *Cultural Impact on International Relations*, Washington DC: CRVP, 2002, p.29.
[66]Graham Allison, 'China Vs. America', *Foreign Affairs*, September/October 2017.
[67]United Nations Human Rights-Office of the High Commissioner, 'Baseline Study on the Human Rights Impacts and Implications of Mega-Infrastructure

of the BRI, primarily from the Beijing-dominated AIIB.

The objective of Chinese investments in developed markets is slightly different from those in developing and underdeveloped countries, where it simply seeks to create a pattern of economic dependency. In European and American markets, China uses its state-owned enterprises to strategically invest in high-tech industries, including robotics, artificial intelligence, 5G telecommunications, renewable energy, and arms industries. Many of these are mandated by Chinese law to share information and resources with the state party, creating what *The Economist* once referred to as the 'visible hand'. As China continues to acquire American firms and technology, the intellectual property and know-how is almost always transferred back to the Chinese government, allowing it to reinvest in its own domestic industry and military strategies. Some American lawmakers have called for tougher rules against the reach of Beijing's 'tentacles' into American industry.

The traditional European powers who were instrumental in framing the norms of global trade, good governance, human rights, and environmental protection also find themselves in a catch-22 situation with Beijing. China has been pouring money into Europe, investing in infrastructure projects, renewable energy sectors and in more sensitive sectors such as robotics and AI. By some estimates, China has bought or invested in assets amounting to at least $318 billion over the past ten years in Europe[68]—economic investments that are now clearly tied to Beijing's political interests. When the Norwegian parliament awarded the Nobel Peace Prize to Liu Xiaobo—a popular Chinese dissident—Beijing froze trade relations with Oslo, going so far as to abandon talks about a free trade agreement.[69] The message from Beijing to Oslo was heard loud and

---

Investment", 6 July 2017, accessed 15 June 2019, https://www.ohchr.org/Documents/Issues/Development/DFI/MappingStudyontheHRRiskImplications_MegaInfrastructureInvestment.pdf.
[68]Andre Tartar, Mira Rojanasakul and Jeremy Scott Diamond, 'How China Is Buying Its Way Into Europe', *Bloomberg*, 23 April 2018.
[69]Ben Blanchard, 'China says free trade talks with Norway should be accelerated', Reuters, 2 August 2018.

clear; when the Dalai Lama signalled his intent to visit Norway in 2014, he was curtly turned back by the prime minister, Erna Solberg. 'The Dalai Lama has visited Norway roughly a dozen times since receiving the prize in 1989—but things are different now... We need to focus on our relationship with China," Norway's foreign minister, Børge Brende, told reporters on 23 April 2014.[70] The situation in Greece was no different; in June 2016, Greece blocked an EU statement at the United Nations criticizing China's human rights record—months after China's COSCO Shipping took over Greece's port of Piraeus. 'China's strategy in Europe is divide and rule,' said Franck Proust, a French member of European Parliament (MEP) in an interview to *Politico*. 'And it's working because the 27 EU member states are incapable of remaining in solidarity with each other.'[71]

The rise of China as an economic powerhouse has enormous implications for the international order. Nowhere else is this more visible than in Asia, where the economic dependency of smaller states on China, and an interdependent and competitive economic policy vis-à-vis the West, has allowed Beijing to re-imagine a new normative order. It is undeniable that China is pushing its own agenda with a velocity and determination that has no parallels in the post-war era. Writing in his widely acclaimed book *The China Dream*, retired PLA colonel Liu Mingfu outlines the Chinese conception: 'In East Asia's tribute system, China was the superior state, and many of its neighbouring states were vassal states, and they maintained a relationship of tribute and rewards... This was a special regional system through which they maintained friendly relations and provided mutual aid. The appeal and influence of ancient China's political, economic and cultural advantages were such that smaller neighbouring states naturally fell into orbit around China, and many of the small countries nominally attached to China's ruling dynasty sent regular tribute... The universal spread of

---

[70]Robert D. Blackwill and Jennifer M. Harris, *War by Other Means*, p. 37.
[71]Laurens Cerulus and Jacob Hanke, 'Enter the dragon', *Politico*, 4 October 2017.

China's civilisation and the variety of nations that sent emissaries to China were simply a reflection of the attractiveness of the central nation, and the admiration that neighbouring countries had for China's civilisation.'[72]

THE SOUTH CHINA SEA: A BATTLE FOR THE SOUL OF THE INTERNATIONAL ORDER

Indeed, Asia is emerging as ground zero for the contest over the rules, norms and power relations that will define the international order. Already, Asia is characterized by two competing hierarchies. The first is the security hierarchy currently dominated by the United States. Since the 1950s, the United States built defence and economic ties with countries in the region through what is commonly referred to as the 'hub and spoke' system. Through security treaties with Japan and Korea, America guaranteed the security of the East Asian order, allowing Japan, Taiwan, and other East Asian 'tiger economies' to liberalize their markets and follow export-oriented development strategies. Today, most of these countries, such as Japan, South Korea, Australia, and the Philippines, now have China as their leading trade partner. While the United States is still indispensable to the world economy, the economic heart of Asia lies in China, a trend that is likely to continue. The proliferation of colossal infrastructure schemes is only the most visible manifestation of the economic power China wields. New and shiny transcontinental rail lines across Vietnam, Cambodia, Thailand, and Laos; massive ports and sea routes passing through Malaysia, Sri Lanka, Pakistan and culminating in Djibouti, all lead back to Beijing.

As a result, the settled patterns of authority and the rules, institutions, alliances, and relationships that govern this arrangement in Asia are in flux. The dominant narrative is aptly described by Gideon Rachman, who writes in his book *Easternisation: War and Peace in the Asian Century*:

---

[72]Liu Mingfu, *The China Dream: Great Power Thinking and Strategic Posture in the Post-American Era*, Beijing: Beijing Mediatime Books Co., Ltd., 2015.

The central theme of global politics during the Obama years has been this steadily eroding power of the West to shape international affairs. This erosion is closely linked to the growing concentration of wealth in Asia—and in particular the rise of China. One of its consequences is a dangerous rise in diplomatic and military tensions within Asia itself, as a rising China challenges American and Japanese power and pursues its controversial territorial claims with renewed aggression.[73]

For those who follow international affairs, the parallels between China's ancient tributary system and its current attempts to hardwire its influence under the aegis of the BRI are undeniable. Hillary Clinton once admitted that 'history teaches that the rise of new powers often ushers in periods of conflict and uncertainty.'[74] In no other area of the world is this more visible than the South China Sea (SCS). Scattered across this 3.5 million-square-kilometre region are numerous shoals, reefs, rocks, and islands, with overlapping territorial claims advanced by Brunei, China, Indonesia, Malaysia, the Philippines, and Vietnam. By virtue of its position, the SCS is one of the most vital trade routes in the world, with estimates suggesting that roughly one-third of the world's commercial shipping passes through its waterways annually—an estimated value of $3.4 trillion.[75] The area is also rich in marine biodiversity, and has enormous prospects for oil and natural gas exploration—with at least 11 billion barrels of oil, and an estimated 190 trillion cubic feet of natural gas.[76]

American strategist Robert Kaplan has no doubts about what the South China Sea means to Beijing. Drawing parallels to the Monroe Doctrine, through which America prevented European powers from

---

[73]Gideon Rachman, *Easternisation: War and Peace in the Asian Century*, London: Penguin Random House, 2016, p. 3.

[74]Ashley J. Tellis, Travis Tanner, and Jessica Keough, *Strategic Asia 2011-12: Asia Responds to Its Rising Powers: China and India*, Washington DC: The National Bureau of Asian Research, 2011, p. 37.

[75]'How Much Trade Transits the South China Sea?', China Power (CSIS), accessed 10 July 2018, https://chinapower.csis.org/much-trade-transits-south-china-sea/.

[76]Jeremy Maxie, 'The South China Sea Dispute Isn't About Oil, At Least Not How You Think', *Forbes*, 25 April 2016.

meddling in its Atlantic shores in the Greater Caribbean, he writes: 'The key geographical fact about the Caribbean is that it is close to America but was far from the great European powers of the age, just as the South China Sea is close to China but far from America and other western powers.'[77]

Since the late 1970s, Beijing has used its growing maritime might to harass and intimidate its smaller neighbours in the SCS. China has often intercepted fishing vessels, oil rigs, and even military naval vessels, using a variety of tactics from physically ramming vessels to blasting them with water cannons. The onset of this aggression can be traced back is what is popularly known as the nine-dash-line, a large dotted area on the South China Sea over which China claims complete sovereignty. This demarcation first made its official appearance in 1947 under the nationalist government of Chiang Kai-shek, and covers almost the entirety of the South China Sea, angling south from the Chinese mainland and curving up across the Strait of Malacca and concluding near the shores of Manila. Since making this claim, Beijing has made it a point to repeatedly highlight that this part of the world was a part of China for millennia, giving it 'historical rights' in the region. In May 2009, Beijing issued an ultimatum to the United Nations stating that, 'China has indisputable sovereignty over the islands in the South China Sea and the adjacent waters, and enjoys sovereign rights and jurisdiction over the relevant waters, as well as the seabed and subsoil thereof.'[78] This declaration set off alarm bells throughout the region, drawing protest from other littoral states, each with claims of its own, including most fervently Vietnam and the Philippines. By all accounts, China's claims fell well short of the United Nations Convention on the Laws of the Sea (UNCLOS), which, as leaders around the world repeatedly state, is an important element of a 'rules-based international order'. But

---

[77]Robert D. Kaplan, *Asia's Cauldron: The South China Sea and the End of a Stable Pacific*, New York: Random House, 2014.

[78]Chris Whomersley, 'The Award on the Merits in the Case Brought by the Philippines against China Relating to the South China Sea: A Critique', *Chinese Journal of International Law*, Vol. 16, Issue 3, September 2017, pp. 387–423.

Beijing remains unmoved.

To cement its claims in the area, China uses a tactic that is now widely known as 'salami slicing'—encroaching upon contested territory bit by bit in a manner that prevents spiralling escalation, but allows Beijing to change facts on the ground. In 2012, for example, Beijing established 'Sansha City' on the Paracel Islands, which were seized by force from Vietnam in 1974. Since then, China has gone on a construction spree, building houses, runways and even deploying a small contingent of paramilitary forces in the area. The Chinese refer to this as the 'cabbage strategy'; Major General Zhang Zhaozhong of the PLA gave an interview to a Chinese news channel in 2013, describing how Beijing surrounds a contested island with circles of fishing boats, commercial ships and navy vessels in a manner that 'the island is thus wrapped layer by layer like a cabbage'.[79] Since then, China has claimed seven such islands, building military installations such as airfields, radar systems and missile defence technologies.

To push back against what the United States perceives to be a direct violation of the UNCLOS (which, hypocritically enough, the US has itself not signed on to), Secretary of State Hillary Clinton addressed a gathering of the ASEAN in 2010, declaring that 'Freedom of Navigation' was an important norm of a rules-based order, and that 'legitimate claims to maritime space in the South China Sea should be derived solely from legitimate claims to land features', in effect rejecting China's nine-dash line. A visibly flushed State Councillor for Foreign Affairs Yang Jiechi left the meeting for an hour or so, coming back only to be honest about China's point of view: 'China is a big country and other countries are small countries, and that's just a fact.'[80] While Yang's honesty left participants in the room stumped, China's script in the South China Sea is almost equivalent to how it treats its citizens at home: order and harmony are enforced by strict hierarchy and compliance. China's vision for

---

[79]Niharika Mandhana, 'China's Fishing Militia Swarms Philippine Island, Seeking Edge in Sea Dispute', *Wall Street Journal,* 4 April 2019.

[80]Ben Lowsen, 'China's Diplomacy Has A Monster In Its Closet', *The Diplomat,* 13 October 2018.

an international system only reflects its own expectations of order.

China, which has always entertained a long view on global systems, has been guided by how historical powers reached the apex of their influence—in November 2003, the then President Hu Jintao directed the Politburo to 'learn from and draw upon the historical experience of the leading nations of the world and their modernization processes,' and 'realise the strategy of catching up and overtaking the leaders in modernization' to fulfil the 'great rejuvenation of the Chinese nation'.[81] His direction to study major sea powers since the fifteenth century culminated in 2006 with the publication of several works on international maritime history as a part of a TV series titled *The Rise of Great Power*.[82] Two themes stood out: economic power generated through foreign trade and the indispensability of sea power to guarantee this growth. Ever since Xi Jinping took office as president, this imperative has been given top priority.

China's retired navy chief, Admiral Wu Shengli, himself a product of China's tumultuous birth in the mid-twentieth century is clear on why China lost the Opium Wars; in his speeches and writings, he has argued that China's century of humiliation was caused by insufficient naval power. From now onwards, 'the sea is no obstacle: the history of national humiliation is gone, never to return', he said. China's ambition could not have come at a better moment; its pursuit of regional hegemony comes at a time when America is wobbling under the throes of Trump's 'America First' rhetoric.[83] Free press and judiciary, human rights, free trade, and enforceable international rules in the Global Commons were the hallmark of an American-led order—the very ideas which took root in Germany and Japan, allowing them to spread around the world. China is

---

[81]C. J. Jenner and Tran T. Thuy (eds.), *The South China Sea: A Crucible of Regional Cooperation or Conflict Making Sovereignty Claims?*, Cambridge: Cambridge University Press, 2016, pp. 295–96.
[82]Id.
[83]Jeremy Page, 'As China Expands Its Navy, the U.S. Grows Wary', *Wall Street Journal*, 30 March 2015.

ambivalent about these values on all counts, and views American presence in the South China Sea as a remnant of its humiliation under foreign rule. In his widely acclaimed book, *Destined for War*, Graham Allison highlights the perils of the 'Thucydides Trap', where a rising power is inevitably destined for conflict with an existing power. Beginning with the rise of Athens, which sparked war with Sparta almost 2,500 years ago, Allison finds that in sixteen cases where a rising power threatened to displace an existing power, twelve of them ended in war. 'Americans urge other powers to accept a "rules-based international order,"' Allison writes. 'But through Chinese eyes, this appears to be an order in which Americans make the rules, and others obey the orders.'[84]

Influenced by American prodding, the Philippines ultimately chose to drag China to a tribunal set up under the United Nations Convention on the Law of the Sea and challenged the validity of the nine-dash line. Almost immediately China promised to ignore the ruling, going so far as to refuse participation in the process itself. Expressing unconcealed contempt for the UNCLOS, Yang Jeichi stated:

> The South China Sea arbitration has been a political farce all along, staged under the cover of law and driven by a hidden agenda. Certain countries outside the region have attempted to deny China's sovereign rights and interests in the South China Sea through the arbitration. They have even brought other countries into the scheme to isolate and discredit China in the international community with a view to holding back China's peaceful development. But such attempts are futile, to say the least, and in so doing, they are only lifting a stone to drop it on their own feet.[85]

After an international tribunal in the Hague ruled that almost all of China's claims under the nine-dash line were invalid, Chinese state

---

[84]Graham Allison, *Destined for War: Can America and China Escape Thucydides's Trap?*, New York: Houghton Mifflin Harcourt, 2017, p. 147.

[85]Howard W. French, *Everything Under The Heavens*, p. 82.

media responded simply by republishing the map unchanged and reaffirming that China's claims are historical and legitimate. China's legal claims are not worthy of mention for any legal power they might actually possess; there is a global consensus that China's claim on these waters is specious under international law. What is worth understanding, however, is China's clear and decisive rejection of the assumptions underlying the established international order, and its deep and abiding sense of historical imperialism—tianxia. In his book *The Tragedy of Great Power Politics*, American political scientist John Mearsheimer once compared Chinese behaviour to that of the US and asked: 'Why should we expect the Chinese to act any differently than the US did? Are they more principled than we are? More ethical? Less nationalistic? China's rise, if anything, follows an established pattern of great powers selectively ignoring rules and norms to serve its own interests.'[86]

While the tribunal's ruling delivered a victory to the Philippines— one that it most certainly cannot enforce—it was never really about the SCS; the real impact was to highlight how challenging China's rise as a global power would be to the received wisdom about the international system.

A RULES-BASED ORDER IN THE INDO-PACIFIC: INDIA AS A NORMATIVE POWER

China's maritime history was never limited only to the South China Sea. From 1405, the intrepid commander Zheng He would sail towards the Indian Ocean with an armada that rivalled even the largest of the European fleets: the largest of his ships was 440 feet long, making Christopher Columbus's 85-foot *Santa Maria* look miniature in comparison. They sailed past India, and through the Persian Gulf, and went as far as present-day Somalia and Kenya in East Africa, carrying about 27,000 soldiers on 250 ships.[87]

---

[86]John J. Mearsheimer, *The Tragedy of Great Power Politics*, New York: W. W. Norton, 2001.
[87]Vinod K. Aggarwal and Sara A. Newland (eds.), *Responding to China's Rise: US and EU Strategies,* London: Springer International Publishing, 2014, p. 60.

Twenty-first century China is no different. Through economic statecraft and military muscle-flexing, Beijing, as has been pointed out, has created a network of physical infrastructure and strategic dependency across the Pacific and Indian Ocean—a network that includes ports in Malaysia, Sri Lanka, Tanzania and Pakistan; oil and gas projects off the coast of Myanmar; and a military base in Djibouti. China intends to create institutions, rules, and norms which give it the ability to enforce its preferences across the region. From territorial reclamations, rejection of maritime-dispute arbitration, establishment of an air-defence identification zone, and confrontations with regional powers, a Sino-centric regional order suggests an authoritarian approach to the region.

Speaking about this region in Washington, former US Secretary of State Rex Tillerson put it quite bluntly: The world's 'center of gravity is shifting to the heart of the Indo-Pacific'.[88] Interestingly enough, even until a few years ago, the phrase 'Indo-Pacific' was scarcely used. Depending on whom you asked, the Pacific Ocean and the Indian Ocean were largely considered two separate spaces, with governments and scholars choosing to use the term 'Asia–Pacific' instead. Eventually, it made its way into the lexicon of scholars, policymakers, and capitals from a wide array of countries including Indonesia, Japan, Australia, and India. In a 2007 speech delivered at the Indian Parliament, Japanese Prime Minister Shinzo Abe spoke of the 'confluence of two seas. The Pacific and the Indian Oceans are now bringing about a dynamic coupling as seas of freedom and of prosperity,' he said. 'A "broader Asia" that broke away geographical boundaries is now beginning to take on a distinct form.'[89]

How world leaders and states conceptualize geography is not a matter left simply to cartographers; it creates a mental map of how powerful nations understand the world. The idea of the Indo-Pacific breaks down the idea of East and South Asia being two separate areas. At the same time, it captures three interrelated patterns of interactions

---

[88]Brahma Chellaney, 'Asia's New Entente', *The Strategist*, 6 November 2017.
[89]Sanjaya Baru, 'The importance of Shinzo Abe', *The Hindu*, 19 December 2012.

between the region's powers: the first is China's declared intention of developing a blue water navy and becoming a transcontinental economic giant. The second is India's emergence as a power to be reckoned with and a possible counterbalance to China. And the third, the role that the United States will play in shaping the contours of the seemingly irresistible shift in power from the Atlantic to Asia–Pacific. Taken together, the ideation of the 'Indo-Pacific region' captures the growing might, geopolitical interests, and normative visions of these powers, and its consequences for what is arguably the most dynamic region of the twenty-first century.

Continuing with his address, Tillerson outlined a vision for the United States and India, arguing that the two countries, 'with our shared goals of peace, security, freedom of navigation, and a free and open architecture—must serve as the eastern and western beacons of the Indo–Pacific. As the port and starboard lights between which the region can reach its greatest and best potential.' Tillerson sought a 'rules-based' order, which by its very definition denotes a predictable legalistic order. It implies that states will behave according to basic norms and standards. Clearly, China's aggression in the South China Sea, and its expansion into the Indian Ocean, is what prompted such calls.

That Tillerson should look to India to maintain this order is rather ironic considering India's ambivalence towards security pacts in Asia early in its history. In fact, in April 1955, Jawaharlal Nehru, prime minister of a poverty-stricken state still reeling from the violence of Partition and having only recently achieved independence, addressed the Asian–African Conference in Bandung. Here he denounced security pacts and great power politics, arguing that institutions such as SEATO and CENTO, the Central and South-East Asian counterparts to NATO, turned countries into camp followers, depriving them of their freedom and dignity. 'It is an intolerable thought to me,' he said, 'that the great countries of Asia and Africa should come out of bondage into freedom only to degrade themselves or humiliate themselves in this way.'[90] Since the articulation of its policy of non-alignment, India has a long history of vetoing the exercise of unilateral power by the West. While India is not a 'revisionist power' that seeks to completely redefine the contemporary international order, it does not seek to simply be 'co-opted into the existing international order that is controlled by the West' as former foreign secretary Kanwal Sibal noted. 'It must find its due place in it in its own right and be in a position to change the rules rather than simply adhere to existing ones.' India is now ready to move from being a rule-taker in the international system to a rule-maker in its own right.

It is unquestionable that India will have an outsized role to play in regional and global governance. As the world's largest democracy, and one of the leading economic powers, India's status on the global high table is increasingly being institutionalized. Gaining a seat on the G20, the global management table post 2008, itself reflected a shift from its usual solidarity with the G77, or the global trade union of developing countries. Even as India continued supporting many of the institutions and norms of the international liberal order, it has simultaneously invested in institutions that have called for a greater voice for emerging powers in global governance such as BRICS and the AIIB, despite the fact that these groupings and institutions were designed fundamentally to challenge some of the biases of the liberal world order. In today's multi-conceptual world, India's foreign policy is best described by what the late Atal Bihari Vajpayee once called 'alignment with all'. It is fair to argue that New Delhi has evolved well beyond non-alignment to what may be dubbed 'multi-alignment'. BRICS itself is a prime example of this. Within this group, India is part of two other 'minilaterals', or mini-multilateral groupings: the Russia–India–China (RIC) grouping, where India engages with two revisionist autocratic powers, and the India–Brazil–South Africa (IBSA) dialogue, where it seeks South–South cooperation with two other regional democratic powers. In

---

[90]Luis Eslava, Michael Fakhri, and Vasuki Nesiah (eds.), *Bandung, Global History, and International Law*, p. 60.

addition, it joined Brazil, South Africa and China in the BASIC grouping for environmental negotiations.

Having said that, Indian leaders have always been acutely aware of India's manifest destiny in Asia. Perhaps an early intimation of India's world view was articulated by the nationalist leader Bal Gangadhar Tilak in his letter to Georges Clemenceau, at the time of the Paris Peace Conference in 1919: 'India is self-contained, harbours no design on the integrity of other states, and has no ambition outside India. With her vast area, enormous resources and prodigious population, she may well aspire to be a leading power in Asia. She should, therefore, be a powerful steward of the League of Nations in the East for Maintaining Peace in the world.'[91] It was as if greatness would come to India if it was left to its own devices, a sentiment which was echoed even by Nehru. In a speech in March 1949, Nehru stated: 'Remember that India, not because of any ambition of hers, but because of the force of circumstances, because of geography, because of history and because of so many other things, inevitably has to play a very important part in Asia.'

It appears that the reverberation of these sentiments was loud enough for Prime Minister Narendra Modi to hear them in 2014. No longer is India a fledgling post-colonial state determined to protect its 'strategic autonomy' in order to avoid capitulating to the machinations of great power politics. It is now a $3 trillion economy, and against all odds, a vibrant, multicultural democracy. It is home to over a billion individuals, has one of the largest standing armies in the world, and is a declared nuclear power. It is unsurprising perhaps, that when the Indian public delivered to the BJP an electoral majority not seen since 1984, Modi exhorted the Indian foreign service 'to help India position itself in a leading role, rather than [as] just a balancing force, globally.' And as a leading power, New Delhi is intent on ensuring that it is an indispensable actor in shaping the future of the Asian century, and the world at large.

---

[91]Urmila Sharma and S. K. Sharma, *Indian Political Thought*, New Delhi: Atlantic Publishers & Distributors, 2001, p. 117.

Prime Minister Modi's visit to Davos in Switzerland, the exclusive and reclusively-located annual gathering of global elites, perhaps best exemplifies this new-found swagger. While the headlines were undoubtedly concerned about India's appeal as an investment destination, it is more worthwhile to note that Prime Minister Modi also made it a point to reaffirm—in unstated contrast to China—India's commitment to globalization, multilateralism and a rules-based international order. That New Delhi was making these commitments is an extraordinary turn of affairs in itself. Modi was conscious that the archetypal Davos man is under fire: communities who are living though the most unequal era in modern history are rapidly losing faith in the idea of globalization, and are increasingly intent on withdrawing into cultural identities. Democracy is declining throughout the world, and trade protectionism is on the rise. Ironically, the origins of these seismic disruptions lie in the very states which carefully crafted and nurtured the international liberal order—the United States and the United Kingdom.

Perhaps, though, the Indian approach was calibrated to respond to the larger geopolitical shifts that are underway—specifically, the new power that has staked its claim to the throne: China. Even as Trump was furiously tweeting his strategy to 'Make America Great Again', President Xi Jinping likened protectionism to 'locking oneself in a dark room' at the WEF in 2017. While China is 'committed to a fundamental policy of opening-up', he said, it 'also shares more of its development outcomes with other countries'.[92] No one would accuse President Xi of failing to back his words with action with initiatives such as its Belt and Road Initiative.

Having said that, leadership with Chinese characteristics is anything but liberal. Beijing is almost too willing to work with non-democratic regimes and regional strongmen, and turning a blind eye to human rights violations. International law applies to China only to the extent that it serves its own interests, evidenced by Beijing's militarization of the South China Sea. It is in the BRI—

---

[92]'Commitment to opening up the Chinese market', *Irish Times*, 31 October 2018.

China's shining model of 'win-win' cooperation—where many of these contradictions are glaringly visible. As we have seen, former Sri Lankan Prime Minister Mahinda Rajapaksa, for example, is currently facing corruption charges over the Hambantota Port, a project which has indebted the island state to Beijing. The United Nations has recorded its hesitations over 'mega-connectivity' projects like the BRI due to limited environmental and labour protection standards. Moreover, as has been noted, in Africa, Beijing's asymmetric trade power and debt-based economic grants has earned it the moniker of a 'new colonial power'.

Piece by piece, China is dismantling the essence of a liberal world order, aided in part by the disruptions in the West. If the 2008 financial crises opened Western-led international financial institutions to criticism, the election of Trump and the Brexit vote have thrown into question their political systems. At the 19th CPC inaugural address, then, President Xi had enough reason to be unabashed about his disdain for Western liberalism. In its place, 'Socialism with Chinese Characteristics for a new era' is the ideology he will continue to sell to the world. Through the BRI, Eurasia and the 'Indo–Pacific'— geostrategic counterpoints to the Euro–Atlantic system—will be his testing ground. Through debt, coercion, force, and bondage, Pax Sinica will be defined by the submissiveness of its beneficiaries and subjects to the Middle Kingdom.

In the shadow of China's hegemonic ambitions, however, another Asian power has been quietly building its own foreign policy consensus. In 2015, New Delhi committed the full force of its political capital towards securing the Paris Agreement on climate change, following almost two decades of thumb-twiddling. If India's position was not entirely surprising, what was less predictable is that it has only strengthened its commitment despite America's withdrawal from the Paris accord. When India lost a maritime dispute with its significantly smaller neighbour, Bangladesh, at an international tribunal, it chose to peacefully comply with the verdict, in contrast to China's own disdain for maritime law in relation to the South China Sea. At the most recent WTO meeting in Argentina, India led the charge to salvage trade talks, in sharp contrast to America's diffidence, and its own earlier reticence in 2008.

More important, perhaps, for the future of the Indo–Pacific order and the world at large, India was the first power to see the BRI for what it is: an exercise in hardwiring influence in the region through economic and military prowess.[93] The sixty-odd nations that have signed on to the BRI are small countries desperate for infrastructure finance and trade. Currently, the promise of Beijing's bank account outweighs concerns of political systems, financial prudence and sovereignty. New Delhi is acutely aware of the adverse effects that China's actions can have on the region: it observed with dismay as Sri Lanka handed over the Hambantota Port to China and when ASEAN was unable to develop a unified response to China's assertiveness in the South China Sea. What truly jarred New Delhi was the construction of new roads and energy projects in Gilgit–Baltistan—a territory that New Delhi has long claimed is India's, occupied illegally by Pakistan, and which China itself acknowledges as disputed.

In May 2017, China hosted a plethora of world leaders to present a comprehensive agenda for the Belt and Road Initiative. A wide-ranging media blitz took place including television programmes, social media campaigns, and cultural events—including children's stories extolling the virtues of Xi Jinping and the BRI. Even international media outlets in America and Europe were introduced to the BRI for the first time. While leaders from these countries were performing a twenty-first-century kowtow to Beijing at the Belt and Road Initiative Forum, India refused to attend. Instead, New Delhi released a press release which cogently argued that connectivity in Asia must be consultative, and guided by internationally-recognized norms such as transparent financial guidelines, principles of good governance, internationally recognized environmental and labour standards, and respect for sovereignty. It was implicit that India believes that the

---

[93]Samir Saran, 'India sees the Belt and Road Initiative for what it is: evidence of China's unconcealed ambition for hegemony', ORF, 19 February 2018.

BRI does not adhere to any of these norms. India's refusal to sign on to China's initiative was not surprising; for a country that has always preferred multipolarity and multilateralism, both globally and regionally, acquiescing in Pax Sinica was never truly an option.

India's invocation of responsible 'norms' was in itself an extraordinary sign of determination and a baseline which other powers seem to have accepted. In October 2017, former US Defense Secretary General James Mattis signalled for the first time that the US harboured concerns about China's BRI initiative. 'In a globalized world, there are many belts and many roads,' he explained in congressional testimony.[94] Speaking at the Indo–Pacific Oration in New Delhi in July 2017, former Australian Foreign Affairs Minister Julie Bishop stated that her objective for the Indo–Pacific is for 'Australia to be an active participant, in partnership with other nations, in ensuring that a predictable international rules-based order is respected and upheld, as the foundation for peaceful cooperation in the region.'[95] The Trump administration's articulation of the Indo–Pacific dream at the East Asia Summit in Manila, went so far as to replicate India's language on 'responsible financing arrangements' and 'good governance' for infrastructure projects.[96]

India's defiance of what it views as Beijing's attempt to cement its hegemony in Asia was not without its costs: months after New Delhi's overt opposition to the BRI, India and China were locked in a dispute over a 69-square-kilometre piece of land located at the tri-junction between India, Bhutan, and China. The trouble began when Chinese workers began construction on the disputed territory in Doklam. India's response was swift—troops were sent into Bhutan to halt road-building. In the intervening seventy-three days, Indian and Chinese troops were locked in an eyeball-to-eyeball stand-off in a low-intensity conflict. Reactions from Chinese state-owned media

---

[94]Wade Shepard, 'Why The Ambiguity Of China's Belt And Road Initiative Is Perhaps Its Biggest Strength', *Forbes*, 19 October 2017.

[95]'We Must Continue to Engage Closely with China: Australian FM', ORF, 27 July 2017.

[96]Sarah Watson, 'India in Trump's Asia', *CogitASIA*, 27 November 2017.

were quick to berate India's actions: 'India didn't learn lessons from 1962 border war', claimed the *Global Times*, threatening that 'if India keeps ignoring China's warnings, war is inevitable.'[97] Of course, the numbers support China's belligerence: its military spending outstrips India's by almost four times, and its economy is nearly five times larger than India's. The underlying theme was simple: China is a bigger country, and India must acquiesce in its subordinate place, on the border, in the region, and in the world. To its credit, India did not blink, and the stand-off was ended diplomatically.

It would be a mistake to view the border dispute purely in terms of territorial sovereignty, when in fact it was principally about who would get to write the rules of the Asian century.[98] Simply put, China's economic rise over the past three decades inevitably altered the balance of power between the two countries, with China coming out decisively on top. Having said that, simply by virtue of India's own economic growth and continental size, it was never likely that New Delhi would be relegated to a bit player in Asia, or indeed the world. The stand-off on Doklam was the harbinger of a larger question that begets exploring: will China call the shots in Asia, dictating to smaller states what behaviour it considers acceptable, or will Asia truly be multipolar, as India desires? This is why India's defiance over the BRI, and again on Doklam, ruffled feathers in Beijing. Since it began its quest for great power status, no country in the world—not even the United States—has had the courage or the temerity to enter an area over which Beijing claims sovereignty and force it to retreat. India's defiance of China was a unique moment. That China stood down, at least for now, made it all the more rare. The spectre of an invincible fire-breathing dragon did not awe India. Instead New Delhi proved that other countries must, and can, stand up to China when their national interests are at stake.[99]

---

[97]'If India keeps ignoring China's warnings, war is inevitable', *Global Times*, 7 August 2017.

[98]Samir Saran and Wang Dong, 'There is standoff between China and India in the Himalayas. Both sides explain', WEF, 16 August 2017.

[99]Samir Saran, 'How India has actually done a great job in dealing with the Dragon',

Undoubtedly, it is this very tension in the Indo–Pacific that has driven a new security formation in the Indo–Pacific, 'the Quad'. The Quadrilateral Security Dialogue (QSD) was an idea that was mooted almost ten years ago in Manila by representatives from India, Japan, Australia, and the United States. The initiative sought to facilitate a conversation between these maritime powers in the context of a rising and assertive China. Ironically, it was in deference to Chinese interests that the original Quad fell apart, with India in the throes of a coalition government that could not justify a security partnership with the US, and Australia struggling to balance its rising economic ties with China and security commitments with the US. Coincidentally enough, it was in Manila last year, where these very Indo–Pacific democracies agreed that, 'a free, open, prosperous and inclusive Indo–Pacific region serves the long-term interests of all countries in the region and of the world at large.'[100] India is poised to form the linchpin of this initiative given its geography and regional influence. Aligning with a 'concert of democracies', as the Quad is often known, is an important indication of the norms India wants to see take root in the Indo–Pacific. 'Indians and Americans don't just share an affinity for democracy. We share a vision of the future,' Tillerson said. 'China, while rising alongside India, has done so less responsibly, at times undermining the international, rules-based order...that both the United States and India stand for,' he added.[101]

In 2005, Beijing was still 'biding and hiding' to paraphrase Deng Xiaoping. It had effectively sold the narrative of China's 'peaceful rise', of a country intent on focusing on its domestic growth. Things changed in 2008 with the onset of the financial crisis and the decline of Western economic power. Today, a more assertive Chinese policy has taken root: from its disputes in the South China Sea, to the strategic impact of the BRI, China's rise seems not entirely peaceful

---

ORF, 2 November 2017.
[100]Premesha Saha, 'The Quad in the Indo-Pacific: Why ASEAN Remains Cautious', ORF Issue Brief, Issue No. 229, February 2018.
[101]Carol Morello, 'Tillerson Chides China While Calling for Greater Ties with India', *Washington Post*, 18 October 2017.

and not entirely domestic-focused, and is raising concerns across Asia and the world. Indeed, each of the Quad's member countries have their own axe to grind with China: Tokyo has been embroiled in a territorial dispute over the Senkaku Islands; Australia is coming to terms with the extent of China's influence operations at home; India is increasingly positioning itself as a strategic competitor following the Doklam stand-off; and the United States seeks to consolidate its influence in Asia. While the Quad has never explicitly referenced China in any of its official statements, the subtext behind this initiative is evident, at least to Beijing. As early as 2014, the *Global Times* cautioned against endorsing the idea of an 'Indo–Pacific' region, writing that Indians would never endorse the idea; and that instead, it was an initiative scripted by the United States and its allies 'to balance and even contain China's increasing influence in the Asia-Pacific region and the Indian Ocean.'[102]

As a result, the Indo–Pacific—which spans the West Indian Ocean and stretches towards the Western Pacific—is now primed to become the battleground for the future of the liberal order. It is clear that within this space, India will increasingly exercise its political, economic and normative influence. At the WEF in 2019, Modi echoed President Xi's sentiments on economic integration, stating that the solution to the backlash against globalization is not isolation, it is in 'understanding and accepting change'. Where China and India converge on economics, the differences in their political outlook could not be more stark: Modi made it clear that India's democracy is a force for stability in a world that is otherwise in 'a state of uncertainty and flux'. Far from being a business visit, it was an indication that India is willing to preserve, and redefine, the liberal world, even as the Western world struggles to maintain it and China attempts to undermine, if not dismantle, it.

If anything, Prime Minister Modi's visit to Davos was a culmination of developments in 2017, and is a natural extension of

---

[102]Gurpreet S. Khurana, 'Trump's New Cold War Alliance in Asia is Dangerous', *Washington Post*, 14 November 2017.

India's declared ambition of emerging as a 'leading power'—a unique phrase which describes a unique civilization. Even as enthusiasm for globalization seems to be waning in the West, both the Indian public and the government continue to support the project. Even as the limits of multiculturalism are becoming apparent in the Atlantic system, India's civilizational bias towards plurality will help preserve it. And even as China attempts to create an autocratic and unipolar Asia, New Delhi's approach will be defined by a natural affinity for multipolarity, democracy, multiculturalism and respect for the rule of law. That Modi's visit followed Xi's—who himself was the first Chinese leader to attend Davos—was no coincidence; it was a statement of intent.

Wang Yi, China's current foreign minister, once called India a 'tribal democracy'. In some ways, he is not wrong: India's democracy is often chaotic and its economic choices do not always match its foreign policy rhetoric. Yet, as this imperfect democracy and its 1.2 billion people transition from a $2 trillion economy to a $5 trillion one in the coming years, the choices India makes and the partnerships it embraces will implicate the future of the world at large.

CHAPTER 6

THE INDIAN IMPERATIVE

There will be no day of days then when a new world order comes into being. Step by step and here and there it will arrive, and even as it comes into being it will develop fresh perspectives, discover unsuspected problems and go on to new adventures. No man, no group of men, will ever be singled out as its father or founder. For its maker will be not this man nor that man nor any man but Man, that being who is in some measure in every one of us... The new order will be incessant; things will never stop happening, and so it defies any Utopian description.

H. G. Wells, *The New World Order* (1940)

Looking at the world in the 1990s, one could be forgiven for being an optimist. The collapse of the Soviet Union marked the demise of communism and heralded the inexorable march of democracy. That Russia had subsequently embraced political freedom under Boris Yeltsin, and that China had committed towards economic integration led observers to believe that the American way of life would soon be universal. Such hubris was characteristic of the post-Cold War thinking. Globalization—many believed—would leave nations with no choice but to liberalize, first economically and then politically. As incomes grew, citizens would demand greater political power and nations would have no choice but to cede to these demands. The world would be increasingly 'flat', to use Thomas Friedman's optimistic phraseology.

Democratic capitalism was seen as the only model for success, and it was assumed that all societies would inevitably choose this path. 'At the end of history,' as Fukuyama famously put it, 'there are no serious ideological competitors left to liberal democracy.'[1] With the end of the Cold War, history as a process of ideological contestation had ended; all nations would embrace free-market economics to make their people rich, and choose democratic governments to make their citizens free. 'What we may be witnessing,' Fukuyama wrote, 'is not just the end of the Cold War, or the passing of a particular period of postwar history, but the end of history as such: that is, the end point of mankind's ideological evolution and the universalization of Western liberal democracy as the final form of human government.' He was undoubtedly inspired by the numbers: From fifty-one democracies in 1988 to sixty-nine by 1992, the world saw a remarkable 66 per cent increase in the number of free countries in just four years around the end of the Cold War.[2] In the global marketplace of ideas, Fukuyama averred, liberal capitalist democratic internationalism had triumphed. The international system itself would be based on respect for sovereignty and the rule of law. New frontiers in human rights were being established. And new institutions were built to promote human rights, ensure collective security and encourage trade and investment such as the United Nations, the World Bank and the World Trade Organization. All of this was underwritten by a network of military alliances between the United States, Europe, and certain Asian states.

Today, the seventy years of (relative) post-war peace, as we have noted throughout the book, it appears, is coming to an end—and the reasons are as multifaceted as they are complex. In many ways, the 'liberal international order' is coming to terms with its own contradictions—or as Richard Haass quips, it is increasingly evident that this order was 'neither liberal nor worldwide nor orderly'.[3] There is merit in Haass's view, even as it is clear that an international order

---

[1]Fukuyama, 'The End of History'.
[2]Max Roser, 'Democracy'.
[3]Richard Haass, 'Liberal World Order, R.I.P.', *Project Syndicate*, 21 March 2018.

based on liberal institutions did come into being after 1945, and that its future is widely seen as being in jeopardy.

As one of the most prominent advocates of the idea of a liberal international order, the late John McCain, put it in *The Economist*, this new order was based on the rejection of all that led to two World Wars: 'It was based not on ethno-nationalism, spheres of influence and might-makes-right imperialism,' he argued, 'but rather on universal values, human rights, rule of law, open commerce and national sovereignty.' This 'world order' was made up of an international structure of institutions, norms, partnerships, and relationships that regulated a global balance of power, promoted collaboration over competition (and managed the latter when it was unavoidable, as in elections to UN bodies), kept world peace and promoted shared prosperity. The major elements that sustained the liberal world order included the rule of law and the supremacy of a rules-based order, freer trade arrangements than in the past, multilateral cooperation, respect for human rights and humanitarian action in favour of refugees and other marginalized groups, and global support for the economic development of poorer countries. The dollar served for all practical purposes as the de facto global currency, the hard currency of first resort for international transactions.

Upholding and implementing these norms were a set of international institutions: the UN system, which involved not only the well-known Security Council and the General Assembly of member states, but organizations directed by the secretary-general and his civil service to conduct peacekeeping operations and promote social and economic development; the major global economic institutions, including the World Bank, IMF, the Bank for International Settlements (BIS), the GATT (later WTO); humanitarian organizations, like UNICEF and UNHCR; regional political and economic organizations, such as the EU, ASEAN, and AU; more informal organizations and processes, from major summit conferences on issues ranging from the environment to the children's rights, to non-UN-sanctioned but globally recognized groupings like the G7 (later G8) to the G77 (soon to include more than 130 member states of the UN) and the G20. Arguably, if more contentiously, the international order also embraced the Truman Doctrine, the Marshall Plan, NATO, the North American Free Trade Agreement (NAFTA), ASEAN, the Warsaw Pact and other regional groupings, all of which functioned within the broad set of rules established in 1945. The international order underpinned by these institutions was liberal in that it sought to make the world safe for free markets and liberal democracy, and that it was based on the rule of law, established through negotiated international treaties and conventions implemented by these international organizations.

Of course, this represents a somewhat idealized picture of the liberal international order, which, truth be told, was not always liberal and in many places far from orderly. The notion of a liberal order rests implicitly on an acceptance of the idea of American primacy, with the United States initially prepared to bear a significant part of the costs, make much of the diplomatic effort (in concert with its allies), and seek to remould a good part of the world in its own image through the advocacy of democratic and market reforms. In return, though, the United States did not totally bind itself to the rules of the system it was upholding. In the name of defending democracy and free markets, it frequently broke the liberal rules it had underwritten, whether of sovereignty or self-determination, human rights or even liberalism itself. The Bay of Pigs invasion, the use of napalm in Vietnam, support for the Pakistani military dictatorship during its genocide in Bangladesh, backing for the repressive policies of the Shah of Iran and an assortment of illiberal Latin American military juntas and African dictatorships, and the overthrow of democratically-elected governments in an appallingly long list of countries (Albania, Argentina, Chile, Cuba, the Dominican Republic, El Salvador, Ghana, Greece, Grenada, Guatemala, Iran, Nicaragua, and South Vietnam) are merely some examples to suggest that violence, coercion, rule-breaking and unprincipled power politics frequently trumped liberal principles.

As Canada's former leader of the Opposition, Michael Ignatieff, put it: 'It means laying down the rules America wants (on everything from markets to weapons of mass destruction) while exempting itself from other rules (the Kyoto Protocol on climate change and the International Criminal Court) that go against its interest.[4] So consistency was not always, and hypocrisy often was, the hallmark of the liberal international order.

Nonetheless, the overall order was maintained as long as the US remained committed to it, and the world prospered in relative peace. But as Senator McCain lamented shortly before his death: 'We have seen the steady erosion of the world order. As many across the globe turned away from universal values, they found comfort in the old ties of ethnicity, race, and sectarianism. They became increasingly resentful of "the other" they saw in immigrants, refugees, and minority groups. They turned inward and embraced nationalism. Some seem to have given up on the liberal order entirely, preferring chaos to a system that does not seem to have worked for them.'[5] In this he was ironically echoing former US Vice President Joe Biden's call in the final Davos session of the Obama administration to 'act urgently to defend the liberal international order'.[6] Scholars and pundits have been even more alarmist: one has spoken of the 'end of the West as we know it', another of the abandonment of 'global leadership' by its 'long-time champion', a third pundit of a 'coming Dark Age'. Professor Patrick Porter, reviewing these quotes, adds: '*Foreign Affairs*, the house organ of the foreign policy establishment, recently asked 32 experts whether the "liberal order is in peril." Most agreed it is, with 26 respondents registering a confidence level of 7 out of 10.'[7]

The reason for all this undoubtedly lies in a significant change in the attitude of the US administration, which is currently retreating behind a wall, both literally and metaphorically, and seems more interested in keeping the world out than in running it. In his book

---

[4]Michael Ignatieff, 'The American Empire: The Burden', *New York Times*, 5 January 2003.

[5]John McCain, 'Words That Matter', *Medium*, 7 December 2017.

[6]Remarks by Vice President Joe Biden at the World Economic Forum, Office of the Vice President, The White House, 18 January 2017.

[7]'Is the Liberal Order in Peril?', *Foreign Affairs*, undated.

Governing the World: The History of an Idea, Mark Mazower explained that the US government made the case for the UN to the American people by preaching 'a pragmatic realism—the new international organization was a vital necessity, even if it would not solve all the world's problems.'[8] The Trump administration has gone further than its predecessors in expressing its disinclination to make this case, preferring to see the world as a series of transactional bilateral relationships and the 'world's problems' as no longer America's principal concern. US support for the UN has never been more lukewarm. The reasons for this development, going well beyond the US, are not hard to discern.

For one thing, the foundations of political liberalism were underwritten by a rising and prosperous Western middle class following World War II—a status quo that is no longer true in the twenty-first century. In fact, between 2005 and 2014, real incomes in developed countries fell or were flat for about 540 million individuals.[9] For many in the West, there is a sense that international liberalism, a project that was encouraged by the relentless thrust of global free market competition and cultural integration, has only served to accentuate inequality and erode government control over social welfare. The numbers bear testament to their intuition: as has been noted, the richest 1 per cent own nearly 82 per cent of the world's wealth and global inequality is at its highest in modern history. In November 2016, an *Economist* poll found that less than half of Americans, Britons, and French believed that globalization was a 'force for good'.[10]

Technology has accelerated the pressures for change. The Panama Papers have illustrated that even political leaders are no longer invulnerable within their borders. Parking money abroad is no longer safe; a single data leak can lead to widespread geopolitical disruption,

---

[8]Mark Mazower, *Governing the World: The History of an Idea*, New York: Penguin Books, 2012.

[9]Richard Dobbs et al., 'Poorer than their parents? A new perspective on income inequality', McKinsey Global Institute, July 2016.

[10]'What the world thinks about globalisation', *The Economist*, 18 November 2016.

a prime ministerial resignation in Iceland can cause chaos; a judicial case in Pakistan can have global consequences. Whether we like it or not, what happens in East Asia or South Africa—from protectionist politics to corruption cases unseating rulers, from trade sanctions to the fight against AIDS—can affect your lives wherever you live. And your own choices anywhere—what you buy, how you vote—can resound far away, as we have all seen with the worldwide reactions and economic tremors following the election of Donald Trump and the ongoing drama of Brexit.

While, overall, globalization has made the world a better, safer, and more prosperous place, it must be admitted that the manner in which benefits have been distributed has been uneven. In the last twenty years in particular, inequalities in income have become stark and many of the promises globalization widely advertised during its heady rush have not actually been delivered. This has led to resentment and rejection from both the left and the right. In the US alone we have seen the Occupy Wall Street movement of those young people claiming to represent the excluded 99 per cent, the insurgency of Bernie Sanders, and then the revolt of the unemployed, bitter, increasingly xenophobic white blue-collar voters who have propelled Trump into the White House. During the time of the US elections, the liberal elite order was so confident that Hillary Clinton, a capable but somewhat controversial candidate, would win, that in one case, PaddyPower, an online betting platform, gave away the winnings to those who had decided to bet on Clinton even before the ballots had been cast. The subsequent vote against Clinton was in large part because she was seen as being part of a globalized elite linked to Wall Street. Globalization has become a bad word.

Since taking office in 2016, Trump has levelled fierce attacks on global institutions and global governance. He has repeatedly attacked the concept of 'globalism', pulled out of the Trans-Pacific Partnership and the Paris Agreement, blocked the appointment of judges to the WTO, imposed tariffs on steel and aluminium in the name of national security, started a trade war with China, withdrawn from the Iran nuclear deal and imposed sanctions on Iranian oil trade.

The 2008 economic crisis seems to have been a turning point—the financial analyst and author Ruchir Sharma refers to our times as BC (Before Crisis) and AC (After Crisis).[11] The pre-2008 BC years were full of optimism, despite smaller economic crises in different parts of the world. There was confidence that the poor were becoming richer, millions of people were rising out of poverty every year, democracy and freedom were inevitable even in the worst dictatorships, and that the world itself had transformed into one 'global village'. It felt like a sort of historic golden age had begun, and there was every reason to be seduced by this narrative when the going was good.

But 2008 changed all that. What we see and hear now is more and more talk about anti-globalization. The numbers speak for themselves. At the peak of what many see as the earlier era of globalization, in 1914, just before World War I disrupted international commerce, trade accounted for about 12 per cent of global GDP. By the year 2000, global exports alone had risen to 20 per cent of global GDP. Those are exports: that meant that the sum total of imports and exports, or global trade as a whole, stood at about 50 per cent of world GDP. In some countries, like Singapore or Belgium, trade was worth much more than 100 per cent of GDP. It has all gone downhill since.

In 2007, the flow of capital reached a record high of $9 trillion with a 25 per cent share of the global economy. In 2014, the year Prime Minister Modi came to power in India as an anti-status quo, anti-ancien regime hero, the flow of capital stood at $1.2 trillion or 2 per cent of the global economy—the same percentage value as in 1980. The world, in terms of numbers, had gone back decades, and global trade has been growing at a pace slower than the global economy, at less than 2.5 per cent. At the time of the crisis, 186 per cent of Singapore's GDP and 60 per cent of Taiwan's were derived from exports. But once the crisis began and global trade took a

---

[11]'India disappoints optimists, and pessimists: economic analyst Ruchir Sharma (IANS Interview)', *Business Standard*, 3 July 2016.

beating, their economies started to shrink at alarming rates, and they began to look to other means of growth rather than relying excessively on global trade.

Meanwhile, in the developed world, populist objections arose to globalization in its current avatar. For instance, China's trade with its Western partners has brought vast benefits to consumers in the West. But it is equally true that large numbers of workers in the West have lost their jobs in the process. The response from leaders has been increasing political denunciation of global trade, hostility—even violence—towards foreigners, and imposition of austerity measures, which also tend to hurt the poor more. The poor and the unemployed then see that they have no stake in the globalized system, demand to know why government policies benefit people in faraway lands with what used to be their jobs, and want to go back to the security of older, more familiar economic ways and the comforts of traditional identity.

Protectionist barriers have begun to go up in those very nations that had for years advocated the free flow of goods, labour, and capital—an irony that would have been funny had it not smelt a great deal like hypocrisy. Trump promises to bring back jobs that have been 'lost' to China. Neighbours have become less welcome in many countries of the West, international banks became increasingly nervous about issuing loans abroad, and, tellingly, in the last decade, according to Freedom House, the number of states in which political rights have been declining has surpassed those in which they have been increasing.[12] Sixty-eight countries around the world find themselves with some degree of loss of freedom in this last decade. The number of democracies has not reduced—but within these democracies, freedom has been slowly but steadily diluted. Institutions we were certain are here to stay seem to be hollowing out into under-performing shells. Populism, nationalism, and authoritarianism are all on the rise.

The wave of rising right-wing populism that is engulfing Europe

---

[12]'Freedom in the World 2019', Freedom House, 2019, https://freedomhouse.org/report/freedom-world/freedom-world-2019.

is illustrative of this trend. Support for anti-system, populist parties in Europe, such as the National Front in France, Syriza in Greece and the Five Star Movement in Italy are only the more absolute examples. This is occurring when there seems to be the real risk of a power vacuum in Europe. While Austria, France, Germany and the Netherlands appear to have bucked the trend, the fact remains that populists in these countries made some of the political largest gains ever. Marine Le Pen's National Front's support has diminished in the final stages of the last two presidential elections but it would be silly to write her off given that her racist National Front has reached the final hurdle twice. Her appeal is based on her mandate of promising to remove France from the European Union and the Eurozone in addition to adopting a hardline stance on immigration and Islam. Her 2017 defeat by Emmanuel Macron does not mean that the forces she represents have begun to retreat altogether.

Similarly, in Germany, Chancellor Angela Markel's decision to allow nearly a million refugees to enter Germany resulted in a serious dent to her popularity and ratings in 2015, while her rivals exploited the paranoia this created. The rise of an almost neo-Nazi German populism is embodied in AfD, a far-right party that excels in generating even more paranoia. Even though Merkel, who is widely seen as the liberal West's last 'tall' leader, succeeded in winning the 2017 elections, the campaign weakened her position significantly, raising doubts on whether she will indeed be able to hold the European Union together or prevent [in Ishaan Tharoor's words] 'a pronounced polarisation on both sides of the Atlantic'.[13]

Populism has already begun undermining the institutions of the liberal international order. As Pratap Bhanu Mehta puts it:

> The liberal order, in part, rested on the conceit that institutional orders can be insulated from politics. The Right has essentially been able to make that argument (which the Left used to make), that insulation is simply a ruse to get particular cultural

---

[13]Ishaan Tharoor, 'It Will be a Total Disaster if Marine Le Pen Wins the National Elections', *Washington Post*, 9 March 2017.

and technological elites power. They have also been able to make the case that this insulation is essentially protecting those elites from popular pressure. These institutions act as a fifth column for the old order. Therefore, it will become easier to attack institutions.[14]

Then there is the matter of geopolitical instability. In early 2016, the prospect of Britain and the US becoming major sources of geopolitical instability would have been received with disbelief or even ridicule, but at the time nobody thought Brexit would pass and Trump would win. Once both those things have happened, the world is not the same. We are all used to North Korea saying and doing crazy things; could the man in the White House writing his angry 3 a.m. tweets surprise us as much as the man in Pyongyang? But while it may appear that the doom of anti-globalization is upon us, our view is that globalization is not retreating but merely in the throes of a major structural (and inevitable) readjustment.

THE RESTRICTING OF GLOBALIZATION

What shape that adjustment will take is still impossible to foretell. Obituaries for globalization are premature: we are not about to unravel the internet, or cut the connections that allow you to move billions with the click of a mouse, or call back the jet planes, or switch off the satellite dishes. Our connections are irreversible, even if the policies that have sustained them can be temporarily halted, and even if countries that were amongst the principal cheerleaders for globalization have now become the ones who are betraying the very principles they preached to us for the last three decades. The need for a recasting of the hallowed liberal international order is acute.

But geopolitics are as important as geo-economics, and one of the great uncertainties of our present times is what an 'America First' foreign policy might mean in practice. America First and the liberal world order, as Haass has pointed out, seem incompatible. Is this

---

[14]Pratap Bhanu Mehta, 'A Darkening Horizon', *Indian Express*, 2 November 2018.

the end of what Ian Bremmer calls 'U.S. hegemony in security, trade, and the promotion of values [which] provided baseline predictability for the global economy?'[15] If so, what will the new unpredictability consist of? American unilateralism could continue to spring a few surprises year after year.

One activity the US has embarked on over the last quarter-century that it may be less inclined to pursue in the new era is that of 'humanitarian intervention'. This was often a thin disguise for regime change, but always justified with lofty principles: Bill Clinton extolled 'democratic enlargement' and George W. Bush championed a 'freedom agenda'. Such principles resulted in the US-sponsored overthrows of President Slobodan Miloševic in Serbia and President Saddam Hussein in Iraq.

In 2000, the international community—gathered together at the level of Heads of State and Government at a Millennium Summit at UN Headquarters in New York—endorsed the idea that they had a collective responsibility to protect civilians whose own governments were unable or unwilling to do so. Sovereignty was all very well, the world leaders agreed, but it came with certain duties to the people in whose name it was exercised, and if sovereign governments couldn't prevent massive human rights abuses (or worse, inflicted them on their own people), then the world had the duty to do something about it. The new doctrine was immediately dubbed 'R2P', short for 'Responsibility to Protect'.

This was a twist to the earlier arguments for 'the right to humanitarian intervention', turning the issue on its head: the principle was no longer about the right of foreigners to intervene in third countries for humanitarian purposes ('le droit d'ingérence', in the French phrase of its staunchest advocates), but rather their responsibility to protect people, if necessary through intervention. The evocative image behind R2P was that of the 1994 genocide in Rwanda, when perhaps a million people died in a mass slaughter

---

[15]Ian Bremmer, 'These Are the Top 10 Risks to the World in 2017', *Time*, 3 January 2017.

conducted by machete-wielding Tutsi militia—a horror that could have been prevented had the international community taken on such a responsibility, and intervened with a few thousand troops, instead of withdrawing the UN Blue Helmets who already happened to be there.[16]

It all sounded very noble and altruistic. The UK's telegenic and hyper-articulate former prime minister, Tony Blair, memorably declared that in the future, the West would go to war in the name of its values, not just of its interests. The wars of the future, Blair and his acolytes argued, would be fought for peace and human rights, not over something as crass as national interests, oil (perish the thought!) or imperial lust for territorial aggrandizement. The only catch in all this was in applying the principle to an actual case. As Rwanda had revealed, governments were all-too-unwilling to risk blood and treasure for the sake of foreign lives. Would armies actually intervene out of disinterested humanitarianism, or only do so when such declared intent in fact masked more cynical motives?[17]

Indeed, the first major military intervention after the Millennium Summit—the Iraq war in 2003—was initially sought to be couched in the language of humanitarianism by its proponents. But this was hotly rejected by the votaries of R2P, who argued that the war was squarely anchored in Washington's geopolitical interests rather than in any real concern for suffering Iraqi civilians. Blairite altruism never quite recovered its credibility in the aftermath of Iraq.[18]

R2P suddenly came to renewed life, though, with aerial military intervention by NATO forces in Libya (and later in Syria). And as we have written earlier, these interventions were considerably more aggressive than originally thought or planned for. This undermined the global consensus around the liberal world order; as Richard Haass explained: 'Russia...judged the 2003 Iraq war and the 2011 NATO military intervention in Libya, which was undertaken in the name

---

[16]Shashi Tharoor, 'War for Peace', *Forbes*, 30 May 2011.
[17]Id.
[18]Id.

of humanitarianism but quickly evolved into regime change, as acts of bad faith and illegality inconsistent with notions of world order as it understood them.[19] When the US intervened in favour of anti-government rebels in Syria, Russia quickly sent aircraft and weapons to the beleaguered Syrian government of President Bashar al-Assad.

The American writer David Rieff, who was once an enthusiastic interventionist in the civil war in Yugoslavia but has since recanted (as he explains in his book, *At the Point of a Gun*), now criticizes 'the messianic dream of remaking the world in either the image of American democracy or of the legal utopias of international human rights law.'[20] This is not just because it isn't easy to do, nor that it involves taking more lives than it saves. It's also, simply, because Rieff, and gradually other Americans, are coming around to the view that intervention isn't right in any circumstances. He even told the *New York Times'* Maureen Dowd that, 'Qaddafi is a terrible man, but I don't think it's the business of the United States to overthrow him. Those who want America to support democratic movements and insurrections by force if necessary...are committing the United States to endless wars of altruism. And that's folly.'[21]

This sounds rather like the traditional non-aligned objection to any interference in the internal affairs of sovereign states. Countries like India, China, and Brazil, which abstained on the Libyan resolution, have long been profoundly allergic to any attempt by countries to impose their will on 'Third World' nations by the force of arms. The experience of colonialism underlies many of these attitudes— nations that have won their freedom after centuries of subjugation by foreigners supposedly acting out of a 'civilizing mission' are understandably none too keen on seeing the same conduct re-emerge under the garb of humanitarianism, or even R2P. And yet those in the developing world who would resist such intervention have no answer to the question—if the world had been prepared to protect

[19]Richard Haass, 'How a World Order Ends', *Foreign Affairs*, January/February 2019.
[20]David Rieff, *At the Point of a Gun: Democratic Dreams and Armed Intervention*, New York: Simon and Schuster, 2005. p. 171.
[21]Maureen Dowd, 'In Search of Monsters, *New York Times*, 12 March 2011.

the Rwandans from genocide in 1994, would you have considered that an inadmissible interference in Rwanda's sovereignty?[22]

The squeamishness is not only on the part of the developing country ideologues. The potential intervenors have their own hesitations. In the 1820s, the sixth US president, John Quincy Adams, declared about America: 'Wherever the standard of freedom and independence has been or shall be unfurled, there will her heart, her benedictions and her prayers be. But she goes not abroad, in search of monsters to destroy...she is the champion and vindicator only of her own.'[23] Adams' statement recognized that the principal duty of a democracy is to its own voters and legislators. The imposition of its values on others is, indeed, not its business.[24]

It doesn't help, of course, that such attempts at imposition have often gone awry, as the years of chaos in Iraq after the American military triumph in 2003 demonstrated. War creates casualties. Often these exceed the beneficiaries. If you want peace, you must prepare for war—only in order not to have to go to war. Once you do, peace is no longer possible; the logic of war renders the very idea absurd, as we are seeing every day in Libya.

This is why the only true warriors for peace are the UN peacekeepers, whose job is to prevent the recurrence of conflict, rather than to engage in conflict in the name of ending it. When the war ends in Syria, in Iraq, in Libya, amidst all the smoke and the rubble will lie one more discredited notion, that of going to war in the name of peace.

The world, as we know it, has largely been shaped by Westphalian principles, as we have noted throughout this book, and the strongest disruption to Westphalian sovereignty is, of course, the rise of a strong China, fuelled by economic prowess, military might, and a renewed eagerness in the application of its hard power. The South China Sea has become the site of a host of territorial disputes that

---

[22]supra note, 16.
[23]John Quincy Adams, 'She Goes Not Abroad in Search of Monsters to Destroy', *American Conservative*, 4 July 2013.
[24]supra note, 16.

open the floodgates to attempts at capturing the region's economic
resources and strategic value. This is not a fleeting moment, but
rather a part of a wider mobilization within the leadership ranks
of China's elite, revealing their willingness to use hard power across
the globe: in the SCS, in Pakistan and Sri Lanka, and across Africa.
To be sure, the extent of Chinese willingness to assert hard power
in the SCS is yet to be fully revealed—though China's willingness
to flex its muscles in its backyard and even to ignore global rules
by supporting hackers to attempt to gain access to critical strategic
intelligence resources is an indication of unsettling global aspirations.
President Xi Jinping, who embarked on his second five-year term
as the country's unchallenged supremo by abolishing the term limits
that had restricted his two immediate predecessors to ten years,
will not want to look weak, including in the face of threats from
a unilateralist America. His commitment to world order certainly
does not include its 'liberal' elements—neither democracy nor human
rights are principles he would care to see applied to his country, nor
are liberal economic principles compatible with the government-led
'state capitalism' driving his country's development. A new global
order led by China would be marked by market authoritarianism
and illiberal values, even while paying lip service to the post-1945
order it would seek to supplant.

China is the only country with a scalable global economic
strategy, but it is experiencing a slowdown, making it simultaneously
the most important and most uncertain driver of change today. Its
current growth is down to 6 per cent—after decades of double-digit
growth—and it seems unlikely to rise above that for the next five
years. (This would hardly be bad news for most of us: China still
adds a Switzerland every year to the global GDP, since its reduced
growth is still about $800 billion and, according to the IMF, it is
on course to be a $15 trillion economy by 2020.) But nations
exporting to China are already feeling the pinch of reduced demand:
the collapse of the global steel industry is directly attributable to the
China slowdown. So Chinese workers are 'stealing' Western jobs, but
Western markets have no consumers unless they're willing to allow

those jobs to go to China.

To maintain control in the face of a slowing economy, China may be tempted to assert nationalism to increase domestic support, such as in territorial disputes in the South China Sea and the Senkaku–Diaoyu islands in the Sea of Japan. For their own corresponding reasons, China's neighbours, facing electorates and domestic pressures, drum up nationalism, raising the stakes in rhetoric and the flexing of muscles. If these actions develop an irrational momentum, they may disrupt major sea lanes of communication and a global modular supply chain that has allowed for the diffusion of wealth away from traditional manufacturers and into less developed countries, threatening the newfound prosperity of emerging markets around the world. Economic interdependence is not necessarily an insurance against instability. China is Japan's largest trading partner and Japan is China's second most important commercial partner,[25] and yet tensions pervade the relationship. It was the institutions of global governance that have so far kept the peace—institutions that need to change, adapt, and be protected with vigour and commitment.

Globalization and strong economic bonds have brought nations closer by giving them a stake in this global system. But when the system itself confronts trouble, its constituents look to protect their own narrow interests, channeling expectations and resentments born from globalization against that very phenomenon. It would appear that there is a decline of the Davos Man or to be more precise, as British journalist Gillian Tett put it, 'The Davos Man has no clothes'.[26] The signs come from the annual survey of global experts that the WEF, no less, conducts. Traditionally, when asked to cite the biggest threats to global stability, participants would single out issues such as climate change. More recently, the same issues have been replaced with income inequality, migration, and interstate conflict—tangible problems that have cropped up in many Western countries. But it also poses an existential problem for the Davos Man and trust in

---

[25]Mathew Johnston, 'China's Top Trading Partners', Investopedia, 9 August 2019.
[26]Gillian Tett, 'Davos Man Has No Clothes', Foreign Policy, 16 January 2017.

the elite is crumbling fast—as former British prime minister, Theresa May, declared after the startling Brexit referendum, '...if you believe you are a citizen of the world, you are a citizen of nowhere. You don't understand what the very word "citizenship" means.'[27]

The fall of the Davos Man and the global revolt by nationalists and traditionalists against a liberal capitalist elite has resulted in the rise of the strongman—Xi in China, Putin in Russia, Modi in India, Erdoğan in Turkey, and now—in what has perhaps shocked the world and its markets the most—the rise of Trump in America. To take the Indian example first, Prime Minister Modi's resounding success in his bid for re-election is indicative of the larger-than-life appeal that he seems to have generated across the country. In Turkey, Erdoğan did better in a repeat election than in the previous one, and has now won a referendum, even if only narrowly, to strengthen his hands. And yet neither seems ready to launch major economic reforms; their priorities seem domestic and political.

While strongmen assert their own national sovereignty, they are sometimes less respectful of other nations' sovereign rights and go against the very intention behind international order. Putin's annexation of Crimea in 2014 and his involvement in the civil unrest in Ukraine, as well as his decisive intervention in Syria, is a case in example. Under Putin, Russia has played its cards well, emerging as a cannot-be-ignored player on the world stage again after its post-Cold War eclipse, threatening also to undermine institutions of global governance painstakingly developed after World War II. Sanctions by the EU and other countries against Russia to get it to toe the global line have not prevented it from flouting the norm. This is despite the fact that these sanctions have affected the rouble and worsened the Russian financial crisis. Strongmen, despite economic losses, can breach previously established conventions—after all, the sanctions against Russia also work to the detriment of the EU's trade with that country—and they can get away with it. But the fact that even a member of the G20—which is charged with the 'management'

---

[27]'Full Text: Theresa May's conference speech', *The Spectator*, 5 October 2016.

of the globalized order—can violate its norms and practices is an indication that anti-globalization has powerful takers who are starting to question their investment in the way things were.

What does the rise of multiple strongmen hold for the global order? How will Trump's America relate to Xi's China and Putin's Russia? A number of commentators have argued that Trump's promise of domestic retrenchment would provide a boost for China and Russia to take the lead in the international arena and that these countries will benefit from the political crisis. But with regard to maintaining the liberal order, Russia and China have different interests. Russia has very little interest in maintaining a liberal order and its concerns are primarily geopolitical in nature. China, on the other hand, as an emerging economy has greater interest in preserving some semblance of the world order and has much to lose from its collapse; what it wants is to manoeuvre itself to a commanding role in that order, shorn of its liberal elements. At the end of the day, it is clear that the global system will need to be reformed—and reformed swiftly if it is to adapt to the tremors we are witnessing today, and to reinvent itself for a changing world.

This is seen in the response to old fashioned globalization by countries that want to be recognized for their own increasing significance in the world and who have been clamouring for some time for old powers to make room at the high table. Take for instance, BRICS, which, in its original embodiment, was identified as those nations whose rapidly growing economies were challenging the size and preponderance of the aristocratic G7. Indeed, in the last fifteen years, Brazil, Russia and India have caught up with the smallest G7 economy (Italy) in terms of nominal GDP, while China has overtaken Japan to become the second largest economy in the world. Together, the nominal GDP of BRICS countries is similar to that of the EU or the US and will in all likelihood overtake both in the not so far away future. By 2040, BRICS will account for more of world GDP than the original G7.[28]

---

[28]Shashi Tharoor, 'Germany's Responsibility: What the World Expects', *Akzente*, 18

But what is it that draws BRICS close as nation states in their organized 'rebellion' against the global order? As it happens, one major attribute all BRICS members share is their exclusion from the places they believe they deserve in the existing world order. Indeed, BRICS is not a collective that is driven together by economic or geopolitical convergence. Instead, BRICS serves as a functional vehicle to articulate demands for alternative models of governance and development—ones that are not tied to Atlantic narratives.[29] The BRICS forum provides a platform for non-OECD leaders to discuss global challenges and coordinate their actions both within and outside existing global institutions. The five countries in the BRICS formation together account for 43 per cent of the world's population, 46 per cent of the global labour force, 30 per cent of the Earth's landmass and an equal share of the world GDP.[30] The share of world merchandise trade of BRICS increased from 7 per cent in 2001 to 17 per cent in 2015. Simply put, they are too big to be ignored anymore, both individually but, in particular, together.

One only has to look at China to get a sense of how much the West, which was the architect of globalization after World War II, is besieged by paranoia about its loss of control over an order of its own making, throwing up strongmen who question the legitimacy of that order now that there are others claiming bigger shares and the power that comes with it. In 1980, the Chinese share of the global economy stood at about 2 per cent while the US represented 23 per cent. In 2017, China's share is now 18.3 per cent on a PPP basis, while the US's is approximately 15.3 per cent. It isn't like any of this is unprecedented—in the early years of the twentieth century, it was the United States that eclipsed Britain, taking the world from an age of Pax Britannica to Pax Americana. They, with their allies, designed a new world order—the one that is now beginning to unravel. Now that another power seems set to exercise a certain

January 2018.
[29]Samir Saran, 'Building new alliances with BRICS', *The Hindu*, 24 March 2016.
[30]Shashi Tharoor, 'BRICS and their Soft Power', *Rising Powers in Global Governance*, 20 December 2016.

dominance in the world, rules will need to be rewritten, creating, naturally, a degree of imbalance in the process. How we negotiate this imbalance is what needs to be seen. And building walls and looking within isn't a step in the right direction.

But this is also an unfamiliar, multipolar world with not just one but many emerging powers, with as many cracks in the existing global edifice. China and India are seeking global influence commensurate with their economic weight, but in very different ways; Brazil and South Africa are emerging as continental powerhouses, and hydrocarbon-fuelled Russia is chafing at its status on the margins of the Western system. BRICS are slowly emerging as an alternative forum that can stand up to the dominant world view of established economies, the principal ones of which merely happen to still dominate the global system because they were the founders of the post-Bretton-Woods global order. BRICS nations might not have mattered in 1945, but today to ignore BRICS is to ignore the turn of history. And to not make room at that high table only contributes to forces that propel sentiments of anti-globalization.

BRICS are emerging at a time when the future of the international system that arose in the immediate aftermath of World War II is increasingly being called into question. After two world wars, numerous civil wars, colonial oppression, and the horrors of the Holocaust and Hiroshima, the farsighted statesmen of the mid-1940s decided that liberal internationalism, based on the UN Charter and allied institutions, was the only way to prevent more carnage. Indeed, for seven decades, that system has largely achieved its goals. It has broadly ensured world peace and prevented a third world war, although at the cost of shifting many conflicts to the global periphery. And it did not benefit only the developed world; it also ensured decolonization, promoted development, and found ways to accommodate the voices of newly emerging countries, even if it has not always accommodated their aspirations.[31]

---

[31]Shashi Tharoor, 'Do the BRICS need a bigger voice in the world?', WEF, 22 June 2015.

That is why it is clear that existing arrangements are no longer adequate, as BRICS have demonstrated in their demand for greater clout and in their willingness to explore a smaller grouping to pool in their resources and push for a new order. The existing world powers, however, will not cede influence so easily even if their leaders complain about the very institutions where such influence is exercised. It is absurd that China's voting power in the World Bank and the IMF was the same as Belgium's till 2016. But the G20's effort to create parity in these institutions between the advanced economies and the emerging and transition countries had ground to a halt. Although US leaders technically agreed to IMF voting reforms at the Pittsburgh meeting of G20 in 2008, the US Congress did not ratify them till a modest change finally occurred in 2015, nearly seven years later.[32]

As has been noted, countries like China and India—unlike, say, Germany and Japan a century ago—are not seeking to overturn the world order, but rather to increase their influence within it, and perhaps there are lessons for the advanced West to take from their approach to seeking redress within the broad framework rather than destabilizing the framework itself. All they want is a place at the high table—they realize that in world affairs, one is either at the table or on the menu! Barring an accommodation in the global order, they have little choice but to build their own system, in their image and in a different mould, channeling globalization through different routes than before.[33]

As countries acquire economic and military power, they start exercising their geopolitical muscle. The challenge for advocates of world order is to accommodate emerging powers within a framework of universal and stable rules and global structures that ensure everyone a fair deal, appropriate for their size, capabilities, and contributions to the international system. The leaders of the developed West will have to reconcile to this, and make way with grace, instead of seeking to

---

[32]Id.
[33]Id.

undermine institutions by refusing accommodations, just because they fear no longer being in a position of privilege in those institutions.[34]

Today's world leaders appear to lack the breadth of vision, and the generosity of spirit, of those who created the post-1945 world order. By clinging stubbornly to the system they dominate and barring the door to new entrants, they have left those outside little choice. Countries like China have shown, through the creation of institutions like BRICSNDB, SCO, the Eurasian Economic Union (EAEU), and AIIB, that in the absence of a level playing field within the existing system, they are prepared to construct their own. Though what the BRICS countries have in common, as we have argued, is their exclusion from the places they believe they deserve in the current world order, it is arguable that that is not enough of a basis for a credible new international system. But, with their economies on course to overtake those of the G7 before 2050, looks can be deceiving. What that might mean for the world order established in 1945 is anybody's guess—what the emerging powers are doing is not withdrawing from globalization as much as calling for a new design for global forces. The institutionalization of the BRICS agenda in the form of the NDB and their common commitment to multipolarity have arguably been the grouping's most significant contributions to global governance. Of course, the next decade will be quite significant for this group of states. As one of us has argued before, the BRICS ideological incoherence may well undermine their agenda if BRICS cannot build on projects like NDB.[35] Nevertheless, there is certainly an appetite amongst them to do this. And if the West chooses to call this 'anti-globalization', it does so at its own peril.

If at all there is anti-globalization it comes from other sources—what the journalist and political commentator Samantha Power has called problems from hell. Look at the rise of non-state actors, particularly in the Middle East, aided by technology. The largest of

---

[34]Id.

[35]Samir Saran, 'The next ten years of BRICS—will the relationship last?', ORF, 5 October 2017.

these, the Islamic State, continues to be a lethal threat despite its loss of territory earlier captured by it in parts of Iraq and Syria. As the 2019 Easter bombings in Sri Lanka confirmed, ISIS's most dangerous weapon is its ability to inspire and support a dispersed network of scattered operations in far-flung places like Colombo, Paris and Brussels and 'lone wolf' copycats anywhere. The pirates of North Africa, separatists in many parts of the world, and extremists of all faiths and ideologies, are also using new and innovative ways to challenge the authority of the state.

Technological change is further weakening many states in the developing world, especially in West Asia and North Africa. Technological change in energy production, the cheaper production of shale oil and gas, undermines the stability of states still deeply dependent on oil and gas exports as their principal source of revenue. Automation of the workplace—robotization and developments in artificial intelligence—will make it even harder to create jobs for growing numbers of young people. At the same time, new communications technologies continue to enhance the ability of angry citizens to find like-minded rebels and to organize themselves in protests. General Abdel Fattah al-Sisi has curbed protest effectively in Egypt, but it is uncertain how long he will be able to; many governments are discovering that 'forced transparency' (from Wikileaks to the Panama Papers) can undermine their authority seriously, if not fatally.

The rise of Trump has revealed the tremendous frustration and discontent on the part of Americans with the globalization that has altered the familiar assumptions of their lives. Indeed, globalization— and today's anti-globalization—is also what people make of it. In 2002 according to a Pew poll, 78 per cent Americans thought foreign trade was of great advantage to the country; by the time of the crisis in 2008, the number had dropped to 53 per cent.[36] Countries that were economic powerhouses and have faced the worst of the crisis—France,

---

[36]Confidence in Obama Lifts US Image Around the World, Pew Global Attitudes Survey 2009, p. 59.

Japan, the US—are the states now negotiating major regional trade agreements in the face of scepticism about globalization. Pew found in 2014 that 66 per cent of respondents in developing countries held the view that international trade creates jobs as compared to 44 per cent in the developed world. Twenty-five per cent in the developed world believed that trade raises wages, as against 55 per cent in the developing world.[37] A Centre for Economic Policy Research report notes that in the first ten months of 2015 alone, G20 countries imposed 443 new trade distortions, 40 per cent more than they had in 2014.[38] When questioned about this, the argument that national circumstances demand such measures permits them to get away with protectionist policies.

Look at rising inequality, for instance. Globalization has created income winners and income losers. Central banks have been flushing out money, which instead of enabling job growth, as intended, finds its way into financial assets owned by the rich (income winners). Since 2008, wage growth has been weak, but returns for the wealthy continue to be stout—in the UK, wages have grown by only 13 per cent but the stock market is up by 115 per cent. Credit Suisse found in a recent study that out of forty-six major economies around the world, wealth inequality was on the rise, before 2007, in twelve of them—today wealth inequality is growing sharply in thirty-five of the forty-six states.[39] Median income for full-time male workers is actually lower in real (inflation adjusted) terms than it was forty-two years ago, and at the bottom, they are comparable to levels sixty years ago (the income losers). Add to this the fact that the total population of billionaires in the world has increased to 2,153, provoking class resentment by this concentration of wealth in the hands of a few. As noted, ninety-five of them live in London alone, and if Brexit was

[37]'Faith and Skepticism about Trade, Foreign Investment', Pew Research Center, 16 September 2014.
[38]Simon J. Evenett and Johannes Fritz, 'The Tide Turns? Trade Protectionism and Slowing Global Growth', Centre for Economic Policy Research, 2015, https://voxeu.org/sites/default/files/file/GTA18_final.pdf.
[39]'Global Wealth Report 2019', Credit Suisse Research Institute.

a vote from which London stood aside by voting 'stay', in a way it was also the rest of the UK voting against London and its elite by preferring to leave. The fundamental problem it would appear then is not globalization itself but as American economist Joseph Stiglitz argues, the manner in which it has been managed.

Economic inequality at home, coupled with the migration crisis in the Middle East, North Africa, and West Asia has proven to be a lethal cocktail that has sprouted nationalist leaders and has challenged the liberal norms that many took for granted. Populists have fed on this anxiety, dislocation, and fear. As many commentators have argued, Trump's rhetorical call to 'make America great again' may well mean 'make America white again', and his promise to 'build a wall' between the United States and Mexico has only heightened this perception. Cultural and economic anxiety, caused by unequal income distribution and shifting race dynamics, has effectively disrupted notions of identity, leading to the rise of xenophobic sentiments. Nearly 69 per cent of Trump supporters feel that immigrants are a burden on society while 64 per cent believe Muslims living in the US should be subject to more scrutiny.[40] In the EU, as has been noted, xenophobia against Muslims and outsiders is at a tipping point, with Viktor Orbán in Hungary, Marine Le Pen in France, the AfD in Germany and an assortment of populists finding electoral support where earlier there was none. 'A multicultural society is a society that has multiple conflicts,'[41] said Le Pen, echoing the sentiment of millions of anxious Europeans.

The unequal distribution of wealth as a result of haphazard globalization, the ease of communication afforded by social media, and the sharpening of ethnic differences has given rise to desire for strongman politics around the world. Political mobilization often fails to respect democratic norms and procedures, and there is a global desire to embrace leaders who can carry out the 'will of the

---

[40]'Campaign Exposes Fissures Over Issues, Values and How Life Has Changed in the US', Pew Research Center, 31 March 2016.

[41]Yonette Joseph, 'In Their Own Words: Marine Le Pen and Emmanuel Macron', *New York Times*, 5 May 2017.

masses'—often in a manner that defies traditional politics. Asian states have proven to be just as vulnerable to this trend. In Myanmar, Aung San Suu Kyi's weak civilian government has silently watched as the military carries out what the United Nations has called 'ethnic cleansing' against the Rohingya—a move that is popular with much of the Burmese public. In the Philippines, Duterte has promised to wipe out inequality, and has launched a war against drugs that is extremely questionable in legality—again with popular support. Indonesia is struggling to contain rising Islamic radicalization and violence against ethnic Chinese. In Turkey, Erdoğan has eroded whatever promise there was of a secular state and is increasingly embracing a more nationalist and conservative outlook for the country. In Russia, Putin has effectively rigged elections, guaranteeing him another term in office. In China, Xi has abolished what few checks and balances there were against retaining the presidency for life. Even in India, Narendra Modi's rise has accompanied a more nationalist and muscular Hindu assertion that has left minorities fearful and the Opposition in disarray.

This is a global phenomenon: Freedom House notes that 'democracy is facing its most serious crisis in decades, as its basic tenets—including guarantees of free and fair elections, the rights of minorities, freedom of the press, and the rule of law—came under attack around the world.'[42] In fact, 2018 marked the twelfth consecutive year in which global freedoms have declined, and seventy-one countries suffered a net decline in political rights and civil liberties, with only thirty-five registering gains. These domestic political drivers have international economic consequences as well: the liberalization of trade, which was the mainstay of globalization, appears to now be offering diminishing returns, especially in the West. In its place, protectionism is on the rise and the possibility of 'trade wars' is gaining steam. That two of the world's largest economies—the United States and China—are preparing a laundry list of tariffs against each other's products and industries is an ominous sign.

---

[42]'Freedom in the World Report 2018', Freedom House.

At the same time, the primary drivers of globalization are no longer Western states, as new powers seek to capture the material benefits and wealth of nations. At the World Economic Forum in 2017, President Xi Jinping emerged as the somewhat unlikely standard-bearer of free trade, criticizing those who 'blame economic globalization for the chaos in our world'. Unlike the free-market-based globalization of the twenty-first century, however, Beijing is promising a new form of trade based on state capitalism—a model that has only served to increase trade friction and encourage protectionism. As Graham Allison observed: 'When, in 2017, members of the World Economic Forum in Davos crowned Chinese President Xi Jinping the leader of the liberal economic order—even though he heads the most protectionist, mercantilist, and predatory major economy in the world—they revealed that, at least in this context, the word "liberal" has come unhinged.'[43]

If liberalism is now eroding in parts of the world that once sought to proselytize it, today it is more obvious that the international system was far from ever being truly international. The post-war order was a patchwork of economic and military alliances between the Atlantic powers in the West, along with Japan, South Korea, and Australia in the East. Other countries, from Africa, Asia, and Latin America, simply did not have the type of agency in this order that would have allowed them to shape global governance to benefit their teeming millions. Rising powers, such as India and China, have long understood this contradiction, along with other regional powers such as Brazil, South Africa, and Russia. China has gone one step farther: through clever institutional statecraft under the aegis of BRI, AIIB, and RCEP, Beijing seeks to rewrite the rules of the game on trade, investment, and security—and in the process, create a new world order that responds to its own interests.

Indeed, it is difficult today to speak of the world as one whole. The fact that there are now 'regional worlds' is because Western powers

---

[43]Graham Allison, 'The Myth of the Liberal Order: From Historical Accident to Conventional Wisdom', *Foreign Affairs*, July/August 2018.

never truly overcame their colonial-era imperial impulse—instead they were merely subsumed in an international order that embedded traditional power structures through multilateral institutions and terms of trade. It is less and less accurate to think of the world as one system; instead, it is obvious that the world is going through a process of regionalization, especially in Asia, and in some cases such as the Middle East, an absence of order all together.

And while the international order is far from being international, today it is not even orderly. Many point to the financial crisis of 2008 as the defining moment—when governments around the world realized that economic integration could spawn adverse network effects. Perhaps its death knell was sounded as early as 2003 when America chose to invade Iraq under the guise of 'humanitarian intervention' and the pretext of weapons of mass destruction. The giddy heyday of American power led some to believe that the United States could reorder the world in its own image through force and disregard for international law if need be—and the results were disastrous. Perhaps it ended when Russia used military force to change the political borders of Europe, or when it chose to interfere with America's democratic processes and institutions in 2016 through cyberspace. Barring the early 1990s, Moscow never truly accepted the premise of American superiority, and is now subverting the institutions and structures in which it has no stake. Or, it might have ended when China chose to militarize the South China Sea in blatant disregard of international law and norms.

At the same time, new governance frameworks to prevent the militarization of the internet, artificial intelligence and space are struggling to emerge. Most devastatingly of all, the old order can no longer maintain peace and prevent the humanitarian crisis that is playing out in vast swathes of the Middle East and North Africa—especially in Syria, Iraq, and Yemen. And while the prospects of a global war are still slim, the United Nations has been unable to respond to multiple and complex crises; and invariably, geopolitical considerations have taken precedence over humanitarian ones.

Observing this state of affairs, some historians are hard-pressed to miss the similarities between today's world and the turn of the twentieth century. This period truly saw the dawn of a global economy; the Industrial Revolution was in full swing and steamships, telegraphy, telephones, canals, and railways were reducing the costs of transportation and communication. While Europe and North America benefited the most from these developments, the structural power and reach of colonial empire meant that these technologies had also diffused to Asia, South America, Central Asia, and, to a lesser extent, Africa. At the same time, trade and investment policy in Europe, specifically Britain, actively encouraged the free movement of capital and goods—especially with the introduction of the 'most favoured nation' concept, liberal immigration policies, and the reduction of trade barriers on agricultural products. Spurred on by the exploitation of raw materials from the colonies, the implicit faith in the gold standard system of international economics and relative peace between the great powers from the mid-1870s until 1914, the first era of globalization heralded the dawn of a new age.

Interestingly, these very ingredients set the foundations for World War I. Perhaps, as economist Dani Rodrik argues in his book *The Globalization Paradox*: 'We cannot simultaneously pursue democracy, national determination and economic globalization. If we want to push globalization further, we have to give up either the nation state or democratic politics.'[44] His analysis holds true today, as well as it applied to the world of nearly a hundred years ago. The distributional effects of globalization in the late nineteenth century created a backlash not dissimilar to the one we face today. In Europe, agriculturalists were pushing for protectionism to avoid competition with American markets; in America, immigration policies became more unwelcoming, with a succession of laws that were enacted to discourage new immigrants, especially from Asia; in Italy, Germany, and some eastern European States, nationalism had emerged as a power force; and the gold standard market system, which protected investors from inflation

[44]Dani Rodrik, *The Globalization Paradox: Democracy and the Future of the World Economy*, New York: W. W. Norton & Company, 2012.

in the global economy, led to sharp recessions and unemployment in Europe at a time when the idea of the welfare state did not exist. Ultimately, globalization collapsed, trade barriers rose, cultural anxiety was heightened, and the end result was a long period of interstate war between the European powers beginning in 1914.

WHAT NEXT?

If we seek with trepidation to avoid the pitfalls of history, the key questions we must ask are: how do global governance frameworks that were shaped in the context of a very different world adapt to today's changes? Technological and demographic shifts, rising powers, new geographic theatres, and balance of power politics are all moving with a velocity previously unknown to the world. Can new countries assume leadership, and will this create a more representative international system? To be fair, attempting to evaluate the future of world order is an elusive endeavour. For one thing, it is necessary to ask: who does a world order serve? The post-world war order served the Atlantic powers, first to stave off the threat from the Soviet Union, and then to expand their normative vision for democracy and free trade. However, this order failed to accommodate the voices and concerns of countries which found their independence after shedding the yoke of colonialism. Looking further back in history, the Congress of Vienna in 1815 helped end the Napoleonic wars and brought peace to Europe in terms of political stability and economic growth. Yet, that same period was marked by the colonization of Asia and a burgeoning African slave trade. At the same time, ever since the Peace of Westphalia in 1648, world order was primarily understood in terms of interactions between states; and the ideation of a 'world order' itself was an Anglo-American conception. Today, not only do we have multiple state and civilizational contenders for leadership in the international system, but such an international order must also accommodate or address international and regional institutions, multinational corporations and nongovernmental organizations, civil society movements, powerful city states and so on.

Today's problem is that the structural preconditions that allow major powers to enforce their normative visions no longer exist. Control over technology, finance, and trade allowed Europe to spread its 'civilizing mission' and colonize the world. A booming post-war economy and new political ideals allowed America to dominate the second half of the twentieth century. These factors of comprehensive national power no longer reside in one geography—instead they are dispersed between states and within them; and all this takes place in a global economy that does not respect borders. No two powers can agree on a common set of rules.

At the same time, transnational corporations and powerful city states are increasingly functioning in parallel to national government policies and international regulations. American cities, for example, have been the frontrunners against climate change despite President Trump's withdrawal from the Paris Agreement. Moscow and Beijing—most widely considered to be at the forefront of subverting the international order—are challenging the rules and norms that do not support their world view. Even the Transatlantic alliance is under pressure—over terms of trade, rules for the digital economy, political values, and security concerns. Other regional powers, such as Japan or Australia, do not have the normative vision, economic resources, military might or political will to determine the outcome of events in global politics.

Clearly, not everyone has benefited the same way from the post-war order; and it is for this reason that they do not seek to defend it. This is not to say, however, that this order did not benefit anyone at all. If anything, today's rising international power—China—was the primary beneficiary of the international liberal order. No other country has gained from integrating with the global economy in the manner that Beijing has. From a GDP of $92 billion in 1970 to $13.6 trillion in 2018, China has steadily enmeshed itself in global value chains and is creatively moving up the industrial production ladder. Already, it is the second largest economy in nominal terms, and the largest in PPP terms. So why is it that it is China that is at the forefront of subverting this order? This question begets another question: what purpose does a world order serve? Collective peace, hegemony, or mutually beneficial multilateralism, or something else?

As we have shown, Beijing believes, whether or not it will say so in so many words, that a twenty-first-century revival of the East Asian tributary system in which China's economic, political, and cultural superiority is recognized might bring harmony; and it is willing to enforce this world view through force and coercion if need be. America, often contradictorily characterized as a 'liberal leviathan', sees value in a 'rules-based order'—albeit rules that are infused with American norms and power structures. At the same time, it seeks to bring the American way of life to every part of the world through global communications and trade and finance networks. Everyone agrees, in principle at least, that great power wars are undesirable. But today's world requires managing complex challenges that go well beyond stability or hegemony, and just like the global economy, these challenges do not respect sovereign boundaries. Climate change, internet governance, artificial intelligence, space missions, human trafficking, tax evasion, international terrorism, the proliferation of drug trafficking, health pandemics, and many more such challenges are all issues that require international cooperation. No twentieth-century framework, or any other historical point of reference, gives an adequate idea of how to responsibly manage these tensions in a world that is more interconnected and interdependent than ever, but suffers from a leadership deficit.

Moreover, if today's international system is best characterized as an extension of the Atlantic system, where will new orders be constructed? Geography is central to building international systems. The Middle Kingdom's tributary system flourished in East Asia, the Westphalian system thrived in Europe, and the post-world war order simply added America plus Japan, Australia, and South Korea to 'globalize' what was already a somewhat coherent European order. Today, it is clear that the twenty-first century will be defined by the collision of three geographies: the Eurasian landmass, the Indo–Pacific maritime system, and the Arctic Ocean.[45] The interaction of global

---

[45]Samir Saran, 'The Collision of these three geographies is creating a new world

economic and migratory flows, the adoption and diffusion of new technologies, and geopolitical imperatives are eroding the artificial geographical boundaries between Europe and Asia and turning these regions into one fluid and dynamic unit. The Indo–Pacific was catalysed by China's rise and expanding maritime influence but was given shape and definition by other powers in the region— namely the US, India, Japan, and Australia (who collectively make up the Quadrilateral Initiative). Simultaneously, communities and markets from Asia and Europe are virtually driving the once separate continents together to create on contiguous supercontinent: Eurasia. The Arctic, meanwhile, is being reborn as an unintended consequence of climate change. And as it continues to melt, it will merge the politics of the Atlantic and the Pacific, as actors in these once dispersed geographies find their interests overlapping. None of these regions should be thought of as separate units—instead, there is a matrix of interdependent drivers that are merging the political, economic, and security relationships in these regions. There is, accordingly, an immense amount of friction and contest between a plethora of powers to define and then manage these geographies.

And yet, these parts of the world are nothing like what Europe and America—or the Anglo-Saxon community—were in the twentieth century. The political and cultural diversity from Japan to Nigeria, and China to Greece, are enormous. The geographical boundaries that the Europeans arbitrarily drew during colonial times have allowed ethnic and religious differences to escalate. Booming populations are young in these parts of the world, but states simply do not have the capacity to address their aspirations. This very diversity will require a different framework altogether, one in which countries will have to work together despite differences in their governance frameworks and capacity, and despite absolutely no agreement on civilizational norms.

At the same time, one has to acknowledge the diminishing appetite for world order approaches in a number of states. As one

order', WEF, 1 November 2018.

commentator put it: 'The United States has made it clear it continues to oppose the creation of a treaty to govern cyberspace. China has reportedly been reneging on its legally binding commitment to ban ozone-depleting substances, diminishing the Montreal Protocol's claim as the "most effective treaty in the world". It appears highly unlikely that the United States, Russia and China will come together to craft a regime for the governance of the Arctic, interested as each is in the economic possibilities that will open up after its ice melts. The WTO has struggled in recent months to incubate negotiations on global e-commerce rules, and localized rules for national and regional digital economies look set to become the norm.'[46] The international system, which created a vast network of laws, treaties, and institutions that underpin the world we take for granted today, finds itself stagnating and rudderless, without patron or protector. It seems to be heading towards 'each nation for itself'.

This may even be the right place to start considering the possibility of the absence of any world order at all, or what Bremmer calls a 'G-Zero' world. In this much at least history is certain: when international politics become zero sum and transactional, putting the absolute interests of one state above another, war ensues. The absence of any rules, institutions, principles, and leadership inevitably creates a trust vacuum and military might dictates every relationship. While an international order might create a stable balance of power, combining legitimacy and enforcement capacity, by no means does it guarantee peace and development. The absence of any order whatsoever almost guarantees tragic outcomes. The first half of the twentieth century, when a fledgling international order existed and collapsed, is testament to this inevitability: great power conflict unleashed unspeakable violence and chaos—and the world must be all the more wary today because of the presence of nuclear weapons, deadly tech-enabled tools of mayhem, and the proliferation of state and non-state actors committed to upending stability and order.

---

[46]Arun Mohan Sukumar, 'What the Age of Narendra Modi Means for Indian Foreign Policy', *The Wire*, 5 June 2019.

THE INDIAN IMPERATIVE[47]

To be fair, the twenty-first century is different from the twentieth century in many meaningful ways. For one thing, no power is capable of enforcing its preferences on a global scale—the age of American unilateralism is well and truly over, and multipolarity is the norm. Second, at the same time, power in the international order is more diffused than it has ever been in history—from corporations to non-state actors (including terrorist networks) to cities, political and economic power is increasingly networked in a manner that defies hierarchical state control. Third, there is a high degree of economic interdependence between the world's major powers—and a high degree of political divergence. Today's supply chains are delocalized— trade and commerce are underpinned by dense and transcontinental networks of economic nodes. Fourth, as a result of this interdependence, today's conflicts are not merely about controlling geographical landmass, but also about controlling the networks of transportation, communication, and energy infrastructure that enable the flow of goods, capital and labour. Finally, compared to the twentieth century, or any other moment in history, institutional frameworks today, whether it is the United Nations, EU, African Union or ASEAN, are more entrenched and find themselves on a more secure institutional footing even as their credibility, adaptability, and effectiveness are increasingly questioned.

The challenge, then, is how to define and then to manage a pluralistic world of different, coexisting, coevolving, and competing versions of modernity. The battlegrounds of today are indeed human mindscapes and their preferences and choices—and these are largely outside most existing institutional purviews and regulatory frameworks.

It is more than clear that the international liberal order will not be able to succeed in the twenty-first century unless it finds new torchbearers and develops new institutions. To many it is obvious that

---

[47]This section is based on ideas from the following sources: Samir Saran, 'India's role in a liberal non-western world', *International Spectator*, 53 No. 1, 2018, pp. 92–108; Shashi Tharoor, *Pax Indica*; Samir Saran, 'As a rising global power, what is India's vision for the world', WEF, 14 August 2018.

these nations must come from Asia and Africa, where politics and economics are scripting a narrative that is very different from the post-war Atlantic system. Despite the volatility of the post-colonial era, most Asian states have avoided an all-out war even in the face of extreme geopolitical tensions. In fact, none of the famous flashpoints, such as India-Pakistan, or China-Taiwan, or North Korea-Japan, have actually erupted in a major conflagration.

Even as nationalist rhetoric continues to flare, it is equally clear that Asian states—with the unfortunate exceptions of India and Pakistan—are in the midst of a connectivity and integration bonanza. Unlike the West, Asian states are overall more favourably disposed towards globalization; as we have seen, they have become the new drivers of economic growth, now accounting for over two-thirds of the world's GDP. When the United States pulled out of the Trans-Pacific Partnership—which President Trump saw as 'a very bad deal for the United States'—Asian states shrugged and went ahead with the deal without America. Indeed, it is in Asia where the world's major powers will be located, and this region will soon account for a majority of the world's population, economic wealth and military might. Gideon Rachman convincingly argues that the 'West's centuries-long domination of world affairs is now coming to a close. The root cause of this change,' he writes, 'is the extraordinary economic development in Asia over the last fifty years. Western political power was founded on technological, military, and economic dominance, but these advantages are fast eroding. And the consequences are now defining global politics.'[48] If countries in Asia can craft a new governance framework to guarantee peace, or at least to prevent large-scale conflict while managing to cooperate on issues that concern them all, they will go a long way towards shaping a new world order.

If Asia is going to be the defining region of our times, it must be intuitively evident that India, which has successfully combined economic growth with its own distinct and unique liberal traditions,

---

[48] Gideon Rachman, *Easternisation*, p. 3.

will indeed be the heir to and guarantor of the international liberal system. While India's economic reforms have paled in comparison to China, the fact remains that with a near $3 trillion economy, India has surpassed several G7 states in sheer economic heft. In fact, projections suggest that by 2030, India will be the second largest economy, behind only China.[49] At the same time, India is a country with one of the world's largest standing armies and a rapidly modernizing naval force; it is a space-faring nation, and is a declared nuclear weapons state. India's young demographics only add weight to its growing profile: by 2027, India will surpass China as the world's most populous state and while the US, China, Japan, and most of the European powers are expected to age significantly by 2050, with median ages hovering around fifty years, India's median age will be around thirty-five years. Even in India, there is a rising consensus on the role that it will have to play. In July 2015, the then Foreign Secretary of India (and now Foreign Minister) Subrahmanyam Jaishankar delivered a speech in which he declared that India was intent on playing the role of a 'leading' instead of a 'balancing' power in Asia, reflecting a newfound swagger.[50]

The current international order has significantly helped India's economic growth while meeting its trade, energy, and security interests. As a result, India now has a stake in practically every major multilateral regime, and its own self-interest can no longer be seen as isolated from the state of affairs around the world. In other words, India must influence the international order, if only to protect its own interests. It is therefore crucial to understand the many pressures and demands that it will have to contend with at home and as an actor in the international system. An interrogation of such expectations will be important to understand the 'Indian imperatives'.

For one thing, India has outlined a goal to achieve a $5 trillion

---

[49]Kuwar Singh, 'India will overtake the US economy by 2030', *Quartz India*, 9 January 2019.
[50]Subrahmanyam Jaishankar, 'IISS Fullerton Lecture by Dr. S. Jaishankar, Foreign Secretary in Singapore', Speech presented at the International Institute for Strategic Studies, Singapore, 20 July 2015.

economy by 2024. Despite occasional hiccups along the way, the resilience of India's economic institutions and structural macro-economic trends appear certain to support this trajectory. The uncertainty, then, lies in the global economic system. In other words, India's ability to sucessfully emerge as a global economic power is dependent on its capacity to create an environment of certainty and predictability in global financial and economic regimes. And while India is increasingly a consequential geopolitical actor, its geoeconomic priorities and postures remain nascent and underdeveloped. This will perhaps be the most crucial Indian imperative. Delhi must now reimagine its own role and stake in global economic governance to pursue its national interests. Its self-imagination as a leading power must reflect in its trade and economic conversations as well. Second, India is yet to complete the twentieth-century project of building social and physical infrastructure even as it must leverage twenty-first century opportunities in the fourth industrial revolution and attendant digital shifts. These are both complex structural transformations, and India will need to engage and partner with different sets of stakeholders to satisfy the governance demands of both. To build hard infrastructure, for instance, India will rely on finance from bilateral partners from East Asia and multilateral institutions like the ADB, AIIB, and NDB (where India and China are substantive stakeholders). Meanwhile, India will likely partner with hubs of technology like the EU, Israel, Japan, and the US to strengthen its technological prowess. However, given global tensions along the lines of technology, finance, and trade, satisfying this imperative will require India to defend and preserve its room to manoeuvre. India cannot afford to sit by as these global arrangments fragment. India must not allow a situation to arise where it will have to make choices about the partners it engages with. A satisfactory regime of the future should allow a robust partnership with OECD countries and an intimate and beneficial partnership with rising powers such as China.

Third, India recognizes that it must slowly shed its role as the leader of the global trade union and sit at the management table. To a large extent, this process is already underway. In the late twentieth century, India was a leading member of the G77, comprised entirely of developing states. At the turn of the century, India was inducted into the G20, a gathering of the world's twenty largest economies. Most recently, in 2019, India was invited as a special guest to the G7, an elite group of mostly Western developed economies. These developments suggest that there is both a demand for India's stake in global governance and a realization in New Delhi that undertaking this responsibility is an Indian imperative. As India's stake in global institutions and processes deepens, so too must its voice in the management of international affairs. Delhi must invest in consensus-building and in support of multilateral efforts and solutions to address global challenges. To do this, India will have to work with constituencies that believe in multilateralism such as the EU and other international institutions that defend and serve a rules-based order.

Finally, India will assume the mantle of the largest liberal democratic economy by mid-century. This designation will bring with it expectations and demands from the world. Put another way, leadership will be thrust upon India, whether it desires it or not. Delhi must recognize now that the preserving the liberal international order will be in India's national interest. It certainly works in India's favour that it is still an emerging power. It is not burdened by the anti-incumbency sentiments that most large powers must contend with. However, this period of opportunity is narrowing for India. Already, Delhi has made clear its ambition of becoming a 'leading power' in the international system. The question is: does India have the will, capacity, and ideas to do so? Great powers provide solutions and roadmaps for others. India as a leading power must take this challenge and deliver on it, for its own sake and to help achieve the global ambition of a better world. From a global perspective, India seems primed to take on this role.

For one thing, India has consistently maintained its democratic credentials coupled with high economic growth rates based on a relatively transparent free market. This remarkable project began nearly seventy years ago, when India broke the chains of colonialism and embarked on an experiment that no country its size had ever successfully accomplished: constitutional democracy. That there was little faith in India's ability to carry out this project is unsurprising. At the time, most of India was illiterate, its per capita GDP was one of the lowest in the world, the linguistic, religious, and ethnic diversity was enormous, the horrors of Partition were still fresh in the memory, its immediate neighbourhood was awash in conflict, and India had inherited one of the most rigid and discriminatory social stratification systems in the world. Today, India has successfully carried out the peaceful transfer of political power every five years barring a brief period of Emergency rule from 1975 to 1977. Multiple political parties dot the Indian landscape, some national, others regional, and still more local. Each of them represents the diverse array of social identities that inhabit the Indian subcontinent. India's constitution guarantees several basic freedoms, including the right to speech and expression, the right to freedom of religion, equality before law, privacy, and prevention of unlawful detention. Affirmative action and a wide range of social reforms have weakened the grip of India's feudal caste system—in fact, the current president of India belongs to a caste that would once have been considered 'untouchable', as did one of his predecessors. Women are also increasingly making their presence felt in politics, business, and media. Civil society is an integral part of India's social contract, with thousands of grassroots organizations, research institutions, and think tanks actively contributing to India's rise.

Even as social justice remains within reach of many Indians, the economy has made steady gains ever since the market liberalization of 1991. From an average growth rate of less than 4 per cent in 1988, to 6 per cent in 1995, a peak of 9.8 in 2007, and a relatively steady rate of close to 7 per cent today (marred by one quarter of 5 per cent growth in mid-2018), India is primed to become one of the world's largest economies in the near future. Indeed, at the time of writing, the World Bank reported that India had already surpassed China in year-on-year growth rates. At the World Economic Forum in 2018, 'India Inc.' was the buzzword, and for good reason: businesses and private sector entrepreneurship are transforming India and the world.

India's economy somewhat inadvertently leapfrogged manufacturing to emerge as a global destination for business process outsourcing operations. India is today a powerhouse in information technology, a process that India's former Prime Minister Vajpayee once called the confluence of 'Saraswati, Lakshmi and Shakti', because it is both 'driven by knowledge' and 'a producer of wealth and prosperity'. India is now home to one of the largest automobile industries in the world, manufacturing roughly 3.8 million cars every year—a figure that puts India behind only Germany and South Korea. India has also become a generic drugs powerhouse, and India's biotech and pharma czars— such as Lupin, Cipla, and Glenmark—have dominated developing markets in Asia and Africa, and are competing in Western markets as well. Though stocks fell dramatically in 2019, these structural factors suggest an inevitable rebound is more than likely.

At the same time, India, interestingly enough, is resisting the anti-globalization trend. Despite being a self-confessed nationalist, Prime Minister Modi remains resolutely committed to globalism and free trade, and his government's new budget speaks of liberalizing foreign direct investment even further. As it happens, India has had some experience, for all of its modern existence, including after Independence in 1947, with constantly battling challenges of competing identities, disruption, poverty, and worse. India strikes many as maddening, chaotic, inefficient and seemingly unpurposeful as it muddles its way through the twenty-first century. But 'India,' as the British historian E. P. Thompson wrote, 'is perhaps the most important country for the future of the world. All the convergent influences of the world run through this society... There is not a thought that is being thought in the West or East that is not active in some Indian mind.'[51] That importance of India is nowhere more apparent today than in the discourse about the country's place and prospects in a trembling world economy—there are lessons from its

---

[51]Shashi Tharoor, 'India: from Midnight to the Millennium and Beyond: The 125th Anniversary Jubilee Lecture', Speech at St. Stephens College, Delhi, 12 November 2005.

past for the wider world at large, and proactive measures to be taken today so that we do not get left behind in a post-global universe.

To be fair, this is only part of the story. Dense populations, rapid urbanization, rapid technological change, young aspirational demographics, and a cacophony of identities all commingle in one of the world's most unequal economies and unresponsive state structures. Since 1982, India's top 1 per cent have seen their incomes grow by nearly 17 per cent, while the bottom 50 per cent have seen their incomes fall by 9 per cent.[52] Today, while the top 10 per cent of India's population controls nearly half its wealth, India's middle class finds itself increasingly frustrated by diminishing opportunities for advancement even as unemployment is at a forty-five-year high. Shifts in technology, from automation to artificial intelligence, will only make these challenges more intractable. Corruption is rife in India, with indexes consistently placing India on a par with less developed nations. Law and order is a prickly subject, often left to the whims and preferences of the police's political masters. Caste and religion continue to play a toxic role in India's public spaces. In the absence of strong political and economic reforms, the combined forces of urbanization, demography, and technology may just create a maelstrom of sectarian hatred that could erupt in violence, driven by the identity politics Indian politicians have too often resorted to.

These development problems, however, are not unique to India— indeed most countries in Eurasia and the Indo–Pacific are going through similar seismic changes and identity-based politics is now as prevalent in richer and more mature economies. These countries will look towards Asian states in search of solutions and leadership, and India's ability to offer it will shape their destinies. Already, China is betting that its own model can provide the answers: in October 2017, President—or Emperor—Xi Jinping proclaimed that, 'The Chinese

---

[52]Lucas Chancel and Thomas Piketty, 'India Income Inequality, 1922-2015: From British Raj to Billionaire Raj', World Inequality Database, Working Paper Series N 2017/11, July 2017, https://wid.world/document/chancelpiketty2017widworld/.

nation, which since modern times began had endured so much for so long, has achieved a tremendous transformation... It means that the path, the theory, the system, and the culture of socialism with Chinese characteristics have kept developing, blazing a new trail for other developing countries to achieve modernization.'[53] Of course, China's model implies the loss of political freedoms, absolute ideological obedience to the ruling party, and a unique blend of state control over industry and mercantilist free markets. But these conditions are not easily replicable elsewhere in the developing world.

Which brings us to our second ingredient: India is located at the centre of our changing mental maps of the world—giving it a unique opportunity to shape the political, economic, and security arrangements that will govern these regions. 'Geography is destiny', goes the popular adage, and India is sitting on prime real estate. Unsurprisingly, even the British understood the significance of India's location. From the Suez Canal to Singapore, British supply lines and naval forces would have been unable to exercise their global reach without India. The 'crown jewel' of the British empire was far more than a labour and resource supplier; it was the central geographic node of Britain's imperial architecture. That the empire collapsed almost immediately after India was lost is no coincidence; Britain could simply no longer sustain a global reach. Even Lord Curzon, perhaps one of India's most notorious viceroys, thought of India as the heart of global geopolitics. Straddling the Indian Ocean with its inverted triangular shape, India has long been a maritime bridge linking Southeast Asia, the Persian Gulf and East Africa. The Indo–Pacific, as this space is now known among the international community, hosts nearly 40 per cent of the world's population, acts as the world's principal inter-state energy supply route and is home to critical hydrocarbon and mineral resources along with a diverse marine biology. At the same time, for centuries before the violent partition of India, the country remained a land bridge to Central

---

[53]'Socialism with Chinese Characteristics enters a new era: XI', *Xinhua*, 18 October 2017.

Asia and the Middle East, allowing the flow of goods, capital, people and ideas. India, therefore, has for centuries fused the politics and economics of two otherwise disconnected civilizational regions. Today, as India is poised to become an economic behemoth, it will straddle a region that will mark the intersection of Eurasian (comprising Europe and Asia) and Indo–Pacific ambitions.

In the late twentieth century, and well before India was considered any sort of power deserving attention, Kissinger recognized that India would emerge as a crucial swing state in the post-Cold War international order. In his book, *Diplomacy*, he writes that India's 'geopolitical interests will impel it over the next decade to share some of the security burdens now borne by the United States in the region between Aden and Malacca'[54]—prophetically, the very region that is expected to be at the centre of world politics in the twenty-first century. Today, it is certainly clear that India's interests span this geography: from oil, energy, and diaspora interests in the Persian Gulf and Central Asia, to trade, investment, and technology interests in Southeast Asia, India is steadily reclaiming its historical role as a melting pot of Eastern civilizations. India is a part of as many of the alphabet soup of groupings as it possibly can be from the South Asian Association for Regional Cooperation (SAARC), to the SCO, as well as observer status at ASEAN and the East Asian Summit. India is willing to cooperate with countries that share similar goals, and compete with those that do not at the same time, such as China and Pakistan in its neighbourhood. Nevertheless, navigating the politics of the Indo–Pacific and Eurasia will be no easy task. The central predicament for New Delhi will be balancing its relationship with the US, Russia, and China. In the Indo–Pacific, for example, Washington is India's primary partner. However, this relationship breaks down in Eurasia—where India's equity lies with Moscow, despite China's long shadow over the region. New Delhi is walking a tightrope between the political realities of Eurasia and

---

[54] Henry Kissinger, *Diplomacy*.

the Indo–Pacific.[55] How India assesses and acts on its interest in these regions will go a long way in defining the world order in the twenty-first century.

Of course, the fact that India straddles the Indo–Pacific and the Eurasian landmass must also serve a larger purpose. And this is the third, and perhaps most crucial, feature of India's importance: it can anchor liberal democracy in a part of the world where American leadership is no longer as welcome, and where China's offering is not universally acceptable. To place the significance of India's rise in context—China's successful economic growth paved the way for the United Nations to celebrate the success of the Millennium Development Goals and India has the capacity to see that it does the same with the Sustainable Development Goals, albeit in a world that is increasingly insecure. If India succeeds in its effort, it will have an economic development model that works with liberal democracy— and a model that is replicable in large portions of the developing world, given contextual similarities.

Indeed, India has a unique cultural ethos to offer to the world: the breath and scope of its religious, linguistic, caste, and tribal diversity have not so far prevented them from coexisting in relative peace. While nearly 80 per cent of India's 1.2 billion citizens are Hindu, India also hosts around 180 million Muslims—the second largest Muslim population in the world, and due to become the largest in 2050. Indeed, India has long sheltered persecuted minorities and religious groups for most of its history. At the same time, India's census lists nearly 122 major languages, while officially recognizing twenty-two of them. It is home to descendants of every imaginable ethnicity, with Mongoloid, African, Arab, and European blood all mingled in the Indian gene pool.

India has evolved a distinctly non-Western form of democracy and religious freedom that have made it an exemplar of the successful management of diversity in the developing world. And the 'Asian

---

[55]Samir Saran, 'Walking the tightrope: between Eurasia and the Indo-Pacific', Valdai Discussion Club, 10 September 2018.

century' will undoubtedly be characterized by a similar congeries of multicultural, multireligious, and multilingual interactions. Perhaps, in a world that is today racked by questions of identity, race, and religion, and where the very idea of multiculturalism is under strain, India can pursue a multidirectional foreign policy that allows it to manage and bridge these complex relations in order to build a more plural world. Indeed, as former Prime Minister Manmohan Singh once remarked: 'We have emerged as a bridge between the many extremes of the world. Our composite culture is living proof of the possibility of a confluence of civilizations. India will always be a nation bridging many global divides.'[56] The Dalai Lama, the spiritual leader of the Tibetans, once argued that, 'India's long tradition of religious tolerance can be a role model for rest of the world.' History is India's guide—it has long assumed the role of mediating between the 'East' and the 'West', and today it can do the same for the multiple countries, democratic or non-democratic, religions, cultures, and civilizations that comprise our world.

Nevertheless, India still has a long way to go; and how it goes about accomplishing the promises of independence will have reverberations around the world. Whether it seeks to export its own model however, is questionable. Former National Security Advisor Shivshankar Menon once said: 'Do we not have a responsibility to spread democracy and fight for our values abroad? Yes and no. Yes, if we have the means to actually ensure that we are able to spread them. And yes if having democrats as our neighbours contributes to the peaceful periphery that we need. But please remember that a people cannot be forced to be free or to practice democracy. They have to come to these values themselves if they are to be lasting. Such a crusade for one's values is often mistaken by others as the pursuit of self-interest couched in high-toned words.'[57]

---

[56]Manmohan Singh, 'Text of Indian PM's Independence Day Address', as reproduced in *Hindustan Times*, 15 August 2007.

[57]Shiv Shankar Menon, Prem Bhatia memorial lecture, 11 August 2011, reproduced by the National Maritime Foundation, http://www.maritimeindia.org/ CommentryView.aspx?NMFCID=1267.

While many in the West would take this to mean that India has no interest in democracy promotion, it is equally arguable that India is less evangelical in its beliefs, and is willing to allow a bottom-up development of democracy, as opposed to 'liberal interventionism'. In 2004, for example, India was a founding member of the United Nations Democracy Caucus—the 'only body within the United Nations system to convene democratic states based on shared values instead of regional affiliation'. New Delhi is also the second largest contributor to the United Nations Democracy Fund, having contributed $31.91 million as of February 2018.[58] Further, India is involved in a India-Brazil-South Africa dialogue— based on a shared commitment of these three 'Southern' nations to democracy—outside of the larger BRICS grouping, which was ironically a vehicle to oppose Western hegemony and interventions. In and around its neighbourhood, especially in Sri Lanka, Nepal, Afghanistan, and Bhutan, India has consistently supported electoral processes, providing capacity-building aid and training and setting up the India International Institute of Democracy and Election Management to formalize this process.

India's approach towards democracy, then, is tempered by its post-colonial commitments to non-intervention as well as the disastrous consequences of America's democracy promotion in other parts of the world. If anything, India may just be able to temper the excesses of Western liberalism and its belief in universalization, and the coercive nature of Chinese state communism and its belief in cultural subjugation, by offering a middle path between these extremes.

Of course, India's political and geopolitical propositions matter just as much in the physical world as they do in the digital one. The world is fast approaching a moment where the boundaries between the real and the virtual will vanish, and the feedback loops between both will create much political, social, and economic friction. India

---

[58]The United Nations Democracy Fund, 'Status of Contributions in US Dollars', https://www.un.org/democracyfund/sites/www.un.org.democracyfund/files/doc_1_status_of_contributions_undef_2019.pdf.

will be the first global power to mature in the midst of these digital transformations. This brings us to our third key feature: by design, India will have to be a key player in the fourth industrial revolution. With over half its population under the age of twenty-seven, India will be tasked with providing paychecks, purpose, and protection to its young and ambitious workforce as they transition to the new industrial realities of a virtual, digital, and automated world. In this, India is similarly placed with emerging economies around the world, who are all searching for a new digital social contract. The consequences of these shifts are still uncertain and how nations shape their economic and political institutions to cope with them will have a significant impact on the continued success of the world order. India's choices and policies will play a crucial role in determining the future of this digital order.

Fourth, India is emerging as a key player in issues of global governance and development. India, however, will be a very different power. The US is now primarily a geopolitical superpower, with its network of alliances and partnerships buttressing its dominance over economic and strategic global affairs. China, meanwhile, is a geoeconomic power, leveraging its central position in global supply chains to underwrite its influence. India, on the other hand, is likely to be the world's first development superpower. Already, India's budget allocations for economic diplomacy have crossed the one-billion-dollar mark, with most aid being directed towards its development partners in Asia and Africa. More than the amounts alone, however, India is inculcating a new ethic for global development partnerships. Unlike Western powers and China, India's development cooperation is dependent on the priorities set by its partners. At the same time, India has committed itself to creating equitable partnerships that follow internationally recognized norms of good governance, reducing the risk of 'debt trap diplomacy', a feature that has become a staple ingredient of China's aid. Having made no attempts to pursue exceptionalism beyond its nuclear deal with the US, India's development story will be embraced with vigour by foreign markets and governments alike.

More importantly, unlike the Atlantic powers or China, India does not seek hegemony over the international system. Writing for the influential magazine *Foreign Affairs* in 1949, an 'anonymous Indian official' had this to say about India: 'Underdeveloped as she is, her organized industrial and military capacity still exceeds that of any nation in the east. She has no traditional enemies, nor has she acquired new ones; she has no vested interest of any sort in world affairs, except an interest in peace, a tradition of friendliness to all, and a readiness to cooperate with others for constructive ends.'[59] Indeed, India's enthusiasm for the United Nations process in the early twentieth century bears testament to this reality. In September 1946, Nehru promised that India would 'play that role in Councils to which her geographical position, population and contribution towards peaceful progress entitle her', committing 'unreserved adherence, in both spirit and letter' to the UN Charter.[60] Many of the freedoms that India's Constitution guarantees are drawn from international agreements and covenants, and its Supreme Court often refers to the UN Charter to decide human rights cases. Even on the international conduct of states, India has adopted principles of the UN Charter that encourage the promotion of peace and security, international law, and the peaceful settlement of international disputes. Clearly, the philosophy of the United Nations has resonated deeply with India's civilization.

As we have mentioned earlier, India has always sought guidance from its traditional belief that the whole world is one family and this is why India rarely sees the global commons in extractive terms, or seeks to dominate other lands through military force. The 1950s and 60s were the heyday of India's internationalism; it participated in the drafting of several key treaties and conventions, such as the Outer Space Treaty, the United Nations Convention on the Law of the Seas, and the Antarctic Treaty, and insisted on placing a special

---

[59]An Indian Official, 'India as a World Power', *Foreign Affairs*, July 1949.
[60]C. S. R. Murthy, 'UNSC: India's membership and the road ahead' *The Hindu*, 30 October 2010.

emphasis on protecting and preserving the 'common heritage of mankind'. Similarly, on the maritime front, India has always acted as a 'net security provider'; and has always resolved disputes peacefully. The Indian Navy, for example, patrols the International Recommended Transit Corridor (IRTC) near the Gulf of Aden, and India has often been the first responder and primary provider of aid during disasters in South Asia like the Indian Ocean earthquake tsunami in 2004, Cyclone Sidr in 2007, and Cyclone Nargis in 2008. As has been noted, when India lost a maritime dispute with Bangladesh, a country several times smaller geographically and economically, it chose to comply with the verdict, in sharp contrast to China's utter disregard for international law and militarization of the South China Sea, and arguably even America's ambivalence towards international law. At all times, India has allowed regional institutions to perform their functions without seeking to subvert them. Successive Indian prime ministers, for example, have articulated that New Delhi believes in 'ASEAN centrality', with respect to the thriving Southeast Asia community. In contrast, China has used economic statecraft and military bullying to play each nation off against the other to serve its own purposes. It is not surprising that Lee Kuan Yew, Singapore's most famous prime minister, had no personal trepidations about India's involvement in Southeast Asia in 2007, noting that there was 'no fear' that India had 'aggressive intentions'.

Today's world is more networked than ever before—and this new world welcomes every nation; the information era has little room for the domination of any superpower, neither the US nor China. (Mohamed Nasheed, the deposed president of the Maldives, said in a documentary about global warming and his efforts to save his country's shorelines: 'You cannot bully us. We are too small; you will be seen as a bully!') We live in a more equal era, which is perhaps what causes an itch in formerly privileged economies and societies. Relationships are contingent and overlap with others; friends and allies in one cause might be irrelevant to another (or even on opposite sides). The networked world is a more fluid place. Countries use such networks to promote common interests, to manage common issues rather than impose outcomes, and provide a common response to the challenges and opportunities they face.

In such a world, as one of us once suggested, India would move beyond nonalignment to 'multi-alignment'. This would be the appropriate strategy for what the political scientists Robert Keohane and Joseph Nye have called a world of 'complex interdependence'. This is a world in which India would belong to, and play a prominent role in, both the United Nations and the G20; both the Non-Aligned Movement (reflecting its 200 years of colonial oppression) and the Community of Democracies (reflecting its sixty-five years of democratic development); both the G77 (the massive gathering of over 120 developing countries) and smaller organizations like the Indian Ocean Rim Association for Regional Co-operation (IOR-ARC); both SAARC and the Commonwealth; both RIC (Russia–India–China) and BRICS (adding Brazil and South Africa); as well as both IBSA (the South–South alliance of India, Brazil and South Africa) and BASIC (the partnership of Brazil, South Africa, India and China on climate change issues which emerged during the Copenhagen talks). India is the one country that is a member of them all, and not merely because its name begins with that indispensable element for all acronyms, a vowel![61]

'Multi-alignment', it is true, is at one level an amoral strategy: it would see India making common cause with liberal democracies when it suited India to do so, and dissenting from them when (as on Myanmar, Iran, and on certain aspects of the Arab Spring) it was expedient for India to preserve relationships that the other democracies could afford to jettison. It is also a promiscuous strategy, since it exempts no country from its embrace; China, a potential adversary with whom we have a long-standing frontier dispute that occasionally erupts into rhetorical unpleasantness, nonetheless is a crucial partner in several of these configurations. It is a strategy of making and running shifting coalitions of interests, which will require some management of complicated relationships and opportunities—

---

[61]Shashi Tharoor, *Pax Indica*.

in policy environments that may themselves be unpredictable. That should not be excessively difficult for governments in New Delhi, which, for more than two decades, have had to spend their time and energy on managing coalitions in Indian domestic politics.

Multi-alignment also constitutes an effective response to the new transnational challenges of the twenty-first century, to which neither autonomy nor alliance offer adequate answers in themselves. An obvious example is dealing with terrorism, which requires diplomatic and intelligence cooperation from a variety of countries facing comparable threats; but also shoring up failing states, combatting piracy, controlling nuclear proliferation and battling organized crime. In addition to such issues there are the unconventional threats to peace that also cross all borders (pandemics, for instance), and the need to preserve the global commons—keeping open the sea lanes of communication across international waters so that trade routes and energy supplies are safeguarded, ensuring maritime security from the Horn of Africa to the Strait of Malacca, protecting cyberspace from the depredations of hostile forces including non-governmental ones, and the management of outer space, which could increasingly become a new theatre for global competition.[62]

India has the demonstrated capacity, the technological and human resources, to contribute to fashioning the international system in all these areas, from cyberspace to outer space. And India certainly possesses the potential and will to defuse geopolitical tension. If anything, India has always sought the democratization of international politics, preferring a world that is at once multipolar, but also formally multilateral. Manmohan Singh summed up India's approach in his very first address to the United Nations General Assembly in September 2004, underscoring the importance of the 'culture of genuine multilateralism', but lamenting the lack of 'a sustained commitment to democratizing the functioning of the United Nations.' What prevents effective multilateralism, argued Singh, was not multipolarity, but a democratic deficit in the functioning

---

[62]Id.

of international institutions. This pursuit of a culture of 'genuine multilateralism' and the 'democratization' of international institutions is also what prompts India to play by the rules of the established—and now flailing—Western powers, as well as setting up and supporting other regional institutions—that are often seen as peer competitors—such as the AIIB and the BRICS' NDB. At the same time, India is equally reticent towards *any* attempts to enforce hegemony. Even as India criticized Western powers for much of its independence, and bandwagoned with China to champion the cause of developing states under the guise of the G77, it has been equally quick to dismiss Beijing's attempts to hardwire its influence in Asia under the Belt and Road Initiative.

Clearly, then, India faces a defining period: it is central to the economic and political shifts that are redistributing wealth and power towards Asia; it is the world's largest democracy in a region that is prone to weak state capacity, religious violence and military dictatorships; it has a seat at the global high table, being a member of the G20, as well as the global trade union, the G77; it is one of the largest suppliers of peacekeeping forces to the United Nations and is instrumental in a vast array of other multilateral institutions. India is reasserting itself for the first time since the 1500s, and is doing so at a time of profound change: politically, China is vying for global leadership; economically, the world is buffeted by the contradictory forces of protectionism and a desire for connectivity and integration; technologically, new production techniques and consumer technologies from developments in artificial intelligence, 3-D printing, and robotics to 5G communications and driverless vehicles, will all have profound consequences on the human civilization.

This leads us to our final feature of India's rise: India will be the world's first post-colonial great power. Ultimately, India's contribution to the world will rest on its ability to construct an international system that works for the world's aspirational masses. For now, India will remain a poor country, but it will get richer. India's sheer demographics and economic size make it impossible to ignore. Its multiple domestic and global identities have a uniquely settling effect: India is evidently comfortable everywhere at once. From past experience, it is easy to see that India's understanding of its own problems has shaped its identity in global politics. Soon after independence, India tirelessly campaigned against colonialism and racism in Africa and other parts of Asia, establishing itself as a moral leader, while serving the UN as a major contributor of peacekeeping troops from the start, a status that continues to this day. Through the 1970s, India sought to establish a 'New International Economic Order', in order to bring economic parity to the world's impoverished millions and their ability to control their natural resources. Throughout the 1990s, India was vehement in its refusal to support agricultural trade policies that did not allow developing countries to adequately support their small and marginal farmers. Nor did it accept intellectual property regimes that would limit its ability to supply cheap and affordable access to healthcare to its own citizens and to those of the world. Through the 2000s, India refused to be cowed down by Western demands for a climate change treaty that did not pay due heed to past environmental damage.

As India has negotiated, it has repeatedly affirmed its desire for greater international equity—never by subverting global institutions and processes, but by attempting to make them more inclusive. India's own democratic choices are arguably far more relevant to the developing countries of Asia, Africa and the Middle East. Unlike the Atlantic powers, where a large bureaucratic and secular state allows for stable and procedural governance, many countries in these regions continue to suffer from colonial institutions, fractured ethnic rivalry, and large, unskilled, and uneducated populations. India's constitutional model of protecting individual and group rights, devolution of political power, and its multiparty system to reconcile various political interests is far more suited to these parts of the world. At the same time, India will also partner with the West to fuel its own economic and technological expansion. India and China, meanwhile, will often find themselves in the same club of countries seeking to ensure the free flow of finance and trade. Delhi will also lead or participate in coalitions that are built to preserve multipolarity, such as the

Quadrilateral Initiative or the Shanghai Cooperation Organization. Indeed, India will be the nation most capable of erasing the boundaries and the binaries between East and West, North and South.

India matters more than ever today because of key choices it made more than half a century ago: the adoption of universal franchise and individual liberty. It matters, because at no point in history has one-sixth of humanity cohesively formed a single political entity after multiple instances of religious, ethnic and linguistic violence. To have continuously strengthened this state, to have governed it through freedom, and to have given it a voice and agency in international affairs is no mean feat. That this voice has served to amplify not only its own interests, but those of smaller nations as well is equally laudable. It matters, because in today's world of competing modernities and fractured identities, India has the legacy, tools, potential, and will to build an order that is capable of subsuming these differences, and offering a story that is compelling, replicable, and sustainable.

The new India can and must play a role in helping shape the global order. The international system of the twenty-first century, with its networked partnerships, will need to renegotiate its rules of the road; countries realize that, in the global system, the rules are either written, imposed, and maintained collectively or by a dominant superpower. As we have noted, India is among those who have been rule-takers for long and who now feel ready to be rule-makers. India is well qualified, along with others, to help write those rules and define the norms that will guide tomorrow's world. Rather than confining itself to being a subject of others' rule-making, or even a resister of others' attempts, it is in the interests of a country like India (and within India's current and future capacity) to take the initiative to shape the evolution of these norms as well as to have a voice in the situations within which they are applied.

At the midnight moment of India's independence in 1947, the country's first prime minister, Jawaharlal Nehru, spoke feelingly of a 'tryst with destiny'. Three-quarters of a century later, a second tryst awaits the nation—and this time it is the destiny of the globe, and not just of India, that beckons.

ACKNOWLEDGEMENTS

While acknowledging all the efforts that have allowed for the publication of a book is always a daunting task, the authors agree that much credit goes to the young minds who participate at the Asian Forum on Global Governance. This forum, which was inaugurated in 2011, is jointly hosted by the Observer Research Foundation (ORF) and the ZEIT-Stiftung Ebelin und Gerd Bucerius. As we move to its eleventh iteration in 2020, about 500 young leaders from over seventy countries have already participated in ten-day-long discussions on global governance.

In many ways, the ideas we have discussed in this book are a product of the conversations and debates that we were fortunate enough to moderate and take part in. We owe much debt and gratitude to all the alumni of the forum and of the Bucerius Summer School, its sister school for young leaders, for their keen insights on big questions before all of us today. This forum itself would not have been possible but for the leadership of Sunjoy Joshi, Michael Göering, Theo Sommer, Sascha Suhrke, and Antje Uhlig.

We would like to acknowledge and thank a very fine young mind, Akhil Deo, for his research assistance. We are very grateful for the long hours he put into helping us complete this journey. His efforts have certainly strengthened our propositions in this book. His journey as a thinker is one that most must follow.

Our thanks also to our editor and publisher, David Davidar, for his keenness to take on this daunting work and bring it to a broader audience, and to his able team, notably Aienla Ozukum and Rosemary Sebastian, for their diligent stewardship of our manuscript. Needless to say, responsibility for any errors of fact or interpretation remains ours alone.

Shashi Tharoor and Samir Saran
New Delhi
September 2019